D1012542

Visitor's Guide
# SOUTHERN GERMANY

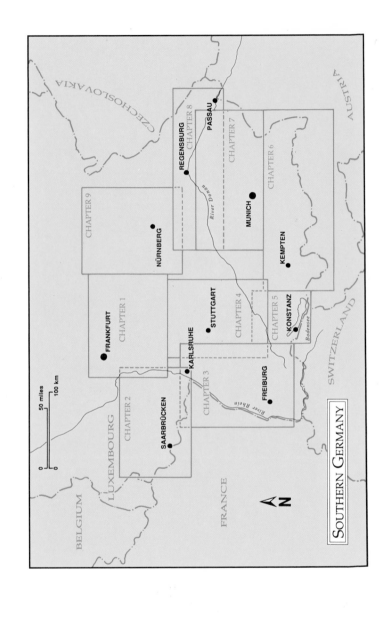

SOUTHERN GERMANY

# VISITOR'S GUIDE
# SOUTHERN
# GERMANY

## GRANT BOURNE
### &
## SABINE KÖRNER-BOURNE

MPC

HUNTER
PUBLISHING INC

Published by:
Moorland Publishing Co Ltd,
Moor Farm Road West,
Ashbourne,
Derbyshire
DE6 1HD
England

© Grant Bourne
& Sabine Körner-Bourne 1991

British Library Cataloguing in
Publication Data:
Bourne, Grant
  Visitor's guide to Southern
  Germany.
  - (Visitor's guides)
  I. Title II. Körner-Bourne, Sabine
  III. Series
  914.304
  ISBN 0 86190 436 2

Published in the USA by:
Hunter Publishing Inc,
300 Raritan Center Parkway,
CN 94, Edison, NJ 08818
ISBN 1 55650 475 6 (USA)

Colour origination by:
Scantrans Pte Ltd, Singapore

Printed in the UK by:
Butler & Tanner Ltd,
Frome, Somerset

Cover photograph: *Brass band at the
Munich Beer Festival*
(Tony Stone Associates Ltd).

Illustrations have been supplied as
follows: H. Alcock: pp 71, 75
(bottom), 78 (both), 79 (bottom), 83
(top), 87; MPC Picture Collection:
pp 15, 27 (top), 34, 39 (bottom), 75
(top), 86 (top), 107 (bottom), 126,
127 (both), 130 (top), 143 (both),
146, 147, 151 (bottom), 154 (both),
203. All other illustrations were
supplied by the authors.

Acknowledgements
The authors would like to thank
the various regional and local
tourist offices for the great amount
of material they put at their
disposal. The city of Saarbrücken,
the Hessischer Fremdenverkehrsverband in Wiesbaden and the
DZT in Frankfurt were especially
generous with information.
Furthermore thanks to Susanne,
Ralf, Steffi and Karsten for
numerous cups of tea and carrying
the tripod.
The authors dedicate this book to
their parents.

MPC Production Team:
Editor: Tonya Monk
Designer: Jonathan Moss
Cartographer: Alastair Morrison

# CONTENTS

## Key to Symbols Used in Text Margin and on Maps

🌳 Parkland

🕭 Church/Ecclesiastical site

🏛 Archaeological site

🏢 Building of interest

🦌 Zoo/Animal park

🏰 Castle/Fortification

🦆 Birdlife

🖼 Museum/Art gallery

✳ Garden

⛰ Beautiful view/Scenery, Natural phenomenon

⛷ Skiing facilities

☀ Other place of interest

🕳 Cave

⛵ Watersports

🚶 Recommended Walk

🚂 Interesting Railway

## Key to Maps

—— Main road

⬭ Lake

══ Motorway

▭▭▭▭ Railway

〰 River

– — – — National Boundary

▭ Town/City

## How To Use This Guide

This MPC Visitor's Guide has been designed to be as easy to use as possible. Each chapter covers a region or itinerary in a natural progression which gives all the background information to help you enjoy your visit. MPC's distinctive margin symbols, the important places printed in bold, and a comprehensive index enable the reader to find the most interesting places to visit with ease. At the end of each chapter an Additional Information section gives specific details such as addresses and opening times, making this guide a complete sightseeing companion. At the back of the guide the Fact File, arranged in alphabetical order, gives practical information and useful tips to help you plan your holiday — before you go and while you are there. The maps of each region show the main towns, villages, roads and places of interest, but are not designed as route maps and motorists should always use a good recommended road atlas.

# INTRODUCTION

For many people 'Romantic Germany' is in fact Southern Germany; the Black Forest, the Bavarian Alps, Rothenburg ob der Tauber and of course Heidelberg. That there is much more to the south than is represented by these world famous names is a fact easily overlooked in the usual travel catalogues and books. The purpose of this guide is not only to cover these famous attractions but also to open the visitor's eyes to those other landscapes and places that are less known but no less deserving of attention.

Summer is of course high season everywhere which means, on the positive side, that all the tourist facilities are certainly open but also that some major attractions can be overcrowded. It might be a good idea to explore less touristed regions like the Saarland, Hunsrück or Swabian Jura at this time. The Alps are obviously a popular destination for skiers in winter but the Black Forest, Bavarian Forest and Swabian Jura can also be particularly beautiful in winters with lots of snow. In spring the weather can be a bit wet, especially in the Allgäu and Bavarian Alps, but then the Bergstrasse to Heidelberg is adorned with pink and white blossoms and Bodensee (Lake Constance) experiences the very first awakenings of spring within view of the snow-clad Alps. Autumn is particularly good for walking as the days are not so hot and, with a bit of luck, the weather is more stable than at other times of the year. Areas covered by broad expanses of deciduous forest like the Saarland, Odenwald, Spessart and Palatinate Forest can be stunningly beautiful at this season. For detailed information on the climate see the Fact File.

The routes in this book have been designed to link places of interest within a region as attractively as possible. It is not necessarily intended that they be completed in a day, nor must they be completed in their entirety. As it is impossible to mention every idyllic valley and each picturesque village the routes should be seen, and serve, as introductions, encouraging visitors to go off and explore on their own and to become even more closely acquainted with the area of their choice. In many places the routes have been linked; either to other routes within a chapter, or to routes in succeeding chapters. Visitors can therefore form their own tours, taking that part of a route they find most appealing. By following the suggested links to routes in succeeding chapters, a large circular tour of Southern Germany could be undertaken. It would move in an anti-clockwise direction from Frankfurt, going first south through Rhineland-Palatinate, east through Baden-Württemberg and then back north through Bavaria.

Please note that the distances given at the start of each route are only approximate and do not include detours from the main route.

# History

It is by no means easy to separate the complex history of the area that has been dealt with as Southern Germany in this book from that of the rest of the country. It is perhaps more sensible to give a brief sketch of Germany's history as a whole, rather than deal with regional history which, when seen out of context, tends to confuse instead of clarify the issue.

### PREHISTORY AND EARLY HISTORY

The geographical entity that is now known as Germany has been inhabited from the very earliest times. The oldest known remains of early man found on German soil are those of *Homo erectus heidelbergensis* (Heidelberg Man) which date back to about 500,000BC. The first Germanic tribes appeared on the scene around 500BC and were to prove a thorn in the side for the Romans from the second century BC. In the middle of the first century BC the Romans were successful in establishing the Rhein as the north-eastern frontier of the Roman Empire. To hold back German advances construction began around AD90 on a 550km (341 mile) long defensive wall with forts, known as the Limes, between the Rhein and the Donau (Danube). This defensive line was breached around AD260 and the Western Roman Empire was finally destroyed by the Eastern Germanic peoples around AD476. The area was dominated by the Franks, a West Germanic tribe, from the sixth century and the Christianisation of the Germans began with the missionary work of Iro-Scottish monks in the late seventh to eighth centuries; monasteries were founded at Würzburg, Regensburg and Reichenau.

## FROM THE CAROLINGIAN EMPIRE TO THE GERMAN EMPIRE (DEUTSCHES REICH)

The Carolingian Empire reached its greatest extent under Charlemagne (AD772-AD814) but after AD843 it fell apart and was succeeded by the so-called Holy Roman Empire. This institution actually dates back to AD800 when Charlemagne was crowned emperor of the West (that area once controlled by the Western Roman Empire) by Pope Leo III, though the name was not used until the mid-thirteenth century. The imperial title, which was inherited by the German kings, was supposed to be elective but in practice medieval Germany was ruled by hereditary dynasties. For the most part the period between the eleventh and thirteenth centuries was characterised by a power struggle between the Emperor and the Pope.

The later Middle Ages saw the rise of the Hanseatic League, led by the city-state of Lübeck, which challenged the power of the princes. After Luther inaugurated the Reformation by nailing his 95 'theses' to the church door in Wittenberg (1517) a long period of religious conflict divided Germany into a mainly Protestant north and Catholic south. The Thirty Years War (1618-48) finally resolved the conflict, but only after large parts of Germany were laid waste and a third of the population was wiped out. Prussia became the dominant German state during the eighteenth century and under Frederick the Great it became a major European power. The Holy Roman Empire was brought to an end by Napoleon in 1806. After Napoleon the German Confederation, was controlled by Austria and Prussia. Prussian victories in the Austro-Prussian War (1866) and the Franco-Prussian War (1870-71) led to the German Empire in 1871.

## FROM WORLD WAR I TO GERMAN REUNIFICATION

After World War I the German Empire was dissolved (1919) to be replaced by the ill-fated Weimar Republic. With the Republic's end in 1933 there was nothing to stand in the way of Hitler and the Nazi dictatorship. After Hitler's defeat in World War II Germany was divided into two separate states: Federal Republic of Germany (West Germany) and the German Democratic Republic (East Germany).

In the wake of radical changes in Eastern Europe communist authority rapidly crumbled in East Germany towards the end of 1989. In May 1990 the first decisive step to German unity was concluded with the signing of the Economic, Monetary and Social Union between the German Democratic Republic and the Federal Republic. Germany was reunited on 3 October 1990 and this day has been declared a public holiday.

## Arts, Culture and Entertainment

German art and culture has a long and impressive history. Of the various periods of art history it was perhaps the Baroque, in terms of architecture, that left the most characteristic mark on Southern Germany. The great master of German painting was, however, Albrecht Dürer of Nürnberg, a Renaissance artist. In the field of literature many of Germany's greatest names came from the south: Goethe, Herman Hesse, Georg Büchner and Hölderlin, to name a few. Bach, Beethoven and Mozart stand for the greatest achievements in German music. The composer Richard Wagner was a good friend of the Bavarian king and is today strongly associated with the Bavarian town of Bayreuth, where the festival of his music is held.

Generally speaking German cities have a wide variety of cultural activities, including theatre, opera and concerts that reach the very highest standards and some very good art galleries and museums. In Southern Germany it is probably Munich that has the most 'exciting' cultural programme of events but Stuttgart and Frankfurt also have much to offer. Tourist offices in all towns and cities always have an up-to-date calendar of events provided for visitors and can often give advice on how to obtain tickets.

## Environmental Issues

Environmental issues have played a significant role in Germany in recent years and it could be said that environmental consciousness is nowhere higher, except perhaps for the Scandinavian countries. The topic that originally galvanized public opinion was that of 'Waldsterben' (the dying forests). The effects of 'acid rain' are quite visible in eastern Bavaria and in every German forest there are information boards dealing with this problem. Exhaust fumes from cars, as well as industry, have been branded responsible for much of this 'acid rain' and partly due to political pressure from the Green Party there has been much discussion of a speed limit (100km, 62 miles) on the German *Autobahn*, though this has not yet eventuated. Most new cars sold in Germany are required by law to have a three-way catalytic converter. World-wide problems like the Greenhouse Effect are dealt with regularly in the newspapers and television with 'typical' German thoroughness. An important forum for environmental issues is the magazine *Natur*.

## Flora and Fauna

Southern Germany lies within the central European zone of decidu-

THE NATIONAL & NATURE PARKS
OF SOUTHERN GERMANY

1. Naturpark Saar-Hunsrück
2. Naturpark Pfälzer Wald
3. Bergstrasse-Odenwald
4. Bayerischer Spessart
5. Hessischer Spessart
6. Hessische Rhön
7. Bayerische Rhön
8. Hassberge
9. Steigerwald
10. Naturpark Frankenwald
11. Fichtelgebirge
12. Naturpark Fränkische
   Schweiz-Veldensteiner Forst
13. Steinwald
14. Hessenreuther and Manteler
   Wald
15. Nördlicher Oberpfälzer Wald
16. Oberpfälzer Wald
17. Oberviechtach-Schönsee
18. Oberer Bayerischer Wald

19. Bayerischer Wald
20. Nationalpark Bayerischer Wald
21. Nationalpark Berchtesgaden
22. Naturschutzgebiet Chiemgauer
   Alpen
23. Naturschutzgebiet
   Karwendelgebirge
24. Naturschutzgebiet
   Ammergebirge
25. Neckartal-Odenwald
26. Frankenhöhe
27. Stromberg-Heuchelberg
28. Naturpark Schwäbisch-
   Fränkischer Wald
29. Naturpark Altmühltal
30. Obere Donau
31. Naturpark Schönbuch
32. Naturpark Augsburg-
   Westliche Wälder

ous forests. The original primeval forests were destroyed or at least greatly altered many centuries ago and coniferous forests which are easier to exploit commercially now dominate over deciduous species. In spite of the damage caused by intensive agriculture such as heavy use of fertilisers to native plant communities there are still many species of wild flowers to be found, especially in areas like the Swabian Jura or the Alps.

Many of the animal species that were once to be found in Germany are long since extinct or are only to be found in zoos. Chamois have been introduced into the Black Forest and moufflon in the Alps. The commonest of the larger animals include several species of deer, wild pigs, foxes and of course rabbits and hares. There are many different species of birds in Southern Germany and a good field guide such as *The Birds of Britain and Europe* published by Collins will prove a useful addition to the luggage of any hobby ornithologist.

## Food and Drink

Everyone knows that Germany is famous for its sausages *(Würste)* as well as beer *(Bier)* and wine *(Wein)*. There are countless varieties of sausage to be found, but *Weisswurst* eaten with sweet mustard is common in Bavaria and Nürnberger Bratwurst is a spicy grilled sausage that is a favourite of crowds at Nürnberg's Christmas Market. German bread is generally very good (best from the bakery rather than the supermarket) and there is a trend to wholemeal *(Vollkorn)* types. A tip for restaurants *(Gasthöfe/Gaststätte)* is to look out for the economical *Mittagstisch* or 'menu of the day'. Note also that restaurants outside the main tourist centres are generally cheapest in Bavaria, as is beer, and that wine is usually cheaper in Rhineland-Palatinate than in Baden-Württemberg or Franconia. In the wine-growing areas look out for what is called a *Strausswirtschaft* and also *Besenwirtschaft* in Baden-Württemberg. These simple restaurants are found in wine-growing towns and villages, run by winegrowers and offer cheap but filling snacks, as well as the chance to try the local wine. They are usually only open in early summer and around harvest time in October, though in some cases they may be open from spring through to autumn.

## Geography and Geology of Southern Germany

Southern Germany is made up of three physical zones: the **South German Uplands** — the southern tip of Hesse, the Saarland, large areas of Baden-Württemberg and northern Bavaria; the **Alpine**

**Plateau** (or Foreland) — south-eastern Baden-Württemberg and southern Bavaria to the Alps, and the **Bavarian Alps**. The main rivers in the south are the Rhein, Donau, Neckar and Main. Southern Germany's neighbours are France in the west, Switzerland to the south, Austria to the south-east and Czechoslovakia in the east.

Of particular interest from the geological point of view are:

The **Hunsrück**. This area forms the southern-most point of the Rhenish Uplands and has an average height above sea-level of between 400 and 500m (1,312 and 1,640ft). It is traversed by a ridge of quartzite hills that reach their highest point in the Erbeskopf (816m, 2,676ft). The present contours of the Hunsrück were formed over 350 million years ago by the waves of the Devonian Sea and there are still many marine fossils to be found in slate mines such as the Grube Herrenberg near Bundenbach.

The **Swabian Jura**. The upland plateau of the Jura or 'Alb' as it is known in German, consists primarily of Upper Jurassic limestones. This permeable rock abounds in karstic formations and features such as dry valleys, caves and underground streams. Like the Hunsrück the area was once covered by a prehistoric sea and fossil ammonites are common in the sedimentary rocks. During the Tertiary Period there was a great deal of volcanic activity and evidence of this can be seen in the northern part of the Jura.

The **Bavarian Alps**. Germany has only a comparatively small section of the European Alps that separate central Europe from Southern Europe. The limestone mountains of the Bavarian Alps were formed by folding processes during the Tertiary Period and glaciation in the Ice Age. The German part of the Alps is divided into two sections, the Allgäuer Alpen in the west and the Oberbayerischen Alpen in the middle and east. The highest point in the Bavarian Alps is the Zugspitze at 2,963m (9,719ft).

In a spirit of generosity this book has often assumed that anything over 350m (just over 1,000ft) is a mountain (*Berg*). The German *Berg* is often used for even lower elevations, though the term *Hügel* or hill does exist it is not considered dramatic enough for local tastes.

# National and Nature Parks

Germany's nature parks (*Naturparks*) are not areas of wilderness in the sense of American National Parks but are landscapes that have evolved in the course of centuries of human settlement and cultivation and have retained a great deal of their natural beauty. Their purpose is not solely to protect what is left of the natural environment but also to serve recreational needs.

*A picture-postcard scene of 'Romantic Germany'*

*The effects of tourism have not altered the quiet village life in Southern Germany*

*This Rathaus in Lindau is adorned with beautiful paintings like so many of the buildings in Germany*

*The German love of art is highly noticeable in their palaces and parks*

Visitors can go from the premise that a *Naturpark* is equivalent to an 'area of outstanding natural beauty'. Furthermore *Naturparks* are almost always excellent for walking, with extensive networks of waymarked trails and good map coverage. Within the larger *Naturparks* are sometimes smaller *Naturschutzgebiete* (nature reserves), where flora and fauna enjoys much stricter protection — picking of wild flowers is forbidden. The few German National Parks *(Nationalparks)* are large reserves where nature is also more strictly protected.

# Politics and Economy

### POLITICS

The Federal Republic consists of 16 Länder (Federal States), five of which are touched upon in this book. The head of state is the Federal President (a primarily representative function) but executive power lies with the Chancellor and his ministers. General elections (Bundestagswahler) for the Federal Government take place every 4 years, as is the case with state government elections (Landtagswahlen). The main political parties are the CDU (Christian Democratic Union), the SPD (Social Democratic Party), the FDP (Free Democratic Party) and the CSU (Christian Socialist Party). The Green Party (die Grünen) has played an important part in recent years and has forced the main-stream parties to take environmental issues more seriously. The present government (since 1990) is a conservative-liberal coalition between the CDU, FDP and CSU.

### ECONOMY

Heavy industries include electrical engineering, iron and steel, cars (especially in Baden-Württemberg and Bavaria) and chemicals. Forestry and tourism, together with the wine industry, are also important factors in Southern Germany. As a whole the economy is heavily export orientated; the main exports include machinery, motor vehicles, electronic goods and chemicals.

# 1

# ON THE MAIN AND NECKAR

---

W ithin this relatively small area, which is roughly defined by
the motorways connecting Frankfurt, Würzburg and
Heidelberg, are not only some of Germany's most famous tourist
attractions but also some of its most picturesque scenery. All three
cities are situated on rivers: the River Main links Frankfurt to
Würzburg, and therefore the state of Hesse to Bavaria, while the
Neckar flows through Heidelberg, in the extreme north of Baden-
Württemberg. All the tours described can be quickly reached from
Frankfurt and provide an excellent opportunity for visitors arriving
by air to gain first impressions of 'Romantic Germany'.

## Route 1 • Frankfurt am Main: Along the Bergstrasse to Heidelberg 79km (49 miles)

The **Bergstrasse** (Mountain Road) gets its name from an old Roman
road, the *Strata Montana*. It runs south along the eastern flank of the
Odenwald — an area of forested hills rather than mountains — and
no doubt earns the somewhat misleading title of 'mountain' road by
virtue of the fact that it is higher than the low lying Rhine valley to
which it runs parallel. A mild climate allows the growth of plants that
one normally associates with Mediterranean regions; almonds and
figs grow along with cherry trees and grapes. Even spring comes
here earlier than elsewhere in Germany and then the hillsides are
awash with pink and white blossoms. At other times of the year the
road's main charm lies in the historic towns and castles that remain
to testify to its importance as an age-old transportation route.

    **Frankfurt** is now one of the world's great financial centres and
with its international airport it is also a major arrival point for foreign
visitors. In World War II severe bombing destroyed most of the old

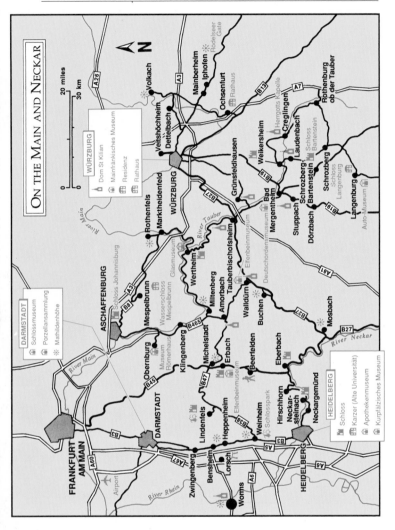

On the Main and Neckar

city so that what can be seen is usually only a copy of the historic original. Skyscrapers are the real symbols of modern Frankfurt, though the restored Römer illustrates the city's bonds to an equally illustrious past.

A good place to start getting to know Frankfurt is by the Baroque **Hauptwache** (Guard-House, 1730) as it is also a junction for the city's

*Frankfurt's modern skyline towers above the old city on the banks of the River Main*

ÄPFELWEINWIRTSCHAFT
Klaane Sachsehäuser

*The district of Sachsenhausen is famous for its apple cider as shown by this wrought-iron sign outside the Apfelweinlokale*

regional train and subway system. The Hauptwache is linked by subway (U-Bahn) to the main railway station (Hauptbahnhof) and trains run directly from the airport into the city. Tickets which are valid for all forms of transport in the city must be bought from one of the blue FVV ticket machines located at tram or train stations. It is only possible to buy tickets from the driver on buses. All-day tickets (24 Stunden Frankfurt) are also available from ticket machines or bus drivers — similar offers are available in most other German cities.

Johann Wolfgang von Goethe (a famous German author) was baptised in **Katharinenkirche** (St Catherine's Church) across the road from the Hauptwache. Only a short distance further is the Catholic **Liebfrauenkirche** (1260-1410) which serves as a waymark to the **Paulskirche** to the south. Shaped as an ellipse with a tower in front the Paulskirche was built between 1789 and 1833. In 1944 the church was completely burnt out but was rebuilt with donations that poured in from all over Germany. The church has a special significance to Germans because between 1848 and 1849 the German National Assembly met here. It represented one of the earliest attempts to set up a democratic constitution in this country. A commemorative plaque is dedicated to John F. Kennedy who spoke in front of the church in June 1963. Just west of the Paulskirche at Grosser Hirschgraben 23 is **Goethehaus**, now a museum with the rooms faithfully restored to their original condition. Goethe was born and lived here until 1775.

Across the Paulsplatz on the Römerberg is old Frankfurt's faithfully restored landmark, the Römer. The three most famous buildings of this Rathaus (town hall) complex are Alt Limpurg, Zum Römer and Löwenstein. The **Kaisersaal** (Imperial Hall) in the upper storey of the house Zum Römer is open to the public. Only a short walk east is the **Kaiserdom** (Imperial Cathedral). It is so called because the German emperors were elected and crowned here. The present building is mainly from the fourteenth and fifteenth centuries. Among its various works of art the most important is a life-size Calvary scene in stone by Hans Backoffen (1509). Near the Römer at Römerberg 27 is a tourist information office where it is possible to pick up free maps of the city, book hotel rooms and tours of the city. The office of the Bürgerauskunft on the Römerberg is more clearly marked than the official tourist office, at least in winter. However, in time for the tourist season, they put out a large sign in front of this office, directing visitors to the proper tourist office a few metres away.

Go towards the Main, pass the **Historisches Museum** whose exhibits include furniture, toys, weapons and textiles. Replicas of the crown jewels of the Holy Roman Empire (the originals are in Vienna) and also a model of the city as it looked in 1912 can be seen here. Cross the River Main over the Eiserner Steg, an iron footbridge. It was originally built in 1868, blown-up in 1945, and put back in place later as a monument to early industrial technology. The Sachsenhausen side of the river is now followed downstream. Here on the **Schaumainkai** or Museumsufer, as it is sometimes called, are seven  museums next to one another.

The **Museum für Kunsthandwerk** (Museum of Arts and Crafts) is divided into four sections: European, Islamic, Far Eastern and a section devoted to books and writing. The building was designed by the American architect Richard Meier.

Housed in a nineteenth-century villa the **Museum für Völkerkunde** (Ethnological Museum) has a huge collection of artefacts from all over the world.

The **Deutsches Filmmuseum** (German Film Museum) offers fascinating insights into the history of film making. The museum has its own movie theatre plus a good café in the basement.

A passage from the Filmmuseum Café leads to the **Deutsches Architekturmuseum** (German Architectural Museum). This is the only museum of its type in the world. The museum's most striking exhibit could be said to be the museum building itself; the exterior is that of a historic villa while the interior is pure twentieth century architecture, a house within a house. The extensive collections of the museum already rank as the largest and most significant in the world. Plans, sketches and models represent the work and ideas of all the worlds greatest architects.

The **Bundespostmuseum** (Postal Museum) is a collection of artefacts connected with postal matters. It also houses telephones as Frankfurt calls itself the birthplace of the telephone, despite the claims of Alexander Graham Bell.

The **Städelsches Kunstinstitut** (Art Institute) was founded in the early nineteenth century by a local banker as an art college. It houses European art from the thirteenth to twentieth century. The collection includes works by Botticelli, Albrecht Dürer, Rembrandt and Rubens.

**Liebighaus** is home to one of the most important collections of sculpture in Europe. The earliest pieces date back to the third millennium BC.

The **Jüdisches Museum** deals with Jewish culture in the German speaking regions of Europe. It is located in the old Rothschild-Palais

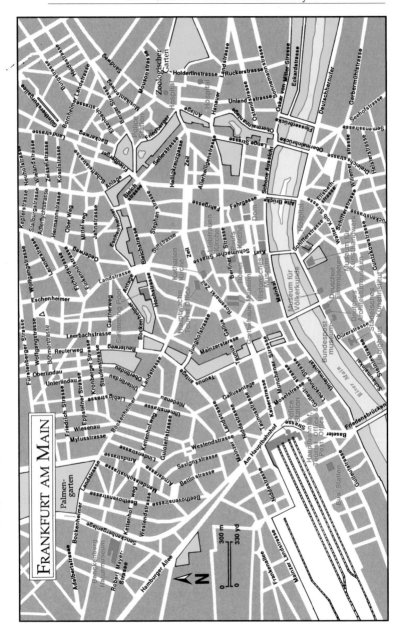

at Untermainkai 14-15, on the opposite bank of the Main from the Deutsches Filmmuseum.

The **Museum für Moderne Kunst** is near the cathedral at Damstrasse 10. One other important museum that should be mentioned is the **Naturmuseum Senckenberg** (Senckenberg Museum for Natural History). It is Germany's largest natural history museum and one of the most important scientific institutions in Europe. It is best reached on lines 6 or 7 of the U-Bahn system from the Hauptwache. Cross back over the Main using the Friedensbrücke, from where it is a short walk to the Hauptbahnhof. Take a tram or the subway back to the starting point.

For a bit of a change from museums and historic places Frankfurt's excellent **Zoologischer Garten** (Zoological Garden), is only 3 minutes by U-Bahn from the Hauptwache. It is one of the most modern zoos in the world. A unique attraction is the Grzimek-Haus where it is possible to observe the behaviour of normally nocturnal animals during daylight hours. The Exotarium simulates animal habitats from all over the world; from polar landscapes with penguins to a south sea coral reef. The opening times are different from the rest of the zoo: daily 10am-10pm throughout the year. The **Palmengarten** (Palm Garden) is well worth a visit. Its large greenhouses contain a wide selection of tropical and sub-tropical flora. In the recently added tropical greenhouse (Tropicarium Wilhelm-Fay-Haus) the complicated ecosystem of a tropical jungle has been perfectly simulated. Included within the area of the Palmengarten is a park with children's playground and restaurant. A small train known as the *Palmenexpress* allows children and adults to get an overview of the park grounds. The district of **Sachsenhausen** is famous for its Apfelweinlokale where apple cider is served and railway fans should inquire about trips on the *Hafenbahn,* a steam train that starts from the Eiserner Steg. Also starting here are boat trips on the Main.

**Darmstadt** is directly south of Frankfurt on the Bundesstrasse 3. Hesses' grand dukes resided here until 1918. Like Frankfurt much of the city was destroyed in World War II but its long tradition as a cultural centre has been kept up to this day. Every year the Georg Büchner Prize — Germany's most important literary prize — is awarded in Darmstadt.

Dominating the Luisenplatz (a car park is located here) is a monument to Grand Duke Ludwig I. A spiral staircase winds to the top of the column from where Darmstadt's Baroque **Schloss** (a palace modelled on Versailles) can be seen. Of especial significance in the **Schlossmuseum** is the *Darmstädter Madonna* painted by Hans

Holbein in 1526. The Grand Dukes **Porzellansammlung** (Porcelain Museum) is at the north end of the Herrngarten and contains a beautiful collection of porcelain, including faience, from the eighteenth and nineteenth centuries. However a visit to Darmstadt is still not complete without seeing the **Mathildenhöhe**. The last Grand Duke, Ernst-Ludwig, created an artists colony on this spot. The most interesting of the buildings in art nouveau style is the **Hochzeitsturm** (Marriage Tower) built in 1905. Set like an exotic jewel amidst these buildings is the Russische Kapelle (Russian Chapel) built in 1899. It was a present from Czar Nicholas II to his wife Alexandra, a sister of the last Grand Duke.

Following the B3 it is a short drive to **Zwingenberg**. This small town lies at the foot of Mount Melibokus. In the old quarter, often signposted in Germany as 'Altstadt', the most interesting sights, apart from the picturesque half-timbered houses, are the 700-year-old Bergkirche, remnants of the town wall and the Marktplatz (market-place) with its beautiful fountain.

Shortly before Bensheim follow a sign pointing left up a narrow road to the ruins of **Schloss Auerbach**, a castle conquered by the French in 1674 after a secret entrance was betrayed to them. The lookout tower on Mount Melibokus (excellent views) can also be reached on this road but must be driven to first because of the one-way traffic system. There is parking by the Schloss and a restaurant. A bit further south and also to be reached by turning left off the B3 is one of the Bergstrasse's major attractions, the **Fürstenlager** (1783-95). It was built as a residence for Landgrave Ludwig I and encompasses a 25 hectare park with exotic plants. **Bensheim** itself has an attractive Altstadt worth exploring and during the first week of September the Bergstrasse's largest Winzerfest (wine-grower's festival) takes place here. A worthwhile detour west along the B47 can be made from Bensheim to Worms and might include a stop in **Lorsch** to see the Carolingian Torhalle — all that remains of a Benedictine abbey established in AD764.

**Worms** is over 5,000 years old and so ranks as one of the oldest towns in Germany. The Burgundians centred a kingdom here around AD405 which was destroyed by the Huns in AD436. The struggle and final demise of the Burgundians is told in the saga of the Nibelungen, an heroic epic from the Middle Ages. During the Middle Ages, Worms developed to become one of the most important towns in Germany. In 1521 Martin Luther defended his writings in front of one of the many Imperial Diets (Reichstage) that took place here. Although the old imperial city had lost virtually all of its significance by the start of the eighteenth century it has recovered to become an important centre of the wine-trade today.

The single most impressive sight in Worms is the **Dom**, which dates back to the eleventh century. It is one of the three great imperial cathedrals on the Rhein, along with those in Mainz and Speyer. Of special interest is the Baroque high altar by Balthasar Neumann. The other sights are scattered like islands of antiquity around the modern town. Posted maps at each place of interest suggest easy to follow circular walks of varying length. Worth searching out is the medieval Jewish cemetery and a synagogue, both of which bear testimony to a once flourishing Jewish community. North of the town centre, about 20 minutes on foot, the Gothic Liebfrauenkirche has given its name to a famous wine grown in the attached vineyards. Only those bottles of Liebfrauenmilch labelled 'Liebfrauenstift-Kirchenstück' are the genuine article.

Continue south on the B3 from Bensheim to the town of **Heppenheim** where the pretty Marktplatz and neo-Gothic parish church are of interest. In fact the church is impressive enough to be known as the 'Cathedral of the Bergstrasse'. Inside the stained-glass windows are very beautiful. From the ruins of Starkenburg, a castle above town, there are good views over the Odenwald and Rhein lowlands.

**Weinheim** is the last stop before Heidelberg. If interest in quaint market-places or crooked streets and houses has not yet waned, then Weinheim is especially nice. The beautiful old Marktplatz is hidden away in the middle of the not so inspiring modern town. Try and park near the spacious grounds of the **Schlosspark** (follow the signs). It is pleasant to walk in the park with its exotic flowers, trees and fountains. A playground and a small aviary are also located here and waymarked paths lead into the adjoining woods.

From the park it is only a short walk downhill to the Marktplatz. The top end is marked by the St Laurentiuskirche, then slopes down to the Rathaus at the bottom. There are several pleasant street cafés located here in summer. The Gerberviertel (Tanners' Quarter) with its many lovely old houses is immediately below in the valley of the Weschnitz stream. At the edge of town is the recreational centre 'Miramar' with its saunas, hot whirlpools, swimming pool and so forth. Above the town, perched on forested slopes, are two castles; Windeck and Wachenburg. The route now continues on the B3 to Heidelberg.

# Route 2 • Heidelberg: The Odenwald
# 195km (121 miles)

The Odenwald is a mountainous area with large patches of forest. A great part of it is taken up by two nature parks; Naturpark Bergstrasse-Odenwald and Naturpark Neckartal-Odenwald. Naturally there are plenty of opportunities for walking and Wanderparkplätze (walker's car parks) are situated next to most clearly marked trails. A recommended walking map is the *RV Wanderkarte 11463 Nationalpark Bergstrasse-Odenwald 1:75,000*.

'Romantic **Heidelberg**'; the name is virtually synonymous with 'Romantic Germany' and should not be missed on any itinerary covering the country's major attractions. The oldest university on German soil is to be found here and today it is still very much a student, as well as a tourist, town. Heidelberg's history goes back a long way but settlement in the general area goes back even further, as is proved by the well preserved jaw bone of *Homo erectus heidelbergensis* (Heidelberg Man), which is over 500,000 years old. The city was lucky to escape destruction in World War II and there is still more than enough left of old Heidelberg to fully justify the term 'romantic'.

After arriving in the city centre it is best to try and find a car park as soon as possible. The many one-way streets and pedestrian zones make traffic a bit confusing. It is possible to drive up to the castle but parking is limited. For those arriving by train it is a good idea to get a map from the tourist information at the Hauptbahnhof. It will not only be useful for picking out sights around the Altstadt, but also for finding those places, like the zoo, which lie on the outskirts of town. A good place to begin a tour of the Altstadt is in the **Marktplatz** which is dominated by the Heiliggeistkirche (1400-63). Across from the church is the Haus zum Ritter (1592) with its beautiful Renaissance front. To get to the castle from the Marktplatz it is either a steep 20 minute walk or a comfortable ride on the Bergbahn (cable railway), which starts from the Kornmarkt just behind the Marktplatz.

A ruin since the French destroyed it at the end of the seventeenth century the **Heidelberger Schloss** (Heidelberg Castle) is situated high above the Neckar river. The various buildings of the castle complex are mainly Renaissance in style, the most important of which are the Ottheinrichsbau (1556-59) and the Friedrichsbau (1601-07). There are regular guided tours through the Friedrichsbau chapel, the Königssaal (Royal Hall) and the Kaisersaal (Imperial Hall). It is also possible to visit the **Apothekenmuseum** (German

*Heidelberg's castle can be reached on foot from the Marktplatz*

*Heppenheim's parish church is worth visiting for its beautiful stained-glass windows*

Apothecary Museum) with its unique exhibits from the past to the present day. Another attraction is the huge wine barrel in the cellar. It could hold 221,726 litres of wine!

Back at the Marktplatz it is a short walk down to the river to the Alte Brücke (Old Bridge) with its Baroque gates. Cross over the bridge to be presented with a classic view of old Heidelberg and the castle. Photos are best made in the late afternoon. Those who wish to get the best overall view of town should walk along the Philosophenweg (Philosophers' Path) on this side of the river — the path is clearly marked.

A few of Heidelberg's other sights can be seen by going from the Marktplatz into the Hauptstrasse. The **Karzer** (Detention Room) at the back of the **Alte Universitätsgebäude** (Old University building, 1713) is where students who took university life a bit too lightly were once locked up. The walls are decorated with interesting graffiti. Opposite the Neue Universität (New University, 1929-32, close to the 'old' building) is the **Universitätsbibliothek** (University Library) with its famous collection of Old German hand-written documents.

A bit further along the Hauptstrasse is the **Kurpfälzisches Museum** (Palatinate Museum). The jaw-bone of Heidelberg Man can be seen here, as well as a masterpiece by Tilman Riemenschneider known as the *Zwölfbotenaltar* (Twelve Apostles' Altar).

From Heidelberg the route now follows the B37 or Burgenstrasse (Castles Road) east along the meandering Neckar river. The jaw-bone of Heidelberg Man was found near the village of Mauer, just south of Neckargemünd. A little further along from Neckargemünd the road climbs steeply up and away from the river to **Dilsberg**. The ruined fortress here commands a wonderful view over the Neckar valley. It seems that during the nineteenth century Heidelberg's students must have been particularly mischievous because there was another detention room in the fortress to supplement the one in Heidelberg.

In order to follow the river return to Neckargemünd and cross the bridge to **Neckarsteinach**. This small town has four castles to its credit, two of which are still lived in. A Naturlehrpfad (nature trail) starting in town goes past all four. Shortly before entering town, to the left, is a car park from where a well marked path leads up to the ruins of Burg Schadeck (Schadeck Castle). Excellent views can be had from the Schwalbennest (Swallow's Nest), which is a look-out tower forming part of the castle complex. By crossing the B37 it is possible to get to the Neckar promenade which leads into town. As the river is very narrow here it is an excellent place to observe the long river barges.

Anybody wishing to combine a cup of coffee with a magnificent panorama should stop at **Hirschhorn** to visit the castle of the same name with its hotel and restaurant. Just below the *Burg* is an old Carmelite Kloster where interesting frescoes can be seen. At

**Eberbach** the B45 offers a shortened alternative to the main route. This attractive stretch of road goes via Beerfelden to Erbach where the main route is rejoined. **Beerfelden** has the macabre honour of possessing Germany's best preserved gallows (1597). The surrounding forest offers very good walking on waymarked trails and in winter there is cross-country skiing along prepared circuits.

The main route continues along the B37 to Mosbach. On the way it is possible to visit **Burg Zwingenberg**, one of the Neckar valley's most beautiful castles. Prince Philip has used the castle as a base for his hunting excursions with the Margrave of Baden. A pleasant walk can be made into the Wolfsschlucht from the castle or from the Cafe Wolfsschlucht on the B37. To enter the Schlucht (gorge) turn right at the castle entrance and walk along the walls to the rear from where a path goes downhill. The Schlucht is about 1km ($^1/_2$ mile) in length. Those who wish could by-pass Mosbach and continue on the B27 south, along the river, to join Route 10 (Chapter 4) at Heilbronn.

Just off the B37 **Mosbach** is particularly interesting for its half-timbered houses. Most of them are to be found in the Hauptstrasse, now a pleasant pedestrian zone, and in the Marktplatz. The most magnificent house of all is the Palmsches Haus (1610) in the Marktplatz. Rather less idyllic, but a part of the landscape nevertheless, is the nuclear power station at Obrigheim, across the river before the turn-off to Mosbach.

After Mosbach the Neckar and the Burgenstrasse are left behind as the route now follows the B27 to Walldürn. Shortly before Walldürn the town of **Buchen** is known for its colourful Fasenacht (carnival) celebrations that take place around Shrove Tuesday. Among the various things of interest to see in town is a gate-tower from the fourteenth century. A little to the south-east, near Buchen-Eberstadt, is a stalactite cavern (Tropfsteinhöhle). It can be visited daily from March through to October.

**Walldürn** is most famous for its Baroque pilgrimage church, Zum Heiligen Blut, but also of interest is the Elfenbeinmuseum (Ivory Museum). An ancient Roman wall *(Limes)* ran very close to the present town. This border wall (much like Hadrian's Wall in England) was meant to keep marauding Germanic tribes out of Roman occupied territory. An instructive walk can be made along the line once followed by the wall by leaving town in the direction of Amorbach and following the green signs to a car park some 2km (1 mile) away. The waymarked trail begins here. Information boards (in German) dot the trail which is about 6km (4 miles) long. Parts of the wall have been reconstructed to give a better idea of how it all was. During summer it is possible to do tours of Walldürn, or further afield, in an old post-coach — inquire at tourist information centre. Route 3 can be joined by taking the B27 via Hardheim to Tauberbischofsheim.

From Walldürn take the B47 (Nibelungenstrasse) to **Amorbach**. The abbey church St Maria (1742-7) is the central attraction not least because of its outstanding Rococo interior decoration. Built by the famous Stumm brothers the church organ is a masterpiece of its kind and a good chance to hear it is during the regular summer concerts. A pamphlet in English describing the church in detail is available at the ticket office. The neighbouring convent buildings have two rooms worth visiting; the Bibliothek and the beautiful Grüner Saal (Green Hall). Also of interest is the parish church St Gangolf (1751-3). Route 4 can be joined by taking the B469 north to Miltenberg.

Further along the scenic B47 the town of **Michelstadt** lies in the heart of the Odenwald. Just before town is Jagdschloss Eulbach, a hunting-seat built in the eighteenth century. Its park is very pretty and includes a mock ruin made from Roman finds in the area. Also in the park are animal enclosures and ponds with rare water-fowl. The prettiest aspect of Michelstadt itself is the Marktplatz with its famous Rathaus. This late Gothic building dates from 1484. A little outside of town to the north-east are some other sights; Schloss Fürstenau is a Renaissance palace with a park and mill and nearby the Einhards-Basilika ranks — along with the Torhalle in Lorsch — as one of the earliest examples of Carolingian architecture.

The neighbouring town of **Erbach** is famed for its ivory carving. The Elfenbeinmuseum exhibits ivory carvings from all over the world but local work received most attention. In the centre of town is a large Schloss with an impressive art collection and hunting trophies. An elaborately carved ceiling from the seventeenth century is particularly noteworthy. Close to town is the deer park Brudergrund.

Continue from Michelstadt on the B47 to **Lindenfels**. It is worthwhile climbing up to the castle ruins above town for fine views over the Odenwald and Weschnitz valley. Immediately below the castle it is possible to make out several round towers which are all that is left of the town's old defensive walls. On the first Sunday of August the most beautiful costumes and folk dances from the Odenwald are on show during the Lindenfels Burgfest. Follow the B38 to Weinheim and then take the B3 back to Heidelberg.

# Route 3 • Würzburg: Along the Romantische Strasse and Burgenstrasse to Langenburg 121km (75 miles)

**Würzburg** is an old bishops' and university town. It also marks the ✳ starting point of the Romantische Strasse (Romantic Road) one of Germany's most famous tourist routes which ends in Füssen in the Bavarian Alps. The Altstadt is enclosed by a ring-road system, with the Main river also providing a border to the west. For those arriving by train the railway station is just north of the Altstadt. Otherwise there are numerous car parks within this old quarter of town.

Because the **Residenz** (1719-44) is centrally located and has a large 🏛 car park in front of it, it makes a good place to start exploring old Würzburg. This immense palace is the masterpiece of Balthasar Neumann (1687-1753), one of Germany's greatest Baroque architects. The interior is interesting not only because of its numerous ornately decorated rooms, but particularly for the monumental staircase by Neumann and the ceiling frescoes by the Venetian artist G.B. Tiepolo. Of artistic note in the palace's attached park is an elaborate wrought-iron entrance gate. Across the road from the Residenz are the Bavarian State Wine Cellars. Weinproben (wine-tastings) take place most days.

Continue from the Residenz along the Hofstrasse, cross the Balthasar Neumann Promenade, to the **Dom St Kilian**. Although the ⛪ result of various styles the cathedral's exterior has managed to preserve much of its Romanesque character. Neumann worked on the Schönbornkapelle which was added in the eighteenth century. Next door to the Dom in the St Kilians-Platz is a basilica known as the Neumünster with its impressive Baroque façade. Proceed a little further on from here then turn left into the Marktplatz. Facing the Marienkapelle (1377-1480) is the beautifully stuccoed front of the Haus zum Falken (1752). A tourist office is located in the same building.

The most direct route to the **Alte Mainbrücke** (Old Main Bridge) is along the Domstrasse which runs west from the cathedral. Near the bridge is a complex of buildings that go to make up the historic 🏛 **Rathaus**. Of especial note is the Wenzelsaal in the first storey of the Grafeneckart-Bau and the Rote Bau (Red Building, 1660) in the western part of the complex. From the bridge are fine views towards the Marienberg fortress perched high on a hill above the Main. A part 🏰 of the fortress complex is the Marienkirche (AD706), one of Germany's oldest churches. The **Mainfränckisches Museum** is housed 🏛

in the former Zeughaus (arsenal) and boasts an outstanding art collection. The greatest attraction here is the large selection of work by Tilman Riemenschneider (around 1460-1531), who was Germany's most gifted sculptor and woodcarver from the late Gothic period. Visible from the fortress on the neighbouring Nikolausberg is the Käppele (1747-50), one of Würzburg's prettiest churches. It was built by Neumann and has a lavish Rococo interior. Cars can park near the fortress.

Würzburg is at the centre of a famous wine-growing region known as Mainfranken. The trademark of a good Franconian wine is a dumpy-shaped bottle called a Bocksbeutel. Unfortunately for local wine-growers the bottle shape is not as exclusive as they would have liked because the Portuguese decided to put out some of their wines in a very similar bottle. A few of the most picturesque of the wine-growing villages are only a short distance from the city.

**Dettelbach** is north-east of Würzburg. Large parts of the town wall still remain and the pilgrimage church of Maria im Sand is especially interesting as a typical example of the so-called 'Julius' style; a mixture of late Gothic, Renaissance and Baroque styles. North-east of here the village of **Volkach** is renowned not only for the Volkacher Madonna by Riemenschneider in its pilgrimage church but also for excellent wines like Volkacher Ratsherr. Volkach's wine-festival is the most important in Bavaria and takes place in mid-August. South-east of Würzburg are the fortified villages of Mainbernheim and **Iphofen**. The Rödelseer Tor (Gate) in Iphofen dates from the fifteenth century and is very photogenic. Also to the south of the city and not far from Mainbernheim the town of **Ochsenfurt** is reputed to have one of the nicest town halls in all Franconia. Finally, just north of Würzburg, **Veitshöchheim** is famous for its Schloss and Rococo park. Route 4 can be joined from Würzburg by following the B8 west to Marktheidenfeld.

Route 3 continues south on the B27 (Romantische Strasse) to **Tauberbischofsheim**. This town on the River Tauber has some very picturesque half-timbered buildings in the Hauptstrasse and Marktplatz. The old quarter of town is marked by two distinctive towers; the round one belongs to the Schloss, while the square one belongs to the parish church of St Martin. Inside the church the altars are of interest, one of them holding a copy of a Grünewald painting depicting the crucifixion. The Romanesque Achatius chapel in nearby **Grünsfeldhausen** is also worth seeing. It was built in 1190 and has an unusual octagonal form.

Take the B290 through Lauda where there are a couple of interesting churches (St Jakobus and St Mary) to **Bad Mergentheim**. This spa town is especially sought out by those suffering from stomach ailments. Closely allied to the history of the town is that of the Order of Teutonic Knights and in the impressive Schloss is a museum devoted to the Order. An outstanding attraction of the Schloss is the Renaissance spiral staircase. By standing in the middle, and looking directly up, it is possible to see on the ceiling a painting depicting the sun. The attached church is a magnificent example of Baroque architecture. In the Marktplatz are many fine old houses, including as usual the Rathaus (1564). In **Stuppach**'s parish church, south on the B19, is a painting by Matthias Grünewald known as the *Stuppacher Madonna*. It is one of the greatest masterpieces of old German painting.

From Bad Mergentheim follow the signs 'Romantische Strasse' and 'Liebliches Taubertal' out of town to reach **Weikersheim**. This part of the Tauber valley is particularly attractive for cyclists as special cycling paths run its length. The pretty village of Weikersheim is the ancestral seat of the House of Hohenlohe. The **Schloss** is for the most part a Renaissance building and can be seen from afar. Of all the many rooms the Rittersaal (Knights' Hall) is especially beautiful. It is in fact considered to be the most magnificent festival hall from the German Renaissance. Connected to the Schloss is a Baroque park which is only accessible by passing through the palace. South of Weikersheim, along the Vorbach river, is the village of **Laudenbach**. Perched high above the village, in the middle of a wood, is the Marienkirche, one of the prettiest churches in the Taubergrund.

Continue along the Tauber river on the Romantische Strasse to **Creglingen**. The carved altar in the Herrgotts-Kapelle is considered to be one of Tilman Riemenschneider's masterpieces. This amazingly detailed work was created around 1505. It is supposed that the figures of the central shrine were done by the master himself, whereas those of the side wings were done by his assistants. In the small church in Detwang another work by Riemenschneider depicts the Crucifixion (1512-13). Rothenburg ob der Tauber is only a few kilometres further on. For a description of this famous town refer to Route 22 (Chapter 9).

From Rothenburg follow the Burgenstrasse via Bossendorf and Leuzendorf to reach Schrozberg. North-west of here, in **Schrozberg-Bartenstein**, is Schloss Bartenstein with its interesting Militär-museum (Military Museum). Continue south through Blaufelden remaining on the Burgenstrasse and finally arrive at Langenburg ob

*These attractive half-timbered buildings are in the Marktplatz at Tauberbischofsheim*

der Jagst, the last destination on this route.

**Langenburg**'s Schloss dates mainly from the sixteenth and seventeenth centuries and, like the village itself, is romantically situated above the Jagst valley. Impressive enough in the distance with its mighty battlements the Schloss also rewards closer inspection; of particular interest is the Renaissance courtyard, together with some lavishly furnished rooms. Next to the Schloss and located in the Marstallgebäude is the Auto-Museum which is a must for vintage car enthusiasts. From the rose garden, where a café is located, there are breathtaking views over the Jagst valley. Below in the village the parish church (1498-99) and a number of quaint half-timbered houses are worth a look.

For those with time a very picturesque excursion from Langenburg is to follow the Jagst river north through Unterregenbach and Mulfingen to **Dörzbach** on the B19. It is only a few kilometres from here back to Bad Mergentheim. Route 10 (Chapter 4) can be joined by following the Burgenstrasse south to Schwäbisch Hall. This road goes under the A6 viaduct which at a height of 180m (590ft) is Europe's highest motorway bridge.

# Route 4 • The Spessart 118km (73 miles)

Germans associate the expansive forests of the Spessart with mysterious legends and tales of marauding robber bands, as recounted in the works of the nineteenth-century author Wilhelm Hauff. Much of what has been preserved of that romance is contained within the boundaries of the Naturpark Bayerischer Spessart. Here the largest remaining stands of beech and oak forest in Germany still seem to cloak ancient towns and castles in the mantle of a bygone age. A recommended walking map is *Wanderkarte Naturpark Spessart, Blatt 3, 1:50,000, Fietz Verlag*.

**Aschaffenburg** likes to title itself 'Gateway to the Spessart' and in the form of the mighty Renaissance palace Schloss Johannisburg it does in fact make a very impressive starting point. Conveniently enough there is parking in front of the Schloss which is worth entering for its art collection containing works by seventeenth-century Dutch and Flemish masters, as well as some fine rooms such as the library. In the palace museum is a unique collection of cork models representing famous buildings from antiquity. The palace's dominating position above the Main river is best appreciated and photographed from the opposite bank.

Connected to the Schloss by a beautiful park is the **Pompejanum**. This incongruous building was built at the wish of King Ludwig I of Bavaria as a copy of a Roman villa excavated at Pompeii. It can only be viewed from the outside. Away from the river in the Stiftsplatz is Aschaffenburg's oldest church, the collegiate church of St Peter and Alexander. Its history goes right back to the late tenth century but it received important additions at later dates. Among the church's many important art works is a *Beweinung Christi* (Lamentation of Christ) by Matthias Grünewald.

Continue south along the Main river through Sulzbach, keeping close to the river until crossing to **Obernburg**, opposite Elsenfeld. This old fortified town is famed for its orchards and the Museum Römerhaus is interesting for its exhibits of Roman finds made in the area. Now the road could be followed either side of the river but it is quieter on the Sulzbach side. In **Klingenberg** it is worth trying excellent local red wines such as Klingenberger Spätburgunder (though drivers should note that it is fairly potent). A good place to take in the attractive panorama of town and river is from the restaurant at the castle above town. Wine-tastings are held in the Haus des Gastes but not only wine connoisseurs would enjoy the wine festival held in August, which is the largest along the Lower Main.

The impression grows stronger that the Main must be one of the most indecisive rivers in Germany as it makes yet another bend, this time to the north, at **Miltenberg**. In spite of the often exaggerated claims of tourist brochures this town can justifiably be called 'Pearl of the Main Valley'. The Marktplatz contains some beautiful half-timbered houses, especially along that section that leads up to the Mildenburg, a medieval castle. In the past the beams of these houses were painted with ox blood, instead of the paint used nowadays. From the Mildenburg's keep are superb views over the Main valley and Spessart. The Gasthaus zum Riesen in the Hauptstrasse is one of Germany's oldest hotels, dating back to 1590. The old Rathaus is from the fifteenth century and was built with local sandstone. Miltenberg celebrates one of the biggest folk festivals along the Lower Main, the Michaelis-Messe, on the last weekend of August.

Follow the Main north-east via Freudenberg to **Wertheim**. The castle ruins high above town are testimony to a long and noble past. For centuries the place was ruled by the counts of Wertheim who are buried in the late Gothic parish church. Their tombstones are finely sculptured works of German Renaissance art. After World War II glass-blowers from Thüringen came to settle here, establishing a profitable industry. A glass museum is housed in one of the town's old half-timbered buildings. Formerly the region of Thüringen belonged to communist East Germany but in 1990 it became one of the five new states in a reunited Germany.

**Marktheidenfeld** is only a bit further north on the River Main. North of here, on the west bank of the Main, the village of **Rothenfels** is interesting for its Rathaus (1598), parish church (1611), and medieval castle. The main route continues on the B8 through the middle of the Naturpark Bayerischer Spessart back to Aschaffenburg.

Roughly half-way to Aschaffenburg, at both ends of the bridge that crosses the A3 motorway, are car parks that serve as starting points for walks of varying length. One of these walks, marked with the pictogram of black boar, is a short nature trail that goes through a stand of ancient oaks, some of which are from 500 to 800 years old.

Before reaching Aschaffenburg the opportunity should not be missed to visit **Wasserschloss Mespelbrunn**. Turn left off the B8 at Hessenthal and follow this road a few kilometres until the sign 'Schloss' points left again. This romantic moated castle, set in thick forest, is one of the most photogenic in Germany. Although it is still lived in some of the rooms may be viewed and it is worth having a look as they offer a unique insight into the lifestyle of an aristocratic family over the centuries. A restaurant is located strategically opposite. Return the same way and then go via Oberbessenbach along the B8 back to the start of this route at Aschaffenburg.

# ADDITIONAL INFORMATION

## *Places of Interest in Frankfurt*

**Goethehaus Museum**
Grosser Hirschgraben 23
Open: April to September, Monday to Saturday 9am-6pm, Sunday 10am-1pm. October to March, Monday to Saturday 9am-4pm, Sunday 10am-1pm.

**Historisches Museum**
Open: Tuesday 10am-5pm, Wednesday 10am-8pm, Thursday to Saturday 10am-5pm. Entrance is free except for special exhibitions.

**Kaisersaal**
Open: Monday to Saturday 9am-5pm, Sunday 10am-4pm.

**Museum für Moderne Kunst**
Open: Tuesday to Sunday 10am-5pm, Wednesday 10am-8pm. Closed Monday.

**Naturmuseum Senckenberg**
Senckenberg-Anlage 25
Open: Monday, Tuesday, Thursday, Friday 9am-5pm; Wednesday 9am-8pm; Saturday/Sunday 9am-6pm. Free tours on Sunday 10.30am and Wednesday 8pm.

**Palmengarten**
Siesmayerstrasse 61 (Entrances at Bockenheimer Landstrasse/ Palmengartenstrasse/ Siesmayerstrasse and Zeppelinallee)
Open: January to February 9am-4pm. March 9am-5pm. April to September 9am-6pm. October 9am-5pm. November to December 9am-4pm. There is an entry fee except on Heiligabend (24 December) and Silvester (31 December), however the greenhouses are closed then.
☎ 212-33382

**The Schaumainkai**
With one exception the museums here are open from Tuesday to Sunday 10am-5pm (staying open until 8pm on Wednesday) and closed on Monday. The Deutsches Filmmuseum is open Tuesday to Sunday 11am-6.30pm. Entry is free to all except the Städel.

**Zoologischer Garten**
Alfred-Brehm-Platz 16
Main entrance Alfred-Brehm-Platz
Open: 16 March to 30 September daily 8am-7pm. 1 October to 15 October daily 8am-6pm. 16 October to 15 February daily 8am-5pm. 16 February to 15 March 8am-6pm. Rhönstrasse entrance open: 16 September to 15 March as main entrance. 16 March to 15 September daily 8am-6pm.

# Useful Information

## Area Code
☎ 069

## Cycle Hire
Per Pedale
Falkstrasse 28 (in Bockenheim)
☎ 707 2363

## Consulates
*UK*
Bockenheimer Landstrasse 51-3
☎ 720406

*USA*
Siesmayerstrasse 21
☎ 753040

*Australia*
Grosse Gallusstrasse 10-14
☎ 20057

## Guided Tours
Ebbelwei-Express
This colourfully painted trollycar takes in the 'apple cider' district of Sachsenhausen. During summer it starts from the Ostbahnhof between 1.30-5.30pm and departs every 30 minutes on Saturday and Sunday. For further information contact the tourist offices or the Stadtwerke Frankfurt
Börneplatz 3
Entrance Kurt-Schumacher-Strasse 8
☎ 213-22236

For information about boat excursions on the Rhein and Main contact the tourist offices or
KD Köln-Düsseldorfer Pavillon at the Eiserner Steg
☎ 282420
A-Ulfried Nauheimer-Wikinger-Linie
☎ 282886

Frankfurter Personenschiffahrt
Anton Nauheimer Primus-Linie,
Mainkai 36 am Eiserner Steg
(departure point)
☎ 281884

Bus tours of Frankfurt as well as walking tours are organised by the tourist office and depart from the tourist information offices at the airport, at the Hauptbahnhof and at the Römer, Römerberg 27. As schedules may change suffice it to say that these tours take place in summer and winter and they are normally available mornings at 10am and afternoons at 2pm. In winter they only take place in the mornings.

Freundeskreis Liebenswertes Frankfurt is a club whose members volunteer their time to escort small groups or individuals around Frankfurt. The tours are normally in English. Contact: Freundeskreis Liebenswertes Frankfurt, Melsunger Strasse 3 ☎ 479361

## Hafenbahn
As the timetable may be subject to variation it is best to inquire at one of the tourist offices. In general the train runs throughout the year on weekends, except in November. From April to December it leaves from the Eiserner Steg, hourly, from 10am-5pm.

Historische Eisenbahn Frankfurt (Hafenbahn)
Postfach 900345
D 6000 Frankfurt 90
☎ 069/436093 or 06171/700714

## Post Offices
The main post office is at Zeil 110. The one at the Hauptbahnhof has longer opening hours.

*A view of Old Miltenberg — the 'Pearl of the Main Valley'*

*The shopping centre at Bad Mergentheim*

## Tax Free Shopping

There is tax free shopping in Frankfurt and other German cities. VAT is refunded to all visitors of Germany who have their place of residence outside the European Community. Savings are between 9-11 per cent depending on the sum of goods purchased. Look out for shops with the TAX FREE sticker.

1. Ask for the Tax Free cheque when making purchases there.
2. Have German customs stamp this cheque on leaving the country. The items purchased may not be used before departure.
3. Europe Tax Free Shopping maintains refund points at all important border crossings, airports, harbours and railway stations where the cheque can be cashed. These refund points are listed on the cheque envelope. The tourist offices in Frankfurt have a booklet detailing this service and listing Tax Free shops in Frankfurt city. (The same applies to tourist offices in other German cities).

## Tourist Information Centres

Hauptbahnhof
Opposite track 23
Open: November to March, Monday to Saturday 8am-9pm, Sunday 9.30am-8pm. April to October Monday to Saturday 8am-10pm, Sunday 9.30am-8pm.
☎ 212 388 49 or 212 8851

Tourist Information Römer
Römerberg 27
Open: Monday to Friday 9am-7pm. Saturday and public holidays 9.30am-6pm. ☎ 212-38708

Bürgerauskunft
Römerberg 32
Open: Monday to Friday 8am-4.30pm.
☎ (069) 212-40000 (Römertelefon)

Tourist Information Flughafen (Frankfurt Airport)
Ankunfthalle (Arrival Hall) B
Open: daily 7am-10pm.
☎ 693153
(No room reservations)

Verkehrsamt
Kaiserstrasse 52
Open: Monday, Wednesday and Friday 8am-12noon.
☎ 212-38800

# Places of Interest in Heidelberg

### Apothekenmuseum

Open: April to October daily 10am-5pm. November to March, Saturday and Sunday only 11am-5pm.

### Grosses Fass (Wine Barrel)

Open: 1 April to 31 October 9am-7pm, 1 November to 31 March 9am-6pm.

### Karzer

Open: Monday to Saturday 9am-5pm.

### Kurpfälzisches Museum

Hauptstrasse 97
Open: Tuesday, Wednesday and Friday to Sunday 10am-5pm. Thursday 10am-9pm.

### Heidelberger Schloss

Open: 1 April to 31 October daily 9am-5pm. 1 November to March daily 9am-4pm.

**Universitätsbibliothek**
Open: Monday to Saturday
8.30am-4.30pm.

**Zoo**
Tiergartenstrasse 3
Open: from 1 April daily 9am-7pm,
from 1 October daily 9am-5pm.
☎ 480041

# Useful Information

**Area Code**
☎ 06621

**Boat Trips**
Season starts: Easter to 15 May,
from 15 September reduced
schedules.

Sight-seeing trips (Rundfahrten) on
the boats last about 40 minutes and
the return trip from Heidelberg to
Neckarsteinach lasts about 3 hours.

Information from: Rhein-Neckar-
Fahrgastschiffahrt ☎ (06221) 20181
or the Tourist Office.

**Cycle Hire**
At the Hauptbahnhof

**Car Breakdown**
☎ 19211 for 24 hour service

**Car Rental**
*Avis*
Bahnhofstrasse 2
☎ 22215

*Hertz*
Bergheimer Strasse 144, ☎ 23435

*Inter Rent*
Bergheimer Strasse 159, ☎ 20845

**Exchange Facilities**
This is available within the
Hauptbahnhof.

Open: Monday to Saturday 7am-
8pm, Sunday 9am-1pm.

**Guided Bus Tour of Heidelberg**
*Start:* Bismarckplatz and
Hauptbahnhof.
*Time:* May to October daily 10am
and 2pm, November to March only
Saturdays 2pm, April daily 2pm.
*Inquiries:* tourist office.
**Markets.**
On Markplatz: Wednesday and
Saturday. On Friedrich-Ebert-Platz,
Tuesday and Friday.

**Post Office**
The main branch is beside the
Hauptbahnhof. Open: Monday to
Friday 8am-6pm. Late counter
(Spätschalter) open: 6-9pm.
Saturday 8am-12noon
(Spätschalter) open: 12noon-3pm,
Sunday 10am-3pm.

**Tourist Office**
Open: Monday to Thursday and
Saturday 9am-7pm, Friday 9am-
9pm, Sunday 10am-6pm in
summer 10am-3pm in winter.
☎ 21341 or 27735
The tourist office publishes
*Heidelberg diese Woche* weekly,
giving information on events,
festivals etc.

# Places of Interest in Würzburg

**Dom St Kilian**
Domstrasse
Open: 1 November-Easter Monday
to Friday 10am-12noon and 2-5pm,
Sundays and public holidays 12.30-
1.30pm and 2.30-6pm. Easter-All
Saints Day Monday to Friday
10am-5pm, Sundays and public
holidays 1-6pm. Guided tours

April to October Monday to Saturday 12noon, Sundays and public holidays 12.30pm. Duration: about an hour.

**Festung Marienberg**
Open: guided tours April to September Tuesday to Sunday 9am-12noon and 1-5pm. October to March, Tuesday to Sunday 10am-12noon and 1-4pm.
☎ 44158

**Mainfränckisches Museum**
Festung Marienburg
Open: April to October daily 10am-5pm. November to March daily 10am-4pm. ☎ 43016

**Residenz** (Picture Gallery)
Open: April to end September daily except Monday 9am-5pm. October to end March daily except Mondays 10am-4pm.

# Useful Information

**Area Code**
☎ 0931

**Boat Trips**
Contact tourist office or: Schiffstouristik Kurth & Schiebe, St-Norbert-Strasse 9, D-8702 Zell ☎ 462982. Landing-place in Würzburg: Alter Kranen, Roter Kiosk (near Congress Centrum) ☎ 58573

Veitshöchheimer Personenschiffahrt Heinrich Herbert, Obere Maingasse 8, D-8707 Veitschöchheim, ☎ 91553. Landing place in Würzburg: Alter Kranen, Weisser Kiosk (near Congress Centrum), ☎ 55633.

Fränkische Personen-Schiffahrt Martin Dörr, Pleicherschulgasse 2, ☎ 55356 or 51722

**Car Rental**
*Avis*
Schürestrasse 2
☎ 50661

**Emergency Dentist** (Zahnarzt)
☎ 19222

**Emergency Doctor** (Arzt)
☎ 19222

**Guided Tours**
*By Bus*
*Start:* Omnibusbahnhof next to Bahnhof.
*Time:* mid-April to October Monday to Saturday 2.30pm, Sundays and public holidays 10.30am.
*Duration:* about 2 hours.
*Tickets:* tourist information at Hauptbahnhof, Haus zum Falken am Markt. On Sunday tickets sold directly on bus.

*On Foot* (in English)
*Start:* Tourist Information Haus zum Falken am Markt.
*Time:* end April to October, Tuesday to Saturday 2pm, not on Sundays and public holidays.
*Duration:* about 2 hours.
*Tickets:* Haus zum Falken.

**Tourist Offices**
Haus zum Falken am Markt
Open: Monday to Friday 9am-6pm. Saturday 9am-2pm.
☎ (0931) 37398

Pavillon am Hauptbahnhof
Open: Monday to Saturday 8am-8pm.
☎ (0931) 37436

Fremdenverkehrsamt
Palais am Congress Centrum
Open: Monday to Thursday 8am-4.30pm. Friday 8am-12noon.
☎ (0931) 37335

# Other Places of Interest

## Amorbach
Former Abteikirche (abbey church) with Bibliothek and Grüner Saal
Open: all year, daily. Guided tours of 35 minutes duration. Entry fee.
For further information contact Fürstliche Leiningsche Verwaltung Schlossplatz 1
☎ (09373) 3061

## Aschaffenburg
*Schloss Johannisburg*
Open: April to end September daily except Mondays 9am-12noon and 1-5pm. October to end March daily except Mondays 10am-12noon and 1-4pm.

## Bad Mergentheim
*Deutschordensmuseum*
(in the Schloss)
Open: March to October, Tuesday to Friday, Sunday & public holidays 10am-12noon and 2.30-5.30pm. November to February, Saturday, Sunday and public holidays only.
☎ (07931) 57209

## Darmstadt
*Schlossmuseum*
Open: Monday to Thursday 10am-1pm and 2-5pm, Saturday and Sunday 10am-1pm.

*Porzellansammlung*
Open: Monday to Thursday 10am-1pm and 2-5pm. Saturday and Sunday 10am-1pm.

## Erbach
*Elfenbeinmuseum*
Neues Bürgerhaus
Erbacher Festhalle

Open: Tuesday to Sunday 10am-12.30pm and 2-5pm.

*Schloss*
Open: April to November Sundays and public holidays 2-6pm.

## Langenburg
*Schloss Langenburg*
Open: Easter to mid-October daily 8.30am-12noon and 1.30-6pm.

*Auto-Museum*
Open: Easter to 1 November. Times as above.

## Mespelbrunn
*Wasserschloss Mespelbrunn*
Open: all year Monday to Saturday 9am-12noon and 1.30-5pm, Sundays 9.30am-6pm.

## Miltenberg
Free guided tours of town
(for individual travellers):
*Start:* Tourist Information Office, Rathaus, Engelplatz.
*Time:* 4 May to 26 October, Mondays and Saturdays 10.30am.

## Obernburg
*Museum Römerhaus*
Römerstrasse 62-64
☎ (06022) 50020
Open: during normal business hours.

## Schrozberg-Bartenstein
*Schloss Bartenstein*
*Militärmuseum*
Open: contact Stadtverwaltung
☎ (07935) 567

## Stuppach
*Church*
Open: daily April to October, 8.30am-5.30pm, November to March 8.30am-12noon and 1.30-5pm.

**Walldürn**
*Elfenbeinmuseum*
Burgstrasse
Open: guided tours take place
when the need arises. Ring at the
door.
☎ (06282) 67107

**Weikersheim**
*Schloss*
Guided tours daily April to
October 8.30am-6pm, November to
March 10am-12noon and 2-4pm.

**Wertheim**
*Glasmuseum*
Mühlenstrasse
☎ (09342) 6866
Open: daily, except Monday 10am-
12noon and 2-4pm. Entry fee.

**Zwingenberg**
*Burg Zwingenberg*
Guided tours May to September,
Tuesday, Friday and Sunday 2-
4.30pm.

# Tourist Information Centres

**Aschaffenburg**
Stadthalle am Schloss
Schlossplatz 1
8750 Aschaffenburg
☎ (06021) 30-230 and -330

Dalbergstrasse 6
☎ 06021/30426 or 23744
For general information about the
Aschaffenburg region contact:
Spessart-Main-Odenwald
Bayernstrasse 18
D-8750 Aschaffenburg
☎ (06021) 394271

**Bad Mergentheim**
Städtisches Kultur- und
Verkehrsamt
Marktplatz 3
6990 Bad Mergentheim
☎ (07931) 57135

**Creglingen**
Verkehrsamt
Postfach 20
6993 Creglingen
☎ (07933) 631 and 70-111. After
hours ☎ (09335) 300

**Darmstadt**
Neues Rathaus
Luisenplatz 55
Open: Monday to Friday 9am-6pm,
Saturday 9am-5pm.
☎ (06151) 132071

Hauptbahnhof
☎ (06151) 132783

**Iphofen**
Rathaus und Heimat- und
Fremdenverkehrsverein
Marktplatz 27
8715 Iphofen
☎ (09323) 3095

**Ochsenfurt**
Fremdenverkehrsbüro
Hauptstrasse 39
8703 Ochsenfurt
☎ (09331) 5855 and 9749

**Rohrbrunn** (near Mespelbrunn)
Tourist Information Franken
Am Rasthof im Spessart-Süd
(On A3 motorway)
Open: Easter to mid-October daily
10am-1pm and 2-7pm.
☎ (06094) 220
(For general information about the
Bavarian Spessart and Franconia)

**Tauberbischofsheim**
Städtisches Kultur- und
Verkehrsamt
Rathaus
Marktplatz 8
6972 Tauberbischofsheim
Postfach 1480
☎ (09341) 80313
For general information about the
Tauberbischofsheim area contact
Gebietsgemeinschaft 'Liebliches
Taubertal'
Landratsamt
Gartenstrasse 1
6972 Tauberbischofsheim
☎ (09341) 82-0

**Veitshöchheim**
Fremdenverkehrsamt
Erwin-Vornberger-Platz
8707 Veitschöchheim
☎ (0931) 9009639

**Volkach**
Verkehrsamt
Rathaus
8712 Volkach
☎ (09381) 40112

**Walldürn**
Städtisches Verkehrsamt
Hauptstrasse 27
Open: Monday to Friday 8.30am-
12noon and Thursday 2-4pm.
☎ (06282) 67107

**Weikersheim**
Kultur- und Verkehrsverein
6992 Weikersheim
☎ (07934) 7272

**Worms**
Neumarkt 14
Open: Monday to Friday 9am-
12noon and 2-5pm, April to
October. Saturday 9am-12noon.
☎ 06241 25045 or 853560

# 2

# *RHINELAND-PALATINATE AND SAARLAND*

---

The three tours in this chapter cover a region which is largely neglected even in the local travel literature. The area described is wedged in between the Mosel (Moselle) and Rhein (Rhine) rivers, with France forming a border to the south. It is perhaps the very proximity of these popular river valleys that has allowed this region to escape relatively unscathed from the effects of mass tourism. The start of the first route in Bad Kreuznach is not much more than an hour from Frankfurt — most of the way on the Autobahn — or a short journey by train from Bingen am Rhein.

## Route 5 • Along The Nahe Valley And Into The Hunsrück 141km (88 miles)

The Nahe river flows into the Rhein at Bingen and those who trouble to follow its valley upstream will be rewarded not only with ancient castle ruins and mines, where precious stones have been quarried for centuries, but also with the peace and beauty of a landscape free of tourist crowds. Sandwiched in between the Nahe and Mosel rivers the sparsely settled heights of the Hunsrück are, if anything, even further off the beaten track, yet they offer in the interplay of village, fields and forest an austere beauty all of their own.

❋    **Bad Kreuznach** claims to be the world's oldest radon-salt-water spa. Radon is a radioactive gas which is used in the treatment of a number of illnesses and it occurs here naturally. What is left of the oldest part of town is to be found along the River Nahe. There is a small car park at one end of the bridge known as the Wilhelms-1brücke, at the other end of which is the Fausthaus. This attractive half-timbered building was temporarily the home of the legendary Dr Faustus. Further upstream is the old Nahe bridge with its famous

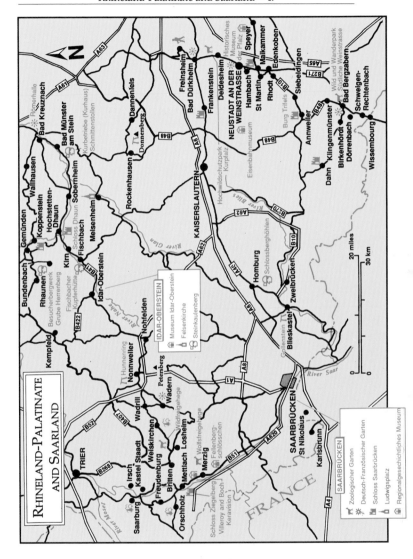

houses on the bridge. It was built in the thirteenth century, while the
houses upon it date partly from the late fifteenth century. On an
island directly below the bridge is Pauluskirche (St Paul's Church)
(1511-32). The Gothic choir bears the name Englische Kirche (English

Church) because it was long used by the once numerous English spa guests. On the 19 June 1843 Karl Marx was married here to Jenny von Westfalen. Also of interest in town is the Römerhalle, with some outstanding exhibits from the time of Roman settlement in the area. Two Roman floor mosaics rank along with that in Nennig on the Mosel as being the most important of their kind north of the Alps.

Only 5km (3 miles) further south, nestled under imposing cliffs topped by the ruins of Rheingrafenstein, is the much smaller spa town of **Bad Münster am Stein**. Near the Kurbetriebe (Kurhaus) which is set in a pleasant garden is a large, elongated construction, used in open-air therapy and known in German as a *Gradierwerk*. Water saturated in radon drips down through the densely packed twigs of the *Gradierwerk* to be blown out by the wind as a fine spray which is inhaled by the spa guests seated next to it. Similar constructions will have been glimpsed in the so-called Salinental (Saline valley) on the way from Bad Kreuznach.

The most direct way to Rheingrafenstein is to cross the Nahe on the small ferry that starts from the river promenade. It is pulled across by the ferry-man with the aid of a rope and docks by the restaurant on the opposite bank. From here it is a pleasant, though fairly steep climb through woods up to the ruins. At the top the panorama is splendid and there are good views of the Ebernburg, a castle now used as a hotel. Back down on the Nahe promenade there are pedalos for hire.

A short excursion from Bad Münster is to drive via Feilbingert to the Lemberger Hütte (a restaurant which is closed on Mondays). Follow the green signs which read first Ebernburg, then Schmittenstollen and Lemberg. The sign '**Schmittenstollen**' eventually indicates a turn-off before the Lemberg, 422m (1,384ft) leading to a disused quicksilver mine. Because tours of the mine are organised privately and their continuation is by no means certain it would be wise to inquire whether it is open at the Kurhaus in Bad Münster. It is also possible to walk down to the mine from the Lemberger Hütte, near a viewpoint on the Lemberg. There are plenty of walks around here and one leads to the Silbersee, a tiny lake just over a kilometre from the restaurant.

For those who already want to join the start of Route 7 take the B48 south to Hochspeyer, near Kaiserslautern, via Alsenz and Rockenhausen. From there take the B37 to Bad Dürkheim. On the way it is worth a detour from Rockenhausen to visit the **Donnersberg** (687m 2,253ft), the highest elevation in the Palatinate. Apart from attractive scenery there is a site of major archaeological importance here; the fortified remnants of a Celtic settlement. It was built in the second century BC and an archaeological trail skirts restored fragments of the fortifications. The Donnersberg has been declared a nature reserve and has an ample network of marked walking paths.

From Bad Münster take the scenic Nahe Weinstrasse (Nahe Wine Road) via Norheim in the direction of Sobernheim. The turn-off is to the right, just before the main part of town, coming from Bad Kreuznach. On the way pass vineyards clutching precariously to the base of sheer cliffs known as the **Rotenfels** (Red Cliffs). Anybody wishing to enjoy the views at the top should follow the sign Traisen/ Rotenfels on the outskirts of Norheim. There is parking near the restaurant-pension Zur Bastei. The path along the cliffs must be one of the most spectacular in all Rhineland-Palatinate.

Cross the Nahe river to Oberhausen an der Nahe over the stone Luitpoldbrücke (1889). From here it is a short scenic drive via Odernheim an der Glan (the railway lines follow virtually the same route) to **Sobernheim**. In town there are a couple of interesting churches, but the main attraction is a little out of town in the Nachtigallental. In this pretty valley is a Freilichtmuseum (Open-Air Museum) which preserves original old buildings once typical for this part of Germany. By following the Glan river south from Odernheim it is possible to visit the historic town of **Meisenheim**. Apart from all the beautiful old houses the main building of interest is the Schlosskirche (1479-1504), a late Gothic church which is considered the most important of its type in this region.

From Sobernheim take the B41 west to **Hochstetten-Dhaun**. Schloss Dhaun holds a commanding position over the Simmer valley. This massive castle was built as a fortress in the twelfth century and after 1729 expanded as a Baroque palace. Parts of the castle are used as a school but the dungeons and park can be visited. They are open from dawn until dusk.

A little outside Hochstetten-Dhaun a turn-off to the right leads past a quarry to **Kirn**. The Altstadt with its cafés and fountains is located near the Hahnenbach stream, making it a pleasant spot to stop and sample a Kirner Pils, just one of the locally brewed beers. Above town the Kyrburg dates back to the twelfth century, but it was completely destroyed in 1734. There is parking at the castle ruins near a rather expensive gourmet restaurant. The ruins are open from dawn to dusk. An alternative to the restaurant would be to picnic amidst the ruins and enjoy superb views over Kirn and the Hahnenbach valley. This area, as indeed the entire Hunsrück, makes

*The ruins of the twelfth-century Kyrburg at Kirn*

*Street musicians entertain the visitors at Bad Münster am Stein*

ideal walking country and it would be more than worthwhile to invest in a *Wanderkarte* (walking map) in order to explore it more thoroughly — inquire at local bookshops for suitable maps. By following the road along the Hahnenbachtal a short-cut can be taken to Rhaunen, a point mentioned further along on this route.

Continue on the B41 to **Fischbach**. Turn right into town and follow the sign 'Historisches Kupferbergwerk' (Copper Mine) in the direction of Berschweiler. This medieval mining complex is unique in Europe. There is even evidence that already the Romans and Celts extracted copper-ore from this area. Entering the mine is a fascinating experience even for those who are not so interested in mining techniques as the mine's cavernous tunnels are covered with glittering crystals. Stalactites have also formed over the centuries which reflect emerald green and turquoise blue in the artificial light. After centuries of exploitation the mine was finally closed down at the end of the eighteenth century. Return to the B41.

**Idar-Oberstein** is one of the oldest centres of the gem cutting and polishing industry in Germany. The Museum Idar-Oberstein (open daily) is well worth visiting for its fascinating collection of precious stones and locally made jewellery. Though modest quantities of precious stones are still mined locally the industry has been kept going with imported stones. This, however, has been enough to allow the town to develop as a leading European centre for the gem trade. The Diamond and Gem Exchange is situated further along the Hauptstrasse. In the same building is the Deutsches Edelsteinmuseum (German Gem Museum). Anyone looking for souvenirs can find jewellery shops all over town.

A bizarre sight directly above the Museum Idar-Oberstein is a white church set in a sheer rock face. A path leads up to the appropriately named **Felsenkirche** (Cliff Church) and the two ruined castles behind it. The church was built between 1482 and 1484 and can be visited from Easter until the end of October. It is also possible to drive up to the castles and walk down to the church. Take the Schlossstrasse up and park in the Strasse am Schlossweiher. A path leads from here to the castles.

Before leaving Idar-Oberstein it is well worth visiting the **Steinkaulenberg** just outside town. This is the only gem mine in Europe which is open to the public. As some of the shafts can only be visited by prior arrangement it is best to ask at the Verkehrsamt first. To join Route 6 go south on the B41 to Nohfelden, then follow the oak leaf symbol of the Hochwaldstrasse to Nonnweiler. The A62 also runs close to Nonnweiler. Connect from B41 just before Nohfelden.

Take the B422 north from Idar-Oberstein. Turn off left to Algenrodt to get to Steinkaulenberg and Katzenloch. Follow the road right, off the B422, to **Kempfeld**, a popular holiday resort in the northern extremities of the Naturpark Saar-Hunsrück. Not far from the village is the Wildenburg, a former ruin that has been partly rebuilt as a restaurant. The keep was completely reconstructed and is now a look-out tower. Near the castle are the impressive remains of a 2,000-year-old Celtic fortress. Also close is a Wildgehege.

From Kempfeld the route continues down the Fischbachtal to **Herrstein**. Follow the sign 'Historischer Ortskern' to a car park. Before 1975 Herrstein did not look much different from other rural Hunsrück villages but during a period of recession a scheme was initiated to give work to local tradesmen. The result is a beautifully restored village centre with houses dating back to the sixteenth century. Another reason why the village is reasonably well pre-served is that during the Palatinate War of Succession, in the sev-enteenth century, the citizens of Herrstein pulled down large parts of their own town wall, in order to show they had no intent of resisting invaders. Marshal Turenne and his troops were convinced by this extraordinary act of self-preservation and they left Herrstein alone.

Return a short way back up the Fischbachtal and turn right to get to **Rhaunen** via Breitental and Sulzbach. There is an interesting Rathaus here and in the Protestant parish church is one of the very first organs built by the Stumm family. The Stumms began making organs in Sulzbach in the early eighteenth century and soon estab-lished a wide reputation which was kept up for 140 years.

Near **Bundenbach**, south of Rhaunen, are the sprawling ruins of the Schmidtburg and a reconstructed Celtic village. Between the two is the **Grube Herrenberg**, a slate mine that has been worked since the sixteenth century. As fossils which date back some 350 million years have been found here the mine will certainly be of interest to amateur palaeontologists. All these sites are closely grouped amidst pictur-esque scenery and are linked by walking trails.

After Rhaunen the quiet country road passes through the villages of Woppenroth and Schlierschied to eventually reach **Gemünden**, a small town lying deep in the Soonwald (Soon Forest). The castle (not open to the public) with its four massive turrets, rises imposingly above town. Here too it is impossible to forget the Hunsrück's fascinating geology. On the edge of town is a geological trail and yet another mine known as the Kaisergrube. It is also a slate mine and next to it is a museum where locally found fossils are on display.

Follow the sign Bad Kreuznach/Argenschwang out of town. The road snakes its way through woods, only occasionally passing a forester's house or a small village. **Koppenstein** is a ruined castle hidden amongst trees a short distance from Gemünden. The keep still stands and from the top there are tremendous views over vast stretches of forest. Further down the road, to the left, is a car park from where a path leads up to the Alteburg. In 1890 a look-out tower was erected here in the form of a medieval castle's keep.

Continue around the villages of Winterbach and Gebroth to reach **Argenschwang**. The castle ruins of the Rosenburg date back to the twelfth century. Just to the north in Spabrücken is an interesting pilgrimage church built between 1731 and 1736. The interior is decorated in Baroque-Rococo style and on the roof are two very picturesque ridge turrets. Follow the Gräfenbach stream to **Dalberg** where there is yet another massive castle hunched over a tiny village. The castle was built in 1150 and was never destroyed in war. With the discovery of gunpowder it lost its significance and slowly started crumbling. Although locals have used it as a stone quarry it is still worth exploring.

Approaching **Wallhausen** the forest now gives way to vineyards which cling to steep valley slopes. In the village the golden opportunity offers itself to sample local wine at the Prinz-Salm-Dalbergisches Weingut, located in the old Schloss. The 'Wein-Cabinet', where wine tastings take place, benefits from the rustic atmosphere of its vaulted cellar. From here it is only a few kilometres via Hargesheim back to Bad Kreuznach.

# Route 6 • The Saarland 91km (56 miles)

Bordering France and Luxembourg the Saarland is Germany's smallest state, with the exception of city-states like Bremen and Hamburg. It has changed hands between France and Germany several times in the course of history and the French influence is reflected not only in the cuisine. Past industries (coal and steel) have given the region an undeservedly bad reputation as far as scenery is concerned. Although the industrial towns are there it is also true that 48 per cent of the land is used agriculturally and some 33 per cent is covered by forest. Again it is a region well worth exploring for those who want to get off the beaten track.

**Nonnweiler** is situated on the fringes of the Naturpark Saar-Hunsrück and is surrounded by conifer and deciduous forests. Just north of the neighbouring town of Otzenhausen, on the Dollberg, are the remnants of the Hunnenring. This Celtic ring fortification is over

2,000 years old and ranks as one of the best preserved prehistoric sights of its kind. Another attraction to the north of Nonnweiler is the Priems-Stausee (a reservoir). To the south the modest heights of the Petersberg (566m 1,857ft) allow for downhill skiing and there are also prepared trails for cross-country skiers. The Bostalsee is another lake to the east which is very popular for water sports. You can camp at the lake.

The route continues along the Hochwaldstrasse (High Forest Road) which is symbolised with a green oak leaf on road signs, through the village of Wadrill, to Weiskirchen. A detour from Wadrill can be made along the pretty Wadrill stream to **Wadern**, the most important town in the area known as the Hochwald. Places of interest include Schloss Dagstuhl (now an old peoples' home) with its attached Schlosskapelle. This chapel has a Baroque interior and serves as a gallery for paintings by the aristocratic artist Octavie de Lasalle von Louisenthal. The Öttinger Schlösschen (1759) now houses the Stadtmuseum (town museum). Swimming is possible at the nearby Noswendelsee.

**Weiskirchen** is a Luftkurort (climatic health resort) and headquarters for the Naturpark Saar-Hunsrück in the Saarland. That should be enough to suggest that it is above all the landscape that is of interest here. Nearby in **Rappweiler** is a 75 hectare Wildfreigehege (game enclosure) in which deer, wisent and moufflon can be viewed in natural surroundings. From here a detour can be made to Losheim where the main attraction is yet another lake. A walk around it would take about an hour. For railway enthusiasts it should be mentioned that an old steam train still runs along a 19km (12 miles) stretch of track. Inquire at the Modell-Eisenbahn Club Losheim or at the Gemeindeverwaltung (town council). Verkehrsverein Losheim, Postfach 1169 ☎ (06872) 6169; MECL-Eisenbahnfreunde, Tulpenstrasse 6, 6646 Losheim ☎ (06872) 3592.

The Hochwaldstrasse continues from Rappweiler through Britten, where the largest ilex plantation in Europe is to be found, to **Mettlach**. This town lies in the most beautiful part of the Saar valley. The old Benedictine abbey buildings (eighteenth century) were bought in 1809 by the Luxembourger industrialist Jean Francois Boch in an auction. Since then the former abbey has been headquarters for the ceramic firm of Villeroy and Boch. Inside is a video-theatre which informs about the firm and its products. In the park is Mettlach's landmark, the Alter Turm (994), and a ceramic sculpture titled *Homo ceramicus mettlachiensis* — the visitor can be left in no doubt that the ceramic industry is the dominating factor here! In

*Hoar frost in the woods of the Soonwald*

*The Saarschleife can be viewed by boat from Mettlach or from the 'Cloef' look-out point*

nearby Schloss Ziegelberg (1879) is the very interesting Keramikmuseum (Ceramic Museum).

From Mettlach's neo-Romanesque parish church a path leads to St Gangolf and then to the ruins of Burg Montclair (fifteenth century). This castle is situated on a tongue of land surrounded by a loop in the Saar river known as the Saarschleife. An earlier castle on the same spot was destroyed by Balduin, the Archbishop of Trier, in 1351.

A short distance away in the village of **Orscholz** follow the signs to the look-out point 'Cloef'. From here there are impressive views over the Saarschleife. Fortunately the canalisation of the Saar has done little to detract from the majestic beauty of the scene. There are restaurants close to the car park and also a small amusement park. Boat trips around the Saarschleife begin from Mettlach.

A longer excursion from Mettlach can be made north via Freudenburg to Saarburg. To the north-east of Freudenburg, near Kastel-Staadt, is a neo-Romanesque chapel built next to the so-called Mönchsklause, a hermit's refuge carved into cliffs high above the Saar river. **Saarburg** itself lies at the confluence of the Leukbach and Saar, but it is the Leukbach which gives the town its unique character. This stream flows through the middle of town, plunging as a 20m (65ft) cascade past picturesque old houses down to the Saar. Above town are the impressive ruins of the over 1,000-year-old Saarburg. Good views can be had from here over rests of the old town walls and the vineyard covered slopes of the Saar valley. Visits can be arranged — ask at the Verkehrsamt — to the Glockengiesserei (bell-foundry) Mabilon in the Altstadt. Bells from this factory are exported all over the world. Across the Saar the wine-growing village of Irsch is reputed to be one of the prettiest in the area, with forest reaching right down to the village outskirts.

Return to Mettlach by crossing the Saar to Beurig and then follow the river south via Serrig. In **Beurig** the pilgrimage church of Maria Heimsuchung is worth a pause. **Serrig** is chiefly famous for its Sekt (German champagne) but Schloss Saarfels and remnants of a Roman settlement are still worth a look.

Take the B51 south from Mettlach to **Merzig**. The town's proudest cultural possession is the Peterskirche (dating around 1200), which is the most important monument from the Romanesque period in the Saarland. Other places of interest are the Stadthaus (1649), the neighbouring Staadt-Marxsche Bürgerhaus (1750) and the Heilig-Kreuz-Kapelle. In the Fellenbergschlösschen is an interesting town museum. North of town, in the Kammerforst, is a wolf enclosure (Wolfsfreigehege). Also worth mentioning is the fact that Merzig's many apple orchards have given rise to a 'Viezfest' that takes place on the first Saturday of October. *Viez* is the local name for apple cider. Continue on the B51 or the Autobahn running parallel to Saarbrücken.

**Saarbrücken** is the capital of the Saarland and is situated right next to the French border. Everything of importance built in the Baroque style stems from the architect F.J. Stengel (1694-1787). The Ludwigskirche (1761) in Alt-Saarbrücken is considered the most important Protestant church in south-west Germany and is Stengel's most mature work. He also planned the Ludwigsplatz and Altes Rathaus. Schloss Saarbrücken was destroyed many times in the course of history and what can be seen today is based on Stengel's Baroque version. The Schloss now contains the Regional-geschichtliches Museum (Museum of Regional History). Worth noting in the St Johann quarter of the city is the Bergwerksdirektion (nineteenth century), neo-Gothic Rathaus and the St Johannkirche, which is once again by Stengel. Another outstanding church in Saarbrücken is the Stiftskirche (1270-1330) in St Arnual.

Among the sights outside the city centre are the zoo, which can be reached with buses 14, 17, 18 and 31, and the Deutsch-Französischer Garten (German-French Garden). This large park has a number of attractions, including the 'Gulliver-Mini-Welt' with its large-scale models of famous buildings from all over the world. It can be reached with the number 11 bus from the Hauptbahnhof. There is another tourist office here.

Perhaps the proximity of the French border has influenced Saarbrücken's reputation for fine cuisine. Whatever the case it has even been claimed that French gourmets cross the border to enjoy the city's specialities. It might also be French *joie de vivre* that plays a part in the Saarbrücker's love of festivities. Early in the year they celebrate carnival (Premabüba), in June and July the Altstadtfest and at Christmas there is a Weihnachtsmarkt, to name just a few.

There are a surprising number of things to be seen in the vicinity of Saarbrücken and what follows is simply a brief summary of some of the most interesting. To the north-east, in **Homburg**, are the Schlossberghöhlen, Europe's largest sandstone caverns. South of here, at Schwarzenacker, are the rests of a Roman settlement. **Blieskastel** is a short distance further south again and on a hill near the town is the Hohberg, central Europe's largest menhir. It is known as the Gollenstein and has been dated as being over 4,000 years old. **Zweibrücken** is also close and this town is famed for its rose garden and the regular equestrian events which are held. South-west of

*Opposite: Ludwigskirche, at Saarbrücken*

Saarbrücken, in the woods of the Warndt, is Karlsbrunn. In 1741 a certain J.N. Eisenhauer emigrated from this village to the USA and one of his descendants became president — Dwight D. Eisenhower. The neighbouring village of **St Nikolaus** is not only a favourite address for children writing to Santa Claus but a popular Nikolaus-Markt (Christmas fair) is also held here on the 6 December.

# Route 7 • The Deutsche Weinstrasse 73km (45 miles)

The **Deutsche Weinstrasse** (German Wine Road) runs along the east flank of Germany's largest nature park, the Naturpark Pfälzer Wald (Palatinate Forest). Innumerable trails criss-cross the nature park's mountainous landscape making it a veritable walkers' paradise. For those who would prefer to walk, rather than drive this route, it is possible to follow the Wanderweg Deutsche Weinstrasse for some 100km (62 miles). It closely follows the motoring route right down to the French border. Good walking maps are put out by the *Fietz Verlag* covering both the Deutsche Weinstrasse and the Pfälzer Wald to a scale of 1:50,000.

The towns and villages of the Weinstrasse are alluring not so much for any outstanding cultural sights, although there is plenty of historical interest, but for the unique atmosphere they generate. The less polished fronts of houses, with grape-vines curling around the doors, the cobbled streets lined with shady trees, the outdoor cafés; these are just some of the ingredients which combine to give an overall impression reminiscent of the Mediterranean, rather than central Europe.

**Bad Dürkheim** is both a spa and wine-growing town. Here it seems that the consumption of alcohol and the pursuit of good health need not be mutually exclusive. The annual Dürkheimer Wurstmarkt (Sausage Fair) in September is reputed to be the largest wine festival in the world. The centre of the festive activities is the 'Riesenfass' (Giant Barrel) with a capacity of 1.7 million litres. The barrel, however, does not store enormous quantities of wine but houses a wine-bar and restaurant instead!

At the Kurhaus in the centre of town is a casino but those who are not interested in gambling can also visit the Johanneskirche, which dates back to the fourteenth century. Just outside town are the ruins of the Hardenburg, once one of Germany's mightiest castles, and

Kloster Limburg both of which are open from dawn until dusk. There is a tavern at this monastery and in summer orchestral concerts and theatrical performances take place here.

A few kilometres north of Bad Dürkheim just off the B271 is the small fortified town of **Freinsheim**. An interesting walk can be taken around the town's medieval walls. The most attractive of the remaining gates is the Eisernes Tor (fifteenth century). Also of interest are the Rathaus (1750) and parish church dating around 1780.

A very picturesque detour from the Weinstrasse into the Pfälzer Wald can be made from Bad Dürkheim by taking the B37 west. Near the point where the detour returns on the B39 to the Weinstrasse is the ruin of **Frankenstein** castle. The castle was erected as a border fortress against Kaiserslautern by the counts of Leiningen in the thirteenth century. The B39 continues to Neustadt.

The main route continues south on the B271. Along the way there are plenty of opportunities to stop and buy wine. **Wachenheim** is famed for its Sekt and the Hochwildschutzpark Kurpfalz a combination of amusement park and zoo. The history of **Deidesheim** goes back nearly 1,300 years and there is still a bit of historical interest to see. The Gasthof Zur Kanne is one of the oldest hostelries in Germany, having offered shelter to pilgrims as far back as 1160. At the Weingut Bassermann-Jordan is an especially interesting Holzfasskeller (wine barrel cellar) which can be viewed on request. Of the numerous local festivals one of the most famous is the Geissbockversteigerung (Goat Auction), during Whitsuntide. According to tradition a billy-goat had to be presented annually by the villagers of Lambrecht to Deidesheim as payment for the right to graze their goats on land belonging to Deidesheim. This tradition is now over 600 years old.

**Neustadt an der Weinstrasse** forms the largest wine-growing community in Germany. In October the Weinlesefest (Harvest Festival) is held, a highlight of which is a huge procession. The old town is quite well preserved and among other things the Gothic collegiate church in the Marktplatz deserves attention. Strangely enough the church is shared by both the Catholic and Lutheran faiths. A wall divides the one section from the other. Next to the railway station is an Eisenbahnmuseum (Railway Museum, open Sundays). There are plenty of Strausswirtschaften (wine-growers' inns) to be found around town in summer. They get their name from the wreath of twigs, or *Strauss*, that usually hangs outside and offer cheap snacks as well as local wine.

A short excursion from Neustadt can be made to the **Hambacher**

**Schloss**. Drive in the direction of Edenkoben, then follow signs pointing uphill to the right. The Schloss has become a symbol of the struggle for democratic rights in Germany. In 1832 some 30,000 people gathered here to protest against feudalism and demand greater political freedom. From the castle terrace there are good views. There is a restaurant here. The Schloss is also a popular starting point for walks in the neighbouring forest. A few kilometres to the east of Neustadt, near **Hassloch**, is the Holiday Park, another amusement park.

A longer excursion from Neustadt is to follow the B39 east to **Speyer**, on the Rhein river. The cathedral is a masterpiece of Roman-esque architecture and is the last resting place of four emperors, four kings, three empresses and a princess. It is also a monument to Germany's imperial history in the Middle Ages. Near the cathedral is the Historisches Museum der Pfalz (Historical Museum of the Palatinate) which also includes a wine museum. To get to the Altpörtel, one of Germany's most beautiful gate-towers, go west from the cathedral along the Maximilianstrasse. It is worth climbing to the top for the excellent views.

The main route continues south from Neustadt through some of the most attractive villages on the Weinstrasse. **Maikammer** has many pretty old dwellings and an interesting parish church (1757) with a Rococo interior. A recommended drive from here is up to the Kalamit (697m 2,287ft), the highest mountain in the Pfälzer Wald. At the top is a look-out-tower and restaurant. The neighbouring village of **St Martin** is especially picturesque and above the village the Kropsburg (thirteenth century) offers good views and wine in its restaurant.

**Edenkoben** is easily reached from St Martin. Worth seeing is the former Cistercian Kloster, now a wine estate with interesting cellars. An excursion from here is up to the Rietburg, a couple of kilometres away in the uplands of the Pfälzer Wald. There is ample parking near the chair-lift, which takes visitors up to this ruined castle. The views from the restaurant at the top are supposed to be the best in the entire Palatinate, at least when it is not hazy. There is a small deer enclosure close by. Schloss Ludwigshöhe, near the foot of the chair-lift, was built for King Ludwig I of Bavaria and has a permanent exhibition of works by the impressionist painter Max Slevogt. Good wines from the area come under the labels 'Heidegarten', 'Kirchberg' and 'Heiligkreuz'.

Only a couple of kilometres away **Rhodt** is yet another pretty wine-growing village. There are good views back to Schloss

*Zweibrücken is famed for its equestrian competitions*

*The welcoming sign above a Strausswirtschaft where local food and drink is available, Neustadt an der Weinstrasse*

*Refreshments at the Hambacher Schloss can be followed by a walk in the nearby forests*

Ludwigshöhe from the top end of the village. Every year at Whitsun the locals celebrate the Kastanienblütenfest (Chestnut Blossom Festival). The Weinstrasse continues on a minor road past Burrweiler and Gleisweiler, until after Albersweiler it joins the B10 to Annweiler.

The main attraction near **Annweiler** is Burg Trifels with its two neighbouring castles Anebos and Münz. Trifels was one of Kaiser Barbarossa's favourite castles and from 1193 to 1194 it also served as a prison for King Richard the Lionheart. It is possible to drive up to the castle, a 15 minute walk from the car park, or to include it in the course of a 2 hour circular walk from town. Annweiler's Catholic church has some beautiful interior frescoes.

From Annweiler join the B48 south to **Klingenmünster**, where there are the ruins of a medieval Benedictine abbey as well as a castle. West of the town via Münchweiler and 8km (5 miles) north-west of

Bad Bergzabern is the Wild und Wanderpark Südliche Weinstrasse. In two large enclosures are a variety of animals, including deer and wild-boars. A Naturlehrpfad (Nature Trail) goes through the Wanderpark and can be walked in about an hour.

**Bad Bergzabern** is the last town of any size on the Weinstrasse. Among the historical sights are the Herzogliches Schloss (sixteenth century, not open to the public) and the Gasthaus zum Engel. A detour west on the B427 to Dahn goes through an area that is littered with ruined castles. **Dahn** has three castles of a type common in this area, so-called 'Felsenburgen' or 'cliff fortresses'. The bizarre rock formations in the vicinity are also an attraction.

To connect with Route 8 (Chapter 3) go east from Bad Bergzabern on the B427 to Kandel. From here connect with the A65/B10 to Karlsruhe, then go south on the B36 to Rastatt — both Karlsruhe and Rastatt are referred to in Route 8. The start of Route 8 at Baden-Baden is only a few kilometres further south, just off the B3.

The last leg of the Weinstrasse continues south on the B38. The pretty village of **Dörrenbach** is worth a detour on the way to **Schweigen-Rechtenbach**, on the French border. It was here that the idea of the Deutsche Weinstrasse originated, as an attempt on the part of local wine-growers to win publicity for their wine in a time of recession. They erected the present Weintor (Wine Gate) in 1936 after an earlier version built of wood was destroyed in a storm. Beyond the gate, in France, the route is continued as the Alsatian Weinstrasse.

# Additional Information

## Places of Interest in Saarbrücken

*Deutsch-Französischer Garten*
Metzer Strasse
Can be reached with buses 11, 12, 14, 19. Buses following line 11 start from Hauptbahnhof and 14 from Rathaus. Open: during the season mid-April to mid-October 8am-6pm.

*Regionalgeschichtliches Museum*
(Museum of Regional History)
In the south wing of the Schloss
Entrance at Talstrasse
Open: Tuesday to Sunday, 10am-

6pm. No entry charge.
☎ (0681) 506-549

*Schloss Saarbrücken*
Schlossplatz 15
Open: free guided tours Wednesday, Thursday, Friday and Saturday 4.30pm. Sundays 11am and 4.30pm.
☎ (0681) 506247

*Zoologischer Garten*
Graf-Stauffenberg-Strasse
6600 Saarbrücken 3
Open: in summer 8.30am-6pm. In winter 8.30am-5pm.
☎ (0681) 812494

# Useful Information

## Accommodation

Youth Hostel (Jugendherberge)
Meerwiesertalweg 31
☎ (0681) 33040

*Camping Grounds*
Campingplatz Saarbrücken 1
Am Spicherer Berg (near Deutsch-
Französischer Garten)
☎ (0681) 51780

Campingplatz Burbach
Saarbrücken 5
Saaranlage
Mettlacher Strasse
☎ (0681) 76121

## Boat Trips

Contact: Familie Hauck
☎ (0681) 34084

Amt für Öffentlichkeitsarbeit,
Kongress und Touristik

Rathaus
Open: Monday to Friday 8.30am-
12noon and 1.30-3.30pm.
☎ (0681) 905-1404, Saturdays 36515

## Bus Tours

April to mid-October Saturday
2.30pm, from Kongresshalle.
☎ (0681) 905-1404

## Concerts

Funkhaus Halberg
Fridays

Kongresshalle
Sundays

Musikhochschule
Wednesdays
The above (classical) concerts are
sponsored by Saarländischer
Rundfunk ☎ (0681) 602-2211,
otherwise contact the tourist office
for further information.

Johanniskirche
Organ concerts (Orgelkonzerte)
For programme information ☎
(0681) 31261 or contact tourist
office.

## Market Days

(Markets usually take place during
the morning).

*St Johanner Markt*
Monday, Wednesday, Friday

*Ludwigsplatz*
Tuesday, Thursday, Saturday

*Marktplatz Dudweiler*
Tuesday, Friday

*Burbacher Markt*
Wednesday, Saturday

*Malstatter Markt*
Tuesday, Friday

*St Arnual*
Thursday

*Flea Market*
St Johanner Markt
Every second Saturday of the
month.

## Travel

*Train Connections*
There is an hourly Intercity
connection to and from
Saarbrücken. For further information ☎ (0681) 19419.

*Flughafen* (Airport)
Saarbrücken Ensheim
The airport is 12km (7 miles) from
the city. There is a bus connection
to the inner-city with line 27. Free
parking at airport. Flight information: ☎ (06893) 83-272.

*Public Transport*
The 24-Stundenkarte (24-Hour
Ticket) is valid for the entire inner-

city. It can be bought from a ticket vending machine or on the bus. Further details can be obtained from the city tourist offices.

## Tourist Offices

**Saarbrücken**
Verkehrsverein
Rathausplatz
6600 Saarbrücken
Open: Monday to Friday 7.15am-12.30pm and 1.30-4.15pm.
☎ (0681) 36901

Verkehrsamt
Trierer Strasse 2
(near railway station)
Open: Monday to Friday 7.30am-8pm. Saturday 7.30am-4pm.
☎ (0681) 3098-222

Verkehrsamt
5510 Saarburg
☎ (06581) 81215 or 81216

Fremdenverkehrsverband Saarland
Postfach 242
D-6600 Saarbrücken
☎ (0681) 35376
(A place to write to for general information)

## *Other Places of Interest*

**Annweiler**
*Burg Trifels*
Open: April to September, Wednesday to Sunday 9am-1pm and 2-6pm. October, November and January to March 9am-1pm and 2-6pm.

**Bad Bergzabern**
*Wild und Wanderpark Südliche Weinstrasse*
Open: March to November 8.30am,

December to February 10am to dusk.

**Bad Kreuznach**
*Römerhalle*
Hüffelsheimer Strasse 5
6550 Bad Kreuznach
Open: daily, except Monday 9am-12.30pm, 2.30-6pm.

**Bad Münster am Stein**
*Kurbetriebe (Kurhaus)*
6552 Bad Münster am Stein-Ebernburg
☎ (06708) 1048

*Schmittenstollen*
☎ (06758) 8404 or (0671) 28347
At the time of writing, open April to October 10am-6pm.

**Bundenbach**
*Besucherbergwerk Grube Herrenberg*
(Slate Mine)
Open: 1 March to end October daily 10am-1pm and 2-5pm.

**Edenkoben**
*Schloss Ludwigshöhe*
Open: April to September 9am-1pm and 2-6pm, October to March 9am-1pm and 2-5pm.

**Fischbach**
(Nahe valley/Hunsrück)
*Fischbacher Kupferhütte* (Copper Mine)
Open: 1 March to mid-November daily 10am-5pm in winter weekends only.

**Gemünden**
*Besucherbergwerk*
*Kaisergrube and museum*
Open: 1 April to 31 October. Closed Monday.
☎ (06765) 1220

## Hambacher Schloss
Open: March to November 9am-5pm.

## Hassloch
*Holiday Park*
Open: end March to start October daily 9am-6pm.
☎ (06324) 5993900

## Homburg
*Schlossberghöhlen*
Open: daily 9am-12noon and 1-5pm.

## Idar-Oberstein
(Nahe valley/Hunsrück)
*Steinkaulenberg* (Gem Mine)
Eugen-Morschhäuser-Stollen
Open: 15 March to 15 November daily 9am-5pm.
Prospecting is possible in the Richard-Märker-Stollen by prior arrangement.
☎ (06781) 47400

*Felsenkirche*
Open: 1 April to 15 October 9am-6pm.

## Merzig
*Fellenbergschlösschen*
Open: Sundays and holidays 2pm-8pm.
Groups may come weekdays by prior arrangement.
☎ (06861) 80-145

*Wolfsfreigehege*
Open: from dawn to dusk and for guided tours.
Contact:
Kreisfremdenverkehrsverband
Merzig-Wadern or
Werner Freund
Auf der Ell
6640 Merzig
☎ (06861) 1051

## Mettlach
*Abbey Park*
Open: during daylight. Admission and car parking free.

*Schloss Ziegelberg*
(Keramikmuseum)
Open: Tuesday to Saturday 9am-12.30pm, 2-5.30pm, Sunday 10.30am-12.30pm, 2-6pm. Closed weekends December to February.
☎ (06864) 81294

*Villeroy and Boch Keravision*
(museum)
In the old abbey
Open: Tuesday to Friday 10am-4pm, Saturday 10am-1pm, Sunday 10am-6pm.
☎ (0684) 81251

## Rappweiler
*Wildfreigehege*
A mile (2km) south-west of Weiskirchen
Open: daily 9am-8pm or dusk if earlier.

## Speyer
*Dom*
Crypt open: Monday to Friday 9am-5.30pm, Saturday 9am-4pm, Sunday 1.30-4.30pm.

*Historisches Museum der Pfalz*
Open: daily 9am-12noon and 2-5pm.

## Wachenheim
*Hochwildschutzpark Kurpfalz*
6706 Wachenheim
☎ (06325) 7805
Open: all year 10am-4pm

*Kurpfalzpark Wachenheim*
Forsthaus Rotsteig
6706 Wachenheim
☎ (06325) 2077
Open: April to October 9am-6pm.

**Wadern**
*Town Museum* (Stadtmuseum)
Öttinger Schlösschen
6648 Wadern
Open: 2.30-5.30pm Sundays and
holidays.
Groups may come weekdays by
prior arrangement.
☎ (06871) 2481 - (12 noon-2pm, or
after 7pm).

**Wallhausen**
*Schloss*
Weingut Prinz zu Salm-Dalberg
6551 Wallhausen
Open: generally any time during
the day. If groups ring beforehand
snacks will be prepared to go with
the wine-tastings.
☎ (06706) 289

# Tourist Information Centres

**Annweiler**
Verkehrsamt
6747 Annweiler am Trifels
☎ (06346) 2200

**Bad Kreuznach**
Kreisverkehrsamt
Salinenstrasse 47
6550 Bad Kreuznach
☎ (0671) 95393

**Dahn**
Fremdenverkehrsbüro
Schulstrasse 29
6783 Dahn
Open: November to April, Monday
to Friday 8.30am-12noon and 2-
4pm, May to October, Monday to
Friday 8.30am-12noon and 2-6pm,
Saturdays 11am-12noon.
☎ (06391) 5811

**Idar-Oberstein**
Vekehrsamt
Bahnhofstrasse 13
6580 Idar-Oberstein
☎ (06781) 27025

**Koblenz**
Fremdenverkehrsverband
Rheinland-Pfalz
Löhrstrasse 103-105
Postfach 1420
5400 Koblenz
☎ (0261) 31079

**Merzig**
Kreisfremdenverkehrsverband
Merzig-Wadern
Poststrasse 12
6640 Merzig
☎ (06861) 73874

**Mettlach**
Verkehrsamt
Rathaus
6442 Mettlach
☎ (06864) 83-0

**Neustadt an der Weinstrasse**
Amt für Fremdenverkehr
Exterstrasse 2
6730 Neustadt an der Weinstrasse
☎ (06321) 855329

**Nonnweiler**
Verkehrsverein
6696 Nonnweiler
☎ (06873) 640 or 634

# 3

# *THE BLACK FOREST*

The Schwarzwald (Black Forest) is one of Germany's greatest tourist attractions. Located in the state of Baden-Württemberg it is a mountainous region filled with picture-postcard villages and valleys. The main charm of the area is the outstanding beauty of its landscape. It almost goes without saying that the Black Forest is an ideal place for walking tours or cross-country skiing. The added attractions of hot springs, Black Forest cake (Schwarzwälder-kirschtorte) and, of course, cuckoo clocks makes the Black Forest almost irresistible for first time visitors to Germany.

## Route 8 • The Northern Black Forest
## 277km (172 miles)

There are numerous hot springs in the Schwarzwald around which spa towns have grown and the most famous of them all is **Baden-Baden**. Even the Romans appreciated the healing qualities and warmth of the town's springs which gurgle up from the depths at a temperature of 69°C. At the Friedrichsbad, which was built in the nineteenth century in the style of a Roman bath, are remnants of a Roman bath from the first to third centuries. International fame came in the nineteenth century, when the presence of royalty and nobility gave Baden-Baden an aura of absolute exclusiveness. Even today there are still plenty of top-class hotels, like the Haus des Kurgastes, awaiting the arrival of visitors with heavy wallets.

Fortunately you do not have to be rich to just stroll about town, enjoying the sights, and to simply absorb the air of elegance and wealth. A pleasant walk is to go along the Lichtentaler Allee which is lined with exotic trees and flowers. On the way it is possible to visit the Kunsthalle where important art exhibitions are held and the

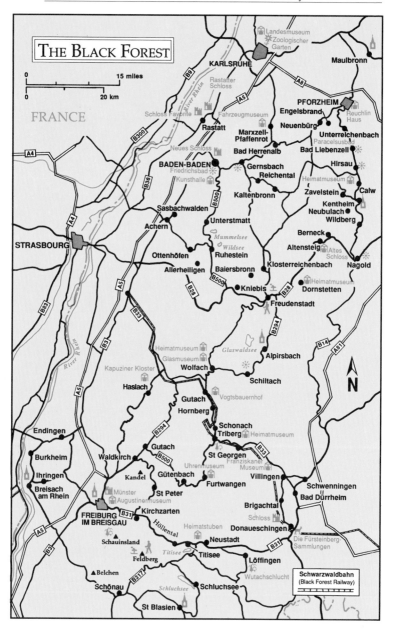

*An air of elegance and wealth can be absorbed while walking around the spa town of Baden-Baden*

Kurhaus (1821-22) in which a casino is located (open to public in the morning). Near the church of St Peter and Paul which has beautiful sepulchres inside, is the Neues Schloss (1437). The climb up to the Schloss is rewarded with good views. Other sights outside town include the Cistercian Kloster Lichtental and the castle ruins of Hohenbaden, Ebersteinburg and Yburg.

Before continuing south an excursion could be made to **Rastatt**, only a few kilometres further north. Just before town to the right off the B3 is Schloss Favorite (1710-12). This palace was built as a summer residence for Margravine Sibylla Augusta of Baden and is situated in an attractive park. The incredibly lavish interior contains among other things, a famous porcelain collection. In Rastatt itself the Schloss (1697-1705) forms the central attraction, in an Altstadt dominated by Baroque buildings. Some might be tempted to travel even further north on the B36 to the city of **Karlsruhe**. Here there is an excellent zoo and a massive Schloss with a spacious park in the English manner. Inside the Schloss is the important Badisches Landesmuseum (Baden State Museum), which has a fascinating collection of war trophies brought back from the Turkish campaigns of Margrave Ludwig Wilhelm of Baden-Baden.

The main route continues south on the B500 or Schwarz-waldhochstrasse (Black Forest High Road) as it is known. There are no settlements of any real size along this stretch of road until Freudenstadt. Here and there a few romantically isolated hostels are all that intrudes upon dense forest scenery. In many places parking is provided near view-points over the Rhein lowlands. Just after Unterstmatt (good skiing in the area) a detour to the right, off the B500, leads to the village of Sasbachwalden, a very pretty place with lots of half-timbered houses.

The Mummelsee, one of the Black Forest's many small lakes, is a few kilometres further on from Unterstmatt. It would be tempting to call the lake 'romantic' or 'idyllic', if it were not for the fact that on weekends there seem to be as many people paddling about on its dark waters, as there are trees growing on its shores. There is an hotel at the lake and an interesting modern chapel. Anglers will have to pack away their rods as the water's mineral content is too high to support fish.

Another detour from the B500 can be made to **Ottenhöfen**. This Luftkurort is terminus for the Achertal steam train. It starts from Achern, down in the Rhein lowlands, and runs from May to October. At Ruhestein yet another road turns off the B500 to wind its way to the Kloster ruins of **Allerheiligen**. The ruins are concealed in thick forest and date back to the thirteenth and fifteenth centuries. Nearby is a large waterfall. From Ruhestein (the name refers to the mountain saddle on the pass road between Achern and Baiersbronn) there is a trail leading to the Wildsee. Take the chair-lift from Gasthaus Ruhestein to the start of a short path that goes through moor to the lake. If the chair-lift is taken only one way the walk takes an hour, otherwise 40 minutes or so are sufficient.

Continue on the B500 which merges into the B28 shortly before Kniebis (a winter sports resort) to **Freudenstadt**. This town is served by rail and enjoys a central position in relation to many other sights in the Black Forest. Although the town was severely damaged towards the end of World War II it was largely rebuilt in the old style. The large Marktplatz is characterised by arcades running in front of the shops, an unusual architectural practice in Germany that may also be seen in the Inn valley in Bavaria. In the woods of the

Parkwald, near town, there are hundreds of kilometres of marked trails. For those who come in winter the ski-slopes are supposed to be good and there are prepared tracks for cross-country skiers as well.

An excursion can be made north of town on the B462, via Baiersbronn, to the Klosterkirche (monastery church) St Gregor in **Klosterreichenbach**. The church was built in the Romanesque manner and dates back to 1085. **Baiersbronn** itself is a large tourist resort with plenty of recreational facilities for both summer and winter visitors. The B462 also forms a very attractive shortened route via Gernsbach back to Baden-Baden.

From Freudenstadt return a short way on the B28, then turn south in the direction of Wolfach. The Wolf valley is one of the prettiest of the Black Forest's many valleys and it is still quite common to see houses built in the traditional style. Many of these places take in guests and would make a pleasant stay. It is quite likely that these family-run Gasthöfe, or Pensionen, would also offer an excellent opportunity to try local specialities like Schwarzwaldschinken (Black Forest ham), Hausmacher-Wurst (home-made sausage), or Obstwässerle (schnapps distilled from various kinds of fruit).

Some 3km (5 miles) south of Klösterle, at Vor Seebach, a sign with a green background points right to the **Glaswaldsee**. Drive along the steeply climbing road, passing on the way some superb examples of traditional Black Forest houses. After about 4km (6 miles) reach a car park. It is about another 20 minutes to the lake on a steep track. The view over this tranquil, beautiful little forest lake is well worth the effort of the climb. The return walk downhill takes only 10 minutes.

Continue south along the main valley via Schapbach and Oberwolfach to **Wolfach**. This pretty town offers a contrast to the rustical buildings of the Wolfach valley in its Baroque Schloss (seventeenth century) and Rathaus (1892). In the Schlosshof (palace courtyard) is the Heimatmuseum with a display of carnival masks. Carnival festivities in February are a colourful affair here and elsewhere in the Black Forest. In Wolfach there are some twelve processions with participants dressed in the beautiful carnival costumes. Wolfach's Glashütte (glassworks) allows visitors to watch the traditional craft of glass-blowing in action. West of Wolfach, in **Haslach**, the former Kapuziner Kloster is a museum dealing with traditional costumes of the Black Forest.

South of Wolfach on the B33, near **Gutach**, is an outstanding open-air museum known as the Vogtsbauernhof. This museum is devoted to the rural culture of the Black Forest and features original buildings

*The work of craftsmen in the Black Forest is prominent in the many carved wooden signs*

*Arcaded shops add character to the Marktplatz in Freudenstadt*

*Opposite: (top) Window boxes along this street in Wolfach are a colourful sight in summer (bottom) Haslach*

from various parts of the region. The entrance is crammed with souvenir shops and there is a restaurant which offers regional specialities.

The most spectacular stretch of the Schwarzwaldbahn (Black Forest Railway) is through the Gutach valley to St Georgen and begins at Hornberg, a short distance south of Gutach. The full journey actually begins in Offenburg, in the Rhein valley, and goes right through to Bodensee (Lake Constance). Some people claim the route follows one of the nicest stretches of mountain railway in Europe. The B33 itself provides a very scenic connection to Triberg, on Route 9 — note the cuckoo-clock shops on this road!

Route 8 continues east from Wolfach, on the B294, along the Kinzig valley to **Schiltach**. The town's many half-timbered houses and cobbled streets make it look very picturesque. This is especially so in the Marktplatz with its Renaissance Rathaus (1594). Also worth looking out for is the Äussere Mühle (1557), the town's oldest half-timbered building. Good views over town can be had from the Häberlesberg. Follow the B294 north, past the ruined castle Schenkenburg (thirteenth century), to Alpirsbach.

In **Alpirsbach** the main attraction is a church that was attached to the old Benedictine monastery. This Romanesque building dates back to the eleventh century and has remained surprisingly pure in style over the centuries, in spite of some additions from the Gothic period. Concerts are held in the Gothic cloister during the summer months. For those who have worked up a thirst, after a walk in the surrounding woods, it might be deemed fortunate that the old Benedictine monks were not only good at building churches but also at brewing beer. There is nothing better to do on a warm summer's day than to sit in one of the local Gaststätte and drink a glass of Alpirsbacher Klosterbräu.

Continue through Lossburg and near Freudenstadt turn right off the B294 to follow the B28 via **Dornstetten**. This is one of the oldest towns in the region and has retained much of its medieval character in the pretty Marktplatz. A Heimatmuseum is located in one of the half-timbered houses. It is especially worth visiting if a demonstration of old crafts happens to coincide with your visit. For much of the rest of the way the road now follows the Schwarzwald Bäderstrasse (Spa Road) which is the B28 until Nagold. Near Pfalzgrafenweiler, in the Weiler Wald, are the tallest fir trees in the northern Black Forest — they approach almost 50m (164ft) in height and are around 200 years old.

The houses of **Altensteig**'s medieval Altstadt are all clustered beneath the Altes Schloss (twelfth century) like vassals paying tribute to their mighty lord. Apart from the Schloss (which is home to the town museum) and the general picture of the Altstadt, the parish church (1775) is particularly worth noting. North of the town at **Berneck** is another picturesque Schloss. An excursion to the Nagoldstausee (storage lake) can be made by going back to the edge of Altensteig and then taking a road to the right. It follows an especially attractive stretch of the Nagold valley to the lake. Bathing is possible near the village of Seewald-Erzgrube.

**Nagold** is on the fringes of the Black Forest. Again old half-timbered houses add a touch of romance to the place. Especially notable is the hotel Alte Post (1697), which is also a good place to try regional cooking. The Remigiuskirche (tenth and twelfth centuries) has some Gothic wall frescoes, while above town Burg Hohen-Nagold (thirteenth century) has been a ruin since it was destroyed in the Thirty Years War. From here the Bäderstrasse follows the B463.

**Wildberg** hosts the oldest folk festival in the northern Black Forest; the Wildberger Schäferlauf (Shepherds Race). As the name implies it all centres around sheep and since 1723 it has taken place nearly every 2 years. The next festival takes place on the third Sunday in July 1992. Traces of the town's 700-year-old history can be seen in the castle ruins, remnants of the medieval town wall and the wooden Rathaus (1480). To the north-west, near **Neubulach**, is a silver mine (follow the Besucherbergwerk sign). Silver and copper mining began here in the eleventh century and only stopped in 1924. The fields around the neighbouring village of Zavelstein are covered with millions of violet-blue crocuses from mid-March until the beginning of April. Back on the B463 to Calw visit **Kentheim** which is home to the Candidus-Kapelle (tenth century), one of the oldest churches in this part of Germany.

An approximation of **Calw's** pronunciation is to pronounce the 'c' as in cake and the 'alw' as in Alf. The town was an important trading place in the Middle Ages, with flourishing industries such as cloth weaving and tanning. Rafting was also an important profession and many of the fir trees felled here were bound together to be floated to Holland, where they were used as ship masts. The town centre preserves a few half-timbered houses from the seventeenth and eighteenth centuries. Haus Vischer (1790) in the Bischofstrasse 48 contains the Heimatmuseum with memorabilia relating to the novelist Hermann Hesse who was born here in 1877. Also of interest is the Nagold bridge (1400), with its small Gothic chapel, and the Rathaus (1673) in the Marktplatz.

*The half-timbered buildings and cobbled streets of Schiltach*

*The Romanesque church at Alpirsbach holds concerts during the summer months in its Gothic cloister*

*The medieval quarter of Altensteig*

*Calw market is a colourful attraction for both visitors and locals*

The romantic monastery ruins of **Hirsau** are only a few kilometres north of Calw. The French destroyed this Kloster in 1692, so there is not a great deal left except for the ruined church (1081-1091), Gothic cloister (1425-94) and the Marienkapelle (1508-16), which houses a museum. In the sixteenth century a Renaissance style hunting lodge was built within the monastery complex, but it also suffered at the hands of the French. In summer open-air performances are held in the Kloster ruins. A nature trail near the car park, opposite the Kloster, leads to an animal enclosure with deer and wild boars which is open from dawn until dusk. Continue north on the B463.

**Bad Liebenzell** is a modern spa town with curative springs that are used for healing rheumatism and various circulatory problems. The Paracelsusbad (mineral baths) is not only open to those taking a cure, but also to the general public. The Kurpark makes a pleasant place for a stroll and there are good views from the town's castle (dating from around 1200). For those who do not wish to continue into the large town of Pforzheim, it is best to turn left, off the B463, at Unterreichenbach. Go via Grunbach and Engelsbrand to Neuenbürg.

**Pforzheim** was almost completely flattened in World War II and the modern town is not one of the most attractive in the Black Forest. Today it is an important gold and jewellery centre and the Reuchlin-Haus in the Jahnstrasse contains an excellent jewellery museum. A very worthwhile detour from here is to follow the B294 north. Turn right at Bauschlott and then go via Ölbronn to the Kloster at **Maulbronn**. This Cistercian monastery was founded in 1147 and has survived the passage of time since the Middle Ages virtually unchanged. Johannes Kepler, Friedrich Hölderlin and Hermann Hesse all studied at Maulbronn. The old mill in the monastery grounds now serves as a youth hostel (☎ 07043 6535). By following the B35 north-west the Baroque Schloss (1720) in **Bruchsal** could be visited.

Continue south from Pforzheim on the B294, which runs close to the railway lines, to **Neuenbürg**. This small town has a large Renaissance Schloss and pretty Marktplatz. Just before Höfen turn right, off the B294, towards **Bad Herrenalb**. Of historic interest in the middle of the town is the ruin of an old Cistercian monastery church from the twelfth century. On the last weekend in August there is a Bahnhofsfest (Railway Festival), a major attraction of which are rides on the Albtalbahn steam train. North of town in the Alb valley are the ruins of Kloster Frauenalb and in **Marxzell-Pfaffenrot** there is a Fahrzeugmuseum (Transport Museum). In winter Bad Herrenalb is a popular ski-resort.

**Gernsbach** is reached via the picturesque village of Loffenau, on a road winding south-west. It is a pretty town with a number of historic buildings such as the Altes Rathaus (1618) and, at the southern end of town, Schloss Eberstein (fourteenth and sixteenth centuries). Those with more time could explore the area around Reichental and Kaltenbronn, further south-east. The landscape here is particularly beautiful, including patches of moor where two nature reserves have been set up around some small lakes. To get to Baden-Baden from Gernsbach cross the Murg stream and go via Unterdorf, Oberdorf and past Ebersteinburg.

# Route 9 • The Southern Black Forest
# 177km (110 miles)

**Freiburg** is situated on the western fringes of the Black Forest in an area known as the Breisgau. A good place to begin a tour of the city is at the Münsterplatz, in the Altstadt (parking near the Rotteckring, or Friedrichring). The Münster Unserer Lieben Frau, is one of the greatest masterpieces of Gothic architecture in Germany. It has been modified at various times over a period of some three centuries, the oldest part of the minster dating back to the Romanesque period, around 1200. The Gothic west tower was completed in 1301. Its filigree-like spire has induced one art historian to call it the 'most beautiful tower in Christendom'. Inside are many fine works of art, including a painting by Hans Holbein the Younger. On the way up the tower which offers excellent views over town at the top, note the huge bell 'Hosanna', cast in 1258.

Around the minster are a number of interesting buildings, including the Kaufhaus (1525-32) and Kornhaus, a reconstruction of a fifteenth-century building destroyed in World War II. On Fridays these historic places make a picturesque background for a colourful market.

Go left past the Kaufhaus into the Buttergasse to reach the Augustinermuseum. This is Freiburg's most interesting museum, with collections of painting, sculpture and folk-art. Not far away is the Schwabentor, a gate-tower and Gasthaus Bären, one of the oldest hotels in Germany. To get to the Rathausplatz follow the Salzstrasse from the museum, turn right into the Kaiser-Joseph-Strasse, then go left into the Bertholdstrasse and continue through the Brunnenstrasse and Rathausgasse. Grouped together in the Rathausplatz is the Altes (Old) Rathaus (1555-9), Neues (New) Rathaus and the Gothic Martinskirche. In the middle of the square is a fountain dedicated to the monk Berthold Schwarz, who discovered gunpowder in the first half of the fourteenth century.

Anybody walking about Freiburg's Altstadt is certain to come across the Bächle. This is a narrow water-filled channel running through the middle of some streets. It was designed in the Middle Ages to provide a handy source of water for combating the frequent fires, but was also used as a forerunner of today's modern sewerage system. Excellent views over the Altstadt can be had from the forested heights of the Schlossberg — either take a cable-car (Gondelbahn) or it is a short walk from the Schwabentor.

A detour west of Freiburg, on the B31, leads to **Breisach am Rhein** The most impressive building here is the Münster St Stephan (thirteenth century), a fortress-like church at the most elevated point in town. Among its many treasures one of the most outstanding is the wooden high altar (early sixteenth century), which is ranked as one of the most important examples of late Gothic German sculpture. The group of hills north-east of town are known as the Kaiserstuhl and are famous for the wine produced from their slopes. In the general area the towns of Burkheim and Endingen, and the wine-growing village of Ihringen are worth visiting.

Another excursion from Freiburg is to **Schauinsland** (1,284m 4,211ft), a mountain to the south. The road is well sign-posted from the city centre but after Günterstal the motorist has to decide whether to use the cable railway (Seilbahn), which starts near here, or to drive the whole distance. The trip with the Seilbahn takes about 15 minutes, but a car would need 40 minutes to the top. From the car park it is another 20 minutes on foot to a look-out tower on the summit. In good weather the view can be breathtaking, this helps explain the mountain's name which literally means — 'look into the countryside'. There is a map posted at the car park showing walking paths in the area.

For those who have come by car the return drive via Hofsgrund, Notschrei and Oberried is very scenic. Near Notschrei at **St Wilhelm** is the Bergwildpark Steinwasen, an enclosure that specialises in mountain animals such as chamois and moufflon. That part of the Black Forest further south, stretching down to the Swiss border, is also very picturesque, and though not discussed in detail here it is well worth exploring.

The main route now follows the B31, which forms part of the Grüne Strasse (Green Road), another tourist road that goes right through to Lake Constance. The Federal Railway follows the same route and one of its most beautiful stretches is through the Höllental

*Gernsbach*

*Pleasure boats awaiting the tourists at Titisee*

(Hell's Valley), shortly after Kirchzarten. The Höllentalbahn (Hell Valley Line) starts at Freiburg and ends in Donaueschingen, although an even shorter stretch could be from Kirchzarten and through the valley to Hinterzarten. Inquire at Freiburg's Hauptbahnhof for more details.

Because the Höllental is so narrow there are only a few places where it is possible to stop and take in the scenery. The first such place is at a spot known as **Hirschsprung**. A bronze statue of a stag on a rocky outcrop above the road recalls the story of how this animal accomplished a mighty leap over the chasm in order to escape pursuing hunters. At the end of the valley it is worth pausing at **Höllsteig**. From here a pleasant walk goes up the Ravenna gorge and another trail leads to the St Oswald-Kapelle, the oldest parish church in this part of the Black Forest. The Hotel Sternen at Höllsteig is supposed to have accommodated Goethe himself. Next to the hotel is a Glashütte, where there are daily demonstrations of glass-blowing. It should be mentioned here, however, that the tranquillity of the Höllental has been all but destroyed by the traffic using the B31.

**Titisee** is a popular tourist resort, further along the B31, on the lake of the same name. The Titisee is the largest naturally formed lake in the Black Forest and visitors are well catered for with a wide range of accommodation, including a couple of campsites. A pleasant stroll along the lake shore goes from Hotel Seehof to the campsites at Seehäusle — there and back takes about an hour. There is a passenger launch service on the lake.

South of Titisee are some other lakes, including the Schluchsee, where the town of the same name has also developed into an important tourist resort. By following the B500 around this lake, and turning off to the right near Häusern, it is possible to visit the Klosterkirche St Blasien, one of the best examples of early Classicism in Germany.

The B317 from Titisee leads to the **Feldberg** (1,493m 4,898ft), the Black Forest's highest mountain. A chair-lift goes from Hotel Feldberger Hof, near the resort of Feldberg, to Seebuck, one of the Feldberg's lower peaks. The real summit has to be reached along a steep path. Fortunately the pretty mountain lake, Feldsee, can only be reached on foot as well, saving it from large crowds. Another good walk is along the Feldberg Naturlehrpfad which is about 20km (12 miles) long. The general area of the Feldberg is also good for skiing.

Some distance further south of the resort of Feldberg, near Schönau, is the Black Forest's second highest mountain, **Belchen** (1,414m 4,639ft). It is closed to motor traffic on Sundays and public holidays from July through to December. This restriction has only been in force since 1990 and is an attempt to reduce the detrimental effect of cars and tourism on the local environment.

The main route continues along the Grüne Strasse, which briefly leaves the B31, to **Neustadt**. This town has long been a centre for the manufacture of the famous Black Forest cuckoo clocks and the Neustädter Heimatstuben (museum) has a number of exhibits dealing with this and other local crafts.

**Löffingen**, just off the B31, is a pleasant town characterised by the stepped gables of its houses and it serves as a starting point for a detour to the Wutachschlucht. The road to this pretty gorge is signposted and there is a car park at the bridge near the Schattenmühle Gasthof. Walk back over the bridge, along the road around the Gasthof, and come to a sign pointing down the valley slope. The trail is some 36km (22 miles) long and can get very muddy, so a pair of good shoes or boots is advisable.

Continue on the B31, turning off at Hüfingen to reach **Donaueschingen** on the edges of the Black Forest. Route 11 (Chapter 4) can be joined by continuing on the B31, then after Geisingen, the B311 to Tuttlingen. In Donaueschingen the main attraction is the Baroque Schloss and park. Located in the park is the so-called Donauquelle, though it is not in fact the source of the Donau, but rather a romantic conception of what it should be like. The real sources of the Donau are the Breg and Brigach rivers, which join to form the Donau near Donaueschingen, but have their springs further west in the Black Forest. In the Karlsbau nearby, is a museum which includes works by Cranach, Holbein and Grünewald. Continue to Villingen either via Bad Dürrheim or along a smaller road going via Brigachtal.

**Villingen's** medieval character is preserved in substantial remnants of the town walls, including three town gates. In the Franziskaner Museum are exhibits dealing with local traditions, as well as prehistoric finds made in the area. Carnival celebrations have a very long tradition here and belong to the most colourful in the entire region. Continue via St Georgen, on the B33, to Triberg.

At **Triberg** is Germany's highest waterfall. It falls in a series of seven cascades some 162m (531ft) to the valley floor. There is an entry fee to see the falls which are open from dawn until dusk. The Heimatmuseum has a fascinating collection of folk art, a clockmaker's workshop and a model of the Black Forest Railway. In the nineteenth century this railway represented a major engineering feat because of the difficult terrain that had to be overcome. Just outside

*Throughout the Black Forest buildings are adorned with flowers, like this hotel in Triberg*

*Opposite: the cascading waterfall at Triberg is the highest in Germany*

*Carved figures in traditional Black Forest costumes*

Triberg, in the direction of Schonach is what is reputed to be the world's largest cuckoo clock — there are others elsewhere in the Black Forest who make exactly the same claim! **Schonach** itself is the starting point for the 100km (62 miles) long Black Forest cross-country ski route.

Continue south from Triberg, on the scenic B500, to **Furtwangen**. This town, along with Triberg, has long been one of the centres of the Black Forest clock industry. Clock-making had its origins in the bad old days when the poor Black Forest farmers had to supplement their meagre incomes by making and selling those cuckoo clocks that have since become so famous. The first Black Forest clock appeared around 1640, but the classic cuckoo clock did not appear on the scene until 1738. The Uhrenmuseum (Clock Museum) in Furtwangen offers an excellent opportunity to study the history of clock-making in more detail.

After Furtwangen take a right turn off the B500, in the direction of Gütenbach. This very beautiful, sometimes spectacular stretch of road, follows the Wilde Gutach stream through the Simonswälder valley to Gutach on the B294. From Gutach it is possible to return directly to Freiburg, otherwise the much more scenic alternative is to go via Waldkirch and up the steep mountain road to the summit of the Kandel (1,242m 4,075ft). In clear weather it is possible to see as far as the Alps. The mountain road continues to the village of **St Peter**, where there is a large Baroque church (1724-7) by the famous architect Peter Thumb. On Sundays, or on certain special occasions, there is a good chance of seeing people dressed in traditional costumes. By taking the road via Eschbach it is no longer far to Freiburg.

# Additional Information

## Places of Interest

### Altensteig
*Altes Schloss*
Open: Sunday 11am-12noon and 2-4pm. Wednesday 2-4pm. Entry is free. Guided tours possible.
☎ (07453) 6633 or 1360

### Baden-Baden
*Friedrichsbad*
Open: Monday and Wednesday to Saturday 8am-10pm, Tuesday 8am-4pm.

*Kunsthalle*
Open: Tuesday and Thursday to Sunday 10am-6pm, Wednesday 10am-8pm.

*Neues Schloss*
Open: Tuesday to Sunday 10am-6pm.

### Bad Liebenzell
*Paracelsusbad*
For more information contact the Kurverwaltung Bad Liebenzell
☎ (07052) 4080 or 408100

### Bruchsal
*Schloss Bruchsal*
Open: all year Tuesday to Sunday 9am-1pm and 2-5pm.
☎ (07251) 742661

## Calw

*Heimatmuseum*
Open: May to October, Monday to
Friday 2-4pm, Sunday 10am-
12noon.

## Donaueschingen

*Schloss*
Guided tours April to September
Monday and Wednesday to
Sunday 9am-12noon and 2-5pm.

*Fürstenberg-Sammlungen*
(In the Karlsbau behind the
Schloss)
Open: all year, except November,
Tuesday to Sunday 9am-12noon
and 1.30-5pm.

## Dornstetten

*Heimatmuseum*
Marktplatz 12
Open: all year, Sundays 2-4.30pm,
May to October Wednesday and
Friday 2.30-4.30pm. No entry
charge.
☎ (07443) 5868 and 6023

## Freiburg im Breisgau

*Augustinermuseum*
Open: Tuesday and Thursday to
Sunday 10am-5pm, Wednesdays
10am-8pm.

*Münster* (The Tower)
Open: March to November,
Tuesday to Saturday 10am-5pm,
Sunday 1-5pm.

## Furtwangen

*Uhrenmuseum*
Open: April to November daily
9am-5pm, December to March
Monday to Friday 9am-12noon and
2-4pm.

## Gutach

*Schwarzwälder Freilichtmuseum
'Vogtsbauernhof'*
Open: April to October daily
8.30am-6pm.

## Haslach

*Kapuziner Kloster*
Open: April to October, Tuesday to
Saturday 9am-5pm, Sunday 10am-
5pm, November to March Tuesday
to Friday 10am-5pm.

## Hirsau

*Museum in the Marienkapelle*
Can only be visited by prior
arrangement. Contact:
Verkehrsamt Calw
☎ (07051) 5671

## Karlsruhe

*Landesmuseum*
In the Schloss
Open: Tuesday, Wednesday and
Friday to Sunday 10am-5.30pm.
Thursday 10am-9pm.

*Zoologischer Garten*
Main entrances: Bahnhofsplatz and
Festplatz/Kongresszentrum
Open: May to September from 8am
otherwise from 9am until dusk.
☎ (0721) 1332939

## Marxzell-Pfaffenrot

*Fahrzeugmuseum*
Open: daily April to September
10am-6pm, October to March 2-
6pm.
☎ (07248) 6262

## Maulbronn

*Kloster*
Open: April to October daily
8.30am-6.30pm, November to
March, Tuesday to Sunday 9.30am-
1pm and 2-5pm.

**Neubulach**

*Silberbergwerk Neubulach*
Open: Saturdays, Sundays and
holidays 9am-5pm from April to
October. During summer holiday
period daily 9am-12noon and 2-
5pm.

**Neustadt**

*Heimatstuben*
Scheurlenstrasse 31
7820 Neustadt
Open: mid-May to September,
Monday to Friday 2-5pm, Saturday
10am-12noon; October to mid-May,
Thursday 2-5pm, Sunday 10am-
12noon.

**Pforzheim**

*Reuchlin-Haus*
Open: Tuesday and Thursday to
Sunday 10am-5pm, Wednesday
10am-8pm.

**Rastatt**

*Rastatter Schloss*
Open: Tuesday to Sunday 9.30am-
5pm. Entry is free. ☎ (07222) 39475

*Schloss Favorite*
Open: Tuesday to Sunday 16
March to 15 November
☎ (07222) 41207

**St Wilhelm**

Between Notschrei and Oberried
*Bergwildpark Steinwasen*
Open: 1 January to 30 April 10am-
5pm, 1 May to 30 September 9am-
6pm.
☎ (07671) 451 or (07602) 1252

**Triberg**

*Heimatmuseum*
Wallfahrtstrasse
Open: mid-May to September 8am-
6pm. Rest of year 10am-12noon
and 2-5pm.

**Villingen-Schwenningen**

*Franziskaner Museum*
Rietstrasse 39
Open: Thursday, Saturday and
Sunday 10am-12noon, Tuesday to
Friday 3-5pm.
☎ (07721) 82408

**Wolfach**

*Glasmuseum*
Glashüttenweg 4
7620 Wolfach
Open: daily 9am-3.30pm. No
charge for children up to 6.
☎ (07834) 751

*Heimatmuseum*
Grosser Schlosshof
7620 Wolfach
Open: May to September, Tuesday,
Thursday and Saturday 2-5pm,
Sunday 10am-12noon, 2-5pm. Rest
of year Thursday 2-5pm and first
Sunday of each month 10am-
12noon, 2-5pm.
☎ (07834) 1433

# Tourist Information Centres

**Alpirsbach**
Kurverwaltung
im Haus des Gastes
Postfach 1129
☎ (07444) 614-281

**Altensteig**
Städtisches Verkehrsamt
☎ (07453) 6633 and 27215

**Baden-Baden**
Kurverwaltung
On Augustaplatz
Open: Monday to Saturday 9am-
10pm, Sunday 10am-10pm.
☎ (07221) 275200

**Bad Herrenalb**
Kurverwaltung
☎ (07083) 7933

**Baiersbronn**
Kurverwaltung
☎ (07442) 2570

**Breisach am Rhein**
Verkehrsamt
☎ (07667) 83227

**Calw**
Verkehrsamt/Kurverwaltung
☎ (07051) 5671

**Donaueschingen**
Karlstrasse 58
Open: Monday to Friday 8am-
12noon and 2-5 or 6pm according
to season. Saturday 9am-12noon.
☎ (0771) 3834

**Feldberg/Schwarzwald**
Town district of Feldberg-Ort
Kurverwaltung
☎ (07676) 250 and (07655) 8019

**Freiburg**
Rotteckring
Open: May to October, Monday to
Wednesday and Saturday 9am-
6pm. Thursday and Friday 9am-
9pm, Sunday and holidays 10am-
12noon. November to April
Monday to Friday 9am-6pm,
Saturday 9am-3pm.
☎ (216) 3286

**Freudenstadt**
Städtische Kurverwaltung
☎ (07441) 864-0

**Furtwangen**
Verkehrsamt
☎ (07723) 61400

**Gernsbach**
Verkehrsamt
Igelbachstrasse 11
☎ (07224) 64444

**Karlsruhe**
Verkehrsverein
Bahnhofsplatz 6
Open: Monday to Friday 8am-7pm,
Saturday 8am-1pm.
☎ (0721) 35530

**Klosterreichenbach/Heselbach**
Kurverwaltung-Nebenstelle
☎ (07442) 2365

**Löffingen**
Kurverwaltung
Rathaus
☎ (07654) 400

**Maulbronn**
Stadtverwaltung
Klosterhof 31
7133 Maulbronn
Open: Monday and Thursday 8am-
12noon and 1-5.30pm, Tuesday and
Wednesday 8am-12noon and 1-
4.30pm, Friday 8am-1.30pm.
Saturday and Sunday 11am-5pm.
☎ (07043) 10317

**Nagold**
Bürgermeisteramt
Marktstrasse 27
☎ (07452) 6810

**Ottenhöfen**
Tourist Information
Kurverwaltung
7593 Ottenhöfen i. Schw.
Postfach 5816
☎ (07842) 2097

**Rastatt**
Stadtverwaltung
Hauptamt ☎ (07222) 385-0

**Schiltach**
Verkehrsamt
☎ (07836) 648

**Titisee**
Kurverwaltung
7820 Titisee
☎ (07651) 8101-04

**Triberg**
Kurverwaltung
☎ (07722) 81230-231

**Villingen-Schwenningen**
Town district of Villingen
Verkehrsamt/Kur-und Bad GmBH
Rietstrasse 8 ☎ (07721) 82311

**Wildberg**
Städtisches Verkehrsamt
☎ (07054) 20122

**Wolfach**
Städtisches Kur-und Verkehrsamt
☎ (07834) 975-33 and 975-34

---

## Travelling in the Black Forest

An interesting possibility for people using public transport in the Black Forest is the Schwarzwald-Bus-Pass. This ticket can be used by any visitor to the Black Forest and is vaild on all railway (DB) buses as well as those bus companies working in conjunction with Federal Railways (Deutsche Bundesbahn). There are reductions for married couples and families and for a period of 7 days it is astonishingly cheap. The pass entitles travellers to unlimited travel in the entire Südschwarzwald (Southern Black Forest) and western region of the Bodensee area or in the entire Nordschwarzwald (Northern Black Forest) and Südpfälzer Raum (region of the Southern Palatinate).

**Contact:**
Geschäftsbereich Bahnbus
Südbaden
Bismarckallee 2A
D-7800 Freiburg im Breisgau
☎ (0761) 214351
and
Nordschwarzwald/Südpfalz
Amalienstrasse 4b
D-7500 Karlsruhe
☎ (0721) 1345945

## Autoreisezug (Motorail) stations in the Black Forest are:

Karlsruhe-Durlach (from/to Berlin, Hamburg, Köln) and Lörrach (from/to Hamburg, Hannover, Bremen, Berlin, Düsseldorf and Köln). The relevant telephone numbers of IC (Intercity) stations in

the Black Forest are:

Baden-Baden
☎ (07221) 61495

Freiburg im Breisgau
(Hauptbahnhof) ☎ (0761) 214346

Karlsruhe (Hauptbahnhof)
☎ (0721) 134346

Offenburg
☎ (0781) 81346

In the Black Forest Intercity (IC) trains stop at: Karlsruhe, Baden-Baden, Offenburg, Freiburg and Pforzheim.

Interregio trains from Kassel (in Northern Germany) stop at Karlsruhe, Rastatt, Baden-Baden, Offenburg, Hausach, Hornberg, Triberg, St Georgen, Villingen and Donaueschingen (every 2 hours).

## Some Tourist Roads in the Black Forest:

**Schwarzwald-Bäderstrasse**
(Black Forest Spa Road)
Length: 250km (155 miles)
This is a circular route in the
northern Black Forest. It starts at
Pforzheim and goes through spa
and health resorts like Bad
Herrenalb, Freudenstadt and Bad
Liebenzell. For further information
and brochure contact:
Gebietsgemeinschaft
Nördlicher Schwarwald e. V.
Am Waisenhausplatz 26
D-7530 Pforzheim
☎ (07231) 17929

**Schwarzwald-Hochstrasse**
(Black Forest Ridge Road)
Length: 65km (40 miles)
This is a very scenic route going
from Baden-Baden to
Freudenstadt. For information and
a brochure contact:
Gastfreundliche Schwarzwald-
Hochstrasse
D-7292 Schliffkopf
☎ (07449) 205

**Schwarzwald-Tälerstrasse**
(Black Forest Valley Road)
Length: 100km (62 miles)
Also very picturesque this route
goes from Rastatt to Alpirsbach.
For information and a brochure
contact:
Kurverwaltung
D-7292 Baiersbronn
☎ (07442) 2570

**Schwarzwald-Panoramastrasse**
(Black Forest Panoramic Road)
Length: 70km (43 miles)
The name does justice to this route
which starts at Waldkirch and goes
via St Peter to Hinterzarten. For
further information and a brochure
contact:
Kurverwaltung
D-7811 St Märgen
☎ (07669) 1066

For general information about all
these roads contact:
Fremdenverkehrsverband
Schwarzwald
Postfach 1660
D-7800 Freiburg im Breisgau
☎ (0761) 31317

Many of the places covered by the
above roads are at least touched
upon in the Black Forest chapter.

# 4

# *WÜRTTEMBERG-HOHENZOLLERN*

---

W üttemberg-Hohenzollern is, like the Black Forest, a part of Baden-Württemberg. The name, however, refers rather to a cultural entity than a geographic region. This is the heartland of Swabia and the people living here are generally referred to as Schwaben (Swabians). The landscape of the Schwäbische Alb (Swabian Jura) is every bit as beautiful as that of the Black Forest, and though of quite a different character, just as rewarding for the visitor.

## Route 10 • Stuttgart and the Region to the North 183km (114 miles)

**Stuttgart** is the capital of Baden-Württemberg and one of the most beautifully situated cities in Germany. Many of the important sights are located in the inner city and are easily reached on foot from the Hauptbahnhof. In the nearby Klett-Passage is a tourist office with useful information about the many cultural events taking place in Stuttgart. Of the various festivals held here, the Christmas Market (Weihnachtsmarkt) is worth mentioning as Germany's largest.

To get to the most representative of the city's squares, the Schlossplatz, simply follow the Königstrasse from the Hauptbahnhof. It was laid out at the end of the eighteenth century and its centre point is a 30m (98ft) high column erected in 1841 for King Wilhelm I on his twenty-fifth Jubilee. Flanking one side of the square is the imposing Neues Schloss (1746-1807). It demonstrates the transitional period from Baroque to Classicist styles and now houses various state ministries. The large park which stretches right back past the main railway station is open to the public. Near the Schloss the Kunstgebäude contains the city art gallery.

South of the Schlossplatz is the much smaller Schillerplatz, where

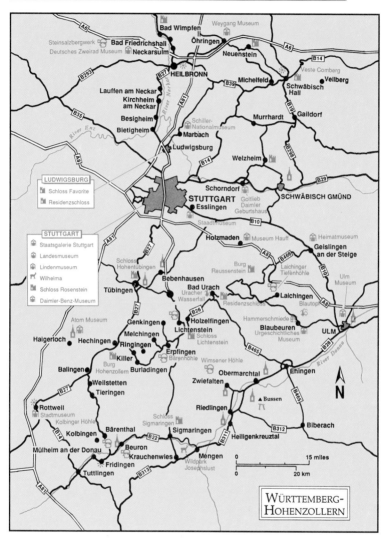

the Weihnachtsmarkt is held. The Altes Schloss was originally a moated castle that dated back to the thirteenth century, but it was modified and enlarged in the Renaissance manner between 1553 and 1570. For centuries it served as residence for the counts and later the Dukes of Württemberg. Especially attractive is the Renaissance courtyard with its three-tiered arcades. The palace contains the **Landesmuseum** dealing with the cultural history of Württemberg. Nearby the Fruchtkasten (1596) is a building that was originally used to store grain but now houses exhibits from Roman antiquity. The neighbouring Stiftskirche (twelfth century) is Stuttgart's oldest church.

North-east of the Neues Schloss (go through the park toward the Konrad-Adenauer-Strasse) is the **Neue Staatsgalerie**. It was designed by the British architect James Stirling and opened in 1984. This impressive example of modern architecture houses the most important collection of Picassos in Germany. Get to the Lindenmuseum with its important ethnological collections, in the Hegelplatz, by going right from the main station and down the Kriegsbergstrasse.

Outside the city centre is Stuttgart's excellent **Wilhelma** zoo — it can be reached on one of the S-Bahn (suburban) lines going from the Hauptbahnhof to the Wilhelmsplatz. **Schloss Rosenstein** is situated in the huge park next to the zoo and houses a natural history museum. Also in this park is the associated Museum am Löwentor. One of its most outstanding exhibits is the skeleton of a prehistoric elephant from the area of the Neckar. Boat cruises on the Neckar to Lauffen start close to the zoo.

Other places of interest include the Daimler-Benz-Museum in Untertürkheim and the Porschemuseum in Zuffenhausen. The suburb of Bad Cannstatt is famed for the Cannstatter Volksfest (Folk Festival) which takes place towards the end of September and rivals Munich's Oktoberfest in size. A little known fact is that Bad Cannstatt possesses the second largest deposits of mineral water in Europe, after Budapest. Twenty-two million litres of water issue forth from the nineteen mineral springs every day.

A pleasant excursion south of Stuttgart can be made along the Neckar to the town of **Esslingen**. The medieval Altstadt is still quite well preserved and is dominated by the Gothic church of St Dionys (thirteenth century). Its two non-matching Romanesque towers give the church its distinctive character. The stained-glass windows in the choir belong to the oldest in all of Southern Germany. Two other important churches are the Paulskirche (1255-68), and the Frauenkirche (1326-1508). The Altes Rathaus contains some beautiful rooms and the town museum. Above the Altstadt is the so-called Burg which is not, however, a castle but the impressive remainders of the old town wall.

Continue north from Stuttgart on the B27 to **Ludwigsburg**. Schloss

Ludwigsburg (1704-1733) was once the residential palace of the dukes of Württemberg and is the largest fully intact Baroque palace in Germany. The immense palace complex consists of 18 connected buildings, with a total of 452 rooms, of which some 50 can be viewed on a guided tour. Duke Eberhard Ludwig had wished to create a palace as magnificent as that in Versailles and he certainly succeeded, at least in terms of magnitude. North of the main palace and park is a comparatively diminutive pleasure seat known as Schloss Favorite (1715-1723). From here a path goes through the Favorite-Park to Schloss Monrepos (1760), a stately home on the edge of a lake — guided tours go through both.

A detour north-east of Ludwigsburg can be made to the pretty town of **Marbach**. Friedrich von Schiller (1759-1805) was born in one of the half-timbered houses still standing here (Geburtshaus Friedrich von Schillers), and it contains a small museum in his memory. The Schiller-Nationalmuseum is devoted not only to the life and work of Schiller but also concerns itself with the works of other great Swabian literary figures.

The main route continues from Ludwigsburg on the B27, which also forms part of the Schwäbische Weinstrasse (Swabian Wine Road). Bietigheim and Besigheim are both picturesque towns worth exploring. The Ku(h)riosum-Brunnen — the name puns with cow and curious — in **Bietigheim** is certainly one of Germany's more original fountains. By turning left off the B27 at Kirchheim am Neckar the amusement park Tripsdrill, near Cleebronn, can be visited. Back on the B27 the town of **Lauffen am Neckar** was the birthplace of the famous poet Friedrich Hölderlin (1770-1843). The character of the land does not seem to have changed much around here, as even in Hölderlin's time he was able to wax lyrical about this 'blessed land', in which 'not a hill' was not covered by vineyards.

**Heilbronn** is a busy industrial town but the word 'industry' might be softened a little if it is added that wine is one of the most important. The general impression made by the Marktplatz with its Rathaus and the Kilianskirche is quite impressive. Take note of the Rathaus clock-tower; every full hour is accompanied by trumpeting angels, charging rams and a crowing rooster! The Kilianskirche had to be rebuilt after extensive damage suffered in World War II but its exquisitely carved high altar from 1498 has survived the centuries. The west tower (1513-29) is considered the first important piece of architecture from the German Renaissance. Heilbronn's wine-festival takes place in autumn and boat trips on the Neckar are possible here.

An excursion could be made north of Heilbronn to **Neckarsulm**, where there is the Deutsches Zweirad Museum (German Two-Wheeler Museum) in the former Deutschordensschloss (Palace of the Teutonic Order). In nearby **Bad Friedrichshall** there is the unique chance of visiting the Steinsalzbergwerk (a working salt mine). Particularly interesting is a huge cavern with reliefs carved from salt. The mine is open during summer and the way is signposted from the middle of town.

**Bad Wimpfen** is close to Bad Friedrichshall and has a very picturesque Altstadt. The town is divided into two parts; Bad Wimpfen im Tal (in the valley) and 'am Berg' (on the hill). The Kaiserpfalz (dating around 1200) in Bad Wimpfen am Berg was the imperial residence of Kaiser Friedrich II. Still remaining are the massive walls, two impressive towers, a chapel and the ruins of some palace buildings. Also worth seeing in this part of town is the Gothic parish church with its beautiful interior. In the lower part of town the collegiate church of St Peter and Paul (tenth century) is the most significant place of interest.

Leave Heilbronn on the B39 and pass through vineyards to reach Weinsberg. Here the route branches left, off the B39, goes under the A6 and A81 motorways to continue in the direction of **Öhringen**, on the route of the Burgenstrasse (Castles Road). The town was already settled in very early times and lay near the Roman wall that stretched from Walldürn to Welzheim — relics from Roman times can be seen in the Weygang Museum. The late Romanesque parish church of St Peter and Paul contains elaborate tombs of the local nobility. Also worthy of attention is a finely carved altar (dating around 1500). Near the former Schloss a large park offers an opportunity to stretch the legs.

**Neuenstein**, to the east of Öhringen, is worth visiting because of its well preserved moated Schloss. It now serves as a museum offering an insight into the lives of the old German nobility. On the ground floor is a huge medieval kitchen. Though the palace dates back to the thirteenth century it has been altered many times over the centuries. Once it even served as an old peoples home.

After Öhringen this route leaves the Burgenstrasse to go southeast via Obersteinbach, Gnadental and Michelfeld (on the B14) to **Schwäbisch Hall**. Salt was won from the springs here already back in Celtic times and in the Middle Ages it made the town so rich that the Heller coin which was minted here, became one of the best known currencies in medieval Germany. Rising above the beautiful Marktplatz with its Baroque Rathaus and the Pranger (pillory) is the

*The Renaissance courtyard of the Altes Schloss, Stuttgart*

magnificent Michaelskirche. Inside are many valuable works of art, including an altar from the school of Riemenschneider. The Neubau (1527) once served as an arsenal and there are still some well preserved remnants of the old town defences. The Gelbinger Gasse has some particularly good examples of the town's old half-timbered houses.

Somewhat out of the main part of town, south along the Kocher stream, is the **Veste Comburg**. This massive 'castle' is clearly visible from afar and it is possible to drive up to it. Originally it was a castle belonging to the counts of Rothenburg-Comburg, before being changed into a monastery complex in the eleventh century. The monastery's church has Romanesque elements, but was partly re-built in Baroque style between 1707 and 1715. Among the church treasures is a huge chandelier from the twelfth century. Its circular form symbolises the walls of Jerusalem with their twelve towers. Also worth noting here is the Eberhardskapelle (1230) and the unique Romanesque gate-house.

Those with time could make a detour south-east to the walled town of **Vellberg**. The fortifications date back to the fifteenth century and include a system of underground passages. Together with the Renaissance Schloss, now a hotel, the overall impression here is of a surprisingly well preserved medieval town. Just across the river from Schwäbisch Hall, near **Wackershofen**, is the Hohenloher Freilandmuseum, where buildings once typical of the area can be seen.

Continue south from Schwäbisch Hall on the B19 to **Gaildorf**. There are still parts of the old town wall and a Schloss (fifteenth century) to be seen here. West of Gaildorf the pretty town of **Murrhardt** lies within the boundaries of the Naturpark Schwäbisch-Fränkischer Wald. It is a beautiful forested region, ideal for walking, and a good way to get a feel for it would be on the Idyllische Strasse (Idyllic Road) which goes through Murrhardt. The Limes Wanderweg (Roman Wall Trail) is a long distance walk and begins here continuing north to Osterburken, north-east of Mosbach. At many places along the way it is possible to see original remnants of the wall, as well as reconstructions.

Follow the B298 south from Gaildorf to **Schwäbisch Gmünd**. The former Free Imperial City is known these days for its important jewellery industry. Of all the historic buildings the Heilig-Kreuz-Münster, dating between 1300 and 1400, is the most important. It is one of the oldest Gothic hall churches in all Southern Germany. Also of interest are the half-timbered houses around the Markt which date back to the sixteenth century, and a few Baroque buildings such as the Rathaus. To the north-west, near **Welzheim** on the Idyllische Strasse, is a partially reconstructed Roman fort. There is also a trail  of some 28km (17 miles) in length which links over a dozen historic timber-mills in the valleys around here. At Lorch, a few kilometres west of Schwäbisch Gmünd, Route 11 can be joined by following the B297 south and then the B10 south-east, to Geislingen.

Continue on the B29 to **Schorndorf**. Sight-seeing here is easy as a marked walk leads to all the main places of interest. Especially attractive is the Marktplatz where the half-timbered building of the  Palmsche Apotheke (Palmsche Pharmacy, 1650) is to be found. Gottlieb Daimler, of Mercedes-Benz fame, was born in the Höllgasse 7 and the house has been arranged as a small museum. From here it is no longer far to Stuttgart, through the wine-growing villages of the Rems valley.

# Route 11 • Around the Swabian Jura
# 303km (188 miles)

The rugged landscape of the Swabian Jura was formed by layers of sedimentary rock laid down millions of years ago during the Jurassic period, when the whole region was covered by water. Later, in the Tertiary period, volcanic activity also helped form the landscape and it was at this time that the numerous cave systems began to form in the soft limestone. So far over a thousand caves have been discovered. For those travelling by train from Stuttgart (via Plochingen), Tübingen makes a good base for exploring the western side of the Jura and Ulm for the Danube valley to the east.

**Geislingen an der Steige** is situated in a valley in the northern reaches of the Swabian Jura. On cliffs high above town are the romantic ruins of Burg Helfenstein, a medieval castle. In town itself the Stadtkirche — a basilica from the late Gothic period — and some old houses in the Hauptstrasse are of interest. Also in the Hauptstrasse is an amusing and very imaginative fountain called the Elefantenbrunnen. The Heimatmuseum, in a beautiful old half-  timbered building, has exhibits relating to the craft of ivory-carving, which used to be practised here.

Follow the Schwäbische Alb Strasse (Swabian Jura Road) in a westerly direction via Deggingen to Wiesensteig. An excursion from here is to take the road in the direction of Neidlingen, but then turn left towards Schopfloch, and after about 2km (1 mile) stop at a large car park. From here it is only a short walk to the impressive ruins of

**Burg Reussenstein**. There are good views from here and a playground is nearby. By continuing through Neidlingen and Weilheim to **Holzmaden**, the Museum Hauff can be visited. This museum is known for its excellent collection of fossils from the Jurassic period. Especially interesting is the complete skeleton of an ichthyosaurus.

The main route continues from Wiesensteig to Westerheim. From here another excursion can be made to the Laichinger Tiefenhöhle (cave) near **Laichingen**. It forms the deepest cave system in Germany, with shafts penetrating down some 100m (328ft). At the entrance is a small museum that is open — like the caves — from Easter until mid-October. Continue from Westerheim via Donnstetten, around the elevation of the Römerstein (874m, 2,867ft) (good views at the top) and through Böhringen to Bad Urach.

**Bad Urach** is beautifully situated in the midst of thickly forested mountainous country. Although the north-west corner of town is somewhat spoiled by the concrete buildings of the spa quarter, the old town centre still has much of its original charm. One of the most attractive buildings in the Marktplatz is the Rathaus (1560-64). In the collegiate church of St Amandus (dated between 1475 and 1500) is a beautiful stone pulpit from the sixteenth century. Next door, the Residenzschloss (Residential Palace), has a number of rooms open to view, as well as a museum. To visit the waterfall nearby follow the B28 to the end of town in the direction of Metzingen and then turn off at the sign 'Uracher Wasserfall' (waterfall). A well marked path leads from the car park to the falls. Another path climbs to the right, past the falls, to the castle ruins of Hohenurach — a walk taking in the falls, and the ruins, would take about 2 hours, there and back.

Leave Bad Urach by first going a very short distance south on the road to Münsingen and then turning right on to a steeply climbing and scenic road towards Bleichstetten and Würtingen. After Würtingen the Jura road passes through Ohnastetten to Holzelfingen. From here take the road south, go around Traifelberg and cross the B312/313 to get to the car park at Schloss Lichtenstein.

**Schloss Lichtenstein** is Baden-Württemberg's answer to the fairytale castles built by King Ludwig II of Bavaria. The original castle, on steep cliffs above the Echaz valley, was torn down in 1802. It would probably have remained a ruin if it were not for the historical novel by Wilhelm Hauff titled *Lichtenstein*, published in 1826. Count Wilhelm of Württemberg was impressed enough by the book to have the castle rebuilt, according to Hauff's description, between 1840 and 1842. There are guided tours through the castle during summer. A marked trail, about 6km (4 miles) there and back, goes from near the

*(Above) The bustling streets and cafés of Tübingen; (Below) The wild flowers of Germany add a splash of colour to the countryside*

castle down to a cave known as the Nebelhöhle — it is also possible to drive via Genkingen. This cave has been open to the public since 1803 and contains beautiful stalactite formations.

Return to the B312-313, turn right, go through Gross-Engstingen on the B313 proper and then turn right again, off the B313, in the direction of **Erpfingen**. After a short distance a road to the right leads to the Bärenhöhle (Bears Cave), one of the most interesting caves in the Swabian Jura. The Bärenhöhle is not only popular because of its limestone formations, but also because of the numerous skeletons of cave bears that were found here. A few of the skeletons have been put back together and can be seen in the course of a guided tour. At the entrance it is possible to buy a detailed booklet in English about the cave. Nearby is a large amusement park for children. The combined attractions of cave and park mean that it can get very crowded here on weekends in summer.

In the Melchingertal (valley) that runs north-west of Erpfingen is a Sommerbobbahn (summer bobsled run). These bobsled runs are quite popular in Germany, with a metal slide replacing snow. A chair-lift goes to the top of the run and the descent can be made on either single or double bobs.

Continue from Erpfingen to Burladingen on the B32, then turn right in the direction of Killer and Hechingen — a pretty alternative route is to go right after Erpfingen to Melchingen, and then via Salmendingen and Ringingen to Killer. Once the B32 connects with the B27 follow the latter in the direction of Rottweil, passing through Hechingen. Leave the dual carriageway of the B27 at the exit Brielhof/Ziegelbach, from where a small windy road goes to **Burg Hohenzollern**. A visitor's car park is situated below the castle, from where it is about another 20 minutes walk uphill — mini buses go up in the high season.

Atop a hill that wins in majesty from the flat country to the north, Burg Hohenzollern is the Swabian equivalent of Schloss Neuschwanstein in the Bavarian Alps. The impression of a medieval castle with turrets and defensive walls is, however, deceptive. It was built only as far back as the nineteenth century, by the romantically inclined Kaiser Friedrich Wilhelm IV, though there was probably already a castle on this easily defended position in the eleventh century — guided tours take place daily.

By returning to Hechingen and taking the B27 north, an excursion can be made to the old university town of **Tübingen**. Those who may have arrived by train from Stuttgart should turn right from the station, go past the post office into the Karlstrasse, and then go over the Eberhardsbrücke, which crosses the Neckar river. The tourist office is located by the bridge which leads into the Altstadt and it should be possible to pick up a town plan marking out suggested tours of the old quarter.

The focal point of the Marktplatz is the Rathaus (1435; extensive changes in 1698 and 1872) with its painted façade and astronomical clock (1511). Nearby in the Holzmarkt is the collegiate church of St George a late Gothic building with an impressive interior. Also here is a bookshop with a plaque out front that commemorates the fact that the great novelist Hermann Hesse worked there between 1895 and 1899. On an elevation behind the Rathaus is Schloss Hohentübingen (sixteenth century). The most famous part of the palace is the Ausseres Tor (Outer Gate) which dates back to 1606. The poet Friedrich Hölderlin lived in the Hölderlinturm, near the Eberhardsbrücke, from 1807 until his death in 1843. Row-boats can be hired near here in summer.

Just north of town on the B27 the former monastery of **Bebenhausen** is worth visiting with its richly decorated church and late Gothic cloister (1471-1496). An added reason for coming here is that the monastery lies at the edge of the Naturpark Schönbuch, a beautiful forested area, ideal for walking.

Another excursion from Hechingen is west to **Haigerloch**, a small town situated in the deeply carved valley of the Eyach river. There are two parts to the town; the Oberstadt (upper town), and the Unterstadt (lower town), down in the valley. The Schloss, in the Unterstadt, dates back to the thirteenth century and was from 1576 residence of the counts of Hohenzollern-Haigerloch. In the attached church are some valuable furnishings, including a Renaissance high altar (1609). Accessible from the Unterstadt is the Atom Museum. In the last months of World War II a nuclear research station, shifted from Berlin, was placed here in a former beer cellar. Today a reconstruction of the nuclear reactor the scientists worked on can be seen, as well as detailed documentation of their activities.

The Oberstadt is of interest above all for the pilgrimage church of St Anna (eighteenth century). Although it does not look much from outside the Baroque interior is quite overwhelming. The stucco work is by the Wessobrunn artist Johann Michael Feuchtmayer.

The main route continues from Hechingen south on the B27 to **Balingen**. This modern Swabian town has little of historical interest left, apart from a couple of churches and the pretty Zollernschloss. The surrounding countryside is, however, very scenic and worth the effort of exploring. East of the town there is excellent walking around

*Opposite: (Top) Carnival time in Rottweil is a colourful celebration;*
*(Bottom) A sixteenth-century half-timbered building*
*in Fridingen an der Donau*

the villages of Burgfelden and Streichen — drive via Frommern, Stockenhausen and Zillhausen. In the Naturschutzgebiet (nature reserve) around the Irrenberg it is possible to find many wild flowers (all protected) once typical of the Swabian Jura. Among these flowers are several species of orchid.

From Balingen there are two possibilities for getting down to the River Donau: the first and simplest route is to go via Rottweil to Tuttlingen; the second and by far the most scenic is to go directly south over the Lochenstein and along the Bäratal. Rottweil is worth at least a detour along the B27 even if the more scenic alternative is chosen.

The most interesting time to visit **Rottweil** is during the period before Lent, when carnival celebrations take place. Rottweil's carnival is one of the oldest and most famous in Southern Germany. The overall impression is that of a genuinely traditional festival — not something simply put on for tourists. Highlight of the festivities is a costumed procession known as the Narrensprung (Fool's March). It always begins at the Schwarzes Tor (Black Gate) on Rose Monday and is repeated the following day. The exact date changes from year to year but it always occurs in February.

Apart from Fasnet, Rottweil also has something to offer in the form of its well preserved Altstadt. Many of the houses date back to the sixteenth or eighteenth centuries and a typical characteristic are the finely decorated bay windows. Of the town's churches the Heilig-Kreuz-Münster (thirteenth to sixteenth centuries) is noted for its richly appointed interior and the Kapellenkirche (fourteenth and fifteenth centuries) is famed for its beautiful late Gothic tower. In the Stadtmuseum (Town Museum) is an interesting selection of exquisitely carved and painted carnival masks. A fact for dog-lovers is that the Rottweiler get its name from this town. They were originally bred in the Middle Ages to guard herds of cattle or flocks of sheep. To get to the Donau go south on the B14 to Tuttlingen.

To get onto the scenic route down to the Donau from Balingen, follow the B463 towards Frommern, but instead of turning towards Albstadt leave the B463 and continue south, past Weilstetten, on a minor road that goes over a mountain known as the Lochenstein. At 963m (3,159ft) the **Lochenstein** is popular for its views, especially in clear autumn weather, and the youth hostel here makes a good base

for walks in one of the most beautiful parts of the Swabian Jura.

After Tieringen the road enters the Bära valley and passes through the villages of Oberdigisheim, Unterdigisheim, Nusplingen and Bärenthal. The valley is picturesque at any time of the year but it is especially pretty in spring when all the wild flowers are out. Walking trails follow much of the Bära valley and a cycle path goes from Tieringen to Beuron. Just outside Bärenthal take the road branching right to Fridingen.

**Fridingen an der Donau** is a very pleasant village. Near the railway station is a look-out tower known as the Gansnest, which offers terrific views over the Donau valley towards Beuron. A couple of kilometres south, a significant portion of the Donau's water disappears into the porous rock of the southern Jura (Donauversickerung), to reappear some 18km (11 miles) south-west in the Aachtopf near Engen. West of Fridingen the village of **Mühlheim an der Donau** still has rests of its medieval fortifications and an imposing Schloss (1751-3). Nearby, to the north, is the **Kolbinger Höhle**, a cave noted for its outstanding limestone formations — open weekends. The stretch of the Donau now to be described — between Fridingen and Sigmaringen — is regarded as the most beautiful on its entire 3,000km (1,863 miles) journey to the Black Sea. Marked walking trails run along both sides of the valley.

Continue north-east to **Beuron**. Kloster Beuron was founded around 1077 and occupies an idyllic position beside a bend in the Donau. The monastery church was built between 1732 and 1738 in Baroque style, with the contributions of great artists like J.A. Feuchtmayer and I.J. Wegscheider. In spite of changes made in the nineteenth century the Baroque interior remains quite overwhelming in its lavish detail. Close to the monastery is a covered wooden bridge that was erected over the Donau in 1803.

An interesting excursion from Beuron is to go south-east, via Leibertingen, to **Burg Wildenstein**. The castle is a short distance outside Leibertingen, on steep cliffs above the Donau. It was extended as a fortress in the sixteenth century and has been beautifully restored as a youth hostel (☎ 07466/411). Paths lead to several viewpoints over the river. There is also a walk of about 12km ($7^1/_2$ miles) that goes from the castle down to Beuron, then follows the river's left bank to the Mauruskapelle. From there it is possible to cross a bridge and to follow a trail back up to the castle.

From Beuron the road winds its way along the Donau, passing several castles, to the town of **Sigmaringen**. Schloss Sigmaringen is spread over a rocky elevation above the river. Most of the present complex dates back to the eighteenth and nineteenth centuries, though remnants of the original medieval castle have survived in places. Open to view are some of the stately rooms along with the Schlossmuseum, which contains exhibits on subjects of prehistory and early history. The palace art collection has a selection of works by Southern German masters and the royal stables (Marstallmuseum) may also be visited. South of Sigmaringen, in the direction of Krauchenwies, is Wildpark Josephslust, a large game-park with animals in a natural forest setting.

Continue on the B32, via Mengen, to Herbertingen and then go north on the B311 to **Riedlingen**. The town has been able to keep much of its medieval appearance with towers, defensive walls and half-timbered houses. The parish church of St George (fourteenth century) contains fragments of late Gothic wall frescoes. East of the town on the Bussen (767m 2,516ft), is a pilgrimage church (1516) and the ruins of a medieval castle. From the top are breathtaking views over Upper Swabia and the Alps. South-west, at **Heiligkreuztal**, is a well preserved Gothic Kloster and directly south, along the Donau, is an area of marshy land where the last colonies of wild storks in this part of Germany can be seen. By taking the B312 east of Riedlingen Route 12 (Chapter 5) can be joined at Biberach. Otherwise continue north on the B312 to Zwiefalten.

**Zwiefalten's** abbey church is one of the greatest achievements of Germany's Baroque period. It was planned by Johann Georg Fischer and built between 1744 and 1765. The ornate interior was partly the work of such renowned artists as Franz Joseph Spengler (ceiling frescoes) and J.M. Feuchtmayer (stucco). Only a few kilometres north of Zwiefalten the **Wimsener Höhle** is well worth visiting. This cave system is filled with water, but boats can penetrate some 700m (2,296ft) inside.

From Zwiefalten go via Zwiefaltendorf to join the B311, and then continue to **Obermarchtal**. The Baroque monastery church was built between 1686 and 1701. The Schmuzer, a famous family of artists and master-builders from Wessobrunn, were responsible for the richly ornamental stucco work. Without a guided tour it is only possible to enter the area below the organ gallery, however a good general impression is possible from here anyway.

Continue on the B311 to **Ehingen** (attractive Marktplatz and some interesting churches) and from there leave this road to follow the B492 to **Blaubeuren**. Apart from the Kloster, the most famous sight here is the Blautopf, one of the largest natural springs in Germany. It is fed by water that has seeped through the porous rock of the

*Opposite: Precipitous white cliffs are characteristic of the beautiful Danube valley*

central Swabian Jura. The Blautopf (Blue Pot) gets its name because of the bluish-green colour of its water. Next to the spring is the restored Hammerschmiede smithy (1804) that can be visited.

Blaubeuren's monastery was established by monks from Hirsau in the eleventh century. The great attraction of the church is a unique high altar (1493), a masterpiece from the late Gothic period. Also of note are the superbly carved choir stalls (1493) by Jörg Syrlin the Younger. In the middle of town the Urgeschichtliches Museum (Museum of Prehistory) has exhibits that go back to the time of Neanderthal Man. Of particular interest is a 33,000 to 35,000-year-old ivory carving that is supposed to be the earliest representation of a human figure yet found. As with all the other finds it comes from caves in the vicinity of Blaubeuren.

From Blaubeuren continue along the B28 to **Ulm**, the birthplace of Albert Einstein. With a tower that reaches a height of 161m (528ft) to the tip of its spire (the tallest church tower in the world) Ulm's Münster (minster) is difficult to be missed. It is possible to ascend the tower and in clear weather the view extends as far as the Alps. Particularly interesting within the minster, apart from the over-whelming effect of its massive proportions, are the choir stalls (1469-74) by Jörg Syrlin the Elder.

In the Fischer (fisherman's) and Gerber (tanner's) quarters south-west of the minster, near the Donau, are numerous half-timbered houses dating back to the sixteenth and seventeenth centuries. The Rathaus (1370), just south of the minster in the Marktplatz, is one of Ulm's prettiest historic buildings. Near the Rathaus Ulm Museum is to be recommended for its excellent collection of art from the area of Upper Swabia. A very photogenic angle over the old quarter of the city can be obtained by crossing the Herdbrücke over the Donau. By following the B10 east Route 18 (Chapter 7) can be joined at Augsburg. This route continues north back to Geislingen, on the B10.

As a footnote it might be added that most of the Swabian Jura is covered by detailed walking maps that should not be hard to obtain locally. The area is divided into five sheets in the series *RV Wanderkarten*: Härtsfeld, Heidenheimer Alb; Kaiserberge, Filstal; Mittlere Alb, Münsinger Alb; Blaubeurer Alb, Ulmer Alb; Donautal, Grosser Heuberg (all 1:50,000).

# Additional Information

## Places of Interest in Stuttgart

**Daimler-Benz-Museum**
Stuttgart-Untertürkheim
Mercedesstrasse 136
Open: Tuesday to Sunday 9am-5pm, closed on public holidays.

**Landesmuseum**
Altes Schloss
Schillerplatz 6
Open: Tuesday and Thursday to Sunday 10am-5pm, Wednesday 10am-7pm.

**Lindenmuseum**
Hegelplatz 1
Open: Tuesday, Wednesday, Friday to Sunday 10am-5pm, Thursday 10am-8pm.

**Porschemuseum**
Stuttgart-Zuffenhausen
Porschestrasse 42
Open: Monday to Friday 9am-12noon and 1.30-4pm.

**Schloss Rosenstein and Museum am Löwentor**
Open: Tuesday, Thursday and Friday 9am-5pm, Wednesday 9am-8pm, Saturday 9am-6pm, Sunday and public holidays 10am-6pm.

**Staatsgalerie Stuttgart**
(Old and New)
Konrad-Adenauer-Strasse 30-32
Open: Wednesday, Friday to Sunday 10am-5pm, Tuesday and Thursday 10am-8pm.

**Wilhelma**
Stuttgart-Bad Cannstatt
Neckartalstrasse
Open: 1 March to 31 March daily 8am-5pm. 1 April to 30 April daily 8am-5.30pm. 1 May to 31 August daily 8am-6pm. 1 September to 30 September daily 8am-5.30pm. 1 October to 31 October daily 8am-5pm. 1 November to 28 February daily 8am to 4pm.

## Useful Information

**Area Code**
☎ 0711

**Car Rental**
*Avis*
Katharinenstrasse 18
☎ 241441

*Hertz*
Hohenstaufenstrasse 18
☎ 643044

*Inter Rent*
Friedrichstrasse 28
☎ 221749

**Duty Dentist**
☎ 780 0266

**Duty Doctor**
☎ 280211

**Pharmacies**
☎ 224310 for information as to which are open outside normal hours.

**Main Post Office**
Rear of the Königsbau on Schillerplatz
Open: Monday to Friday 8am-6pm. Saturday 8am-12noon.

**Taxis**
☎ 566061

**Tourist Information Centre**
Touristikzentrum 'i-Punkt'
Klett -Passage
Am Hauptbahnhof
Open: January to 31 December,
Monday to Saturday 8.30am-10pm.
January to 30 April, Sundays and
public holidays 1-6pm. May to 31
October, Sundays and public
holidays 11am-6pm. November to
31 December, Sundays and public
holidays, 1-6pm. Closed New
Year's Day, Easter Monday and on
the 25 and 26 December.
☎ (0711) 2228-240/241

Write for information to:
Verkehrsamt der Stadt Stuttgart
Lautenschlagerstrasse 3
Postfach 105044
D-7000 Stuttgart 1

## Other Places of Interest

**Bad Friedrichshall**
*Steinsalzbergwerk* (Salt Mine)
Open: May to mid-October,
Tuesday to Friday 2.30-4pm.
Saturday, Sunday and holidays
9am-4pm.

**Bad Urach**
*Residenzschloss*
Open: Tuesday to Sunday 10am-
5pm.

**Blaubeuren**
*Hammerschmiede*
Open: daily 9am-6pm.

*Urgeschichtliches Museum*
Karlsstrasse 21
Open: daily, except Mondays.

**Burg Hohenzollern**
Near Hechingen
Open: daily April to october 9am-

5.30pm, November to March 9am-
4.30pm.

**Erlebnispark Tripsdrill**
Near Cleebronn
Open: end of March until 1
November 9am-6pm.
☎ (07135) 4081

**Erpfingen**
*Bärenhöhle*
Open: 1 April to October daily
8.30am-5.30pm. In winter only
Sundays.

**Esslingen**
*Stadtmuseum* (Town Museum)
Open: Monday to Saturday 2-4pm.
Sunday 10.30am-12noon.

**Geislingen an der Steige**
*Heimatmuseum*
Open: during summer Wednes-
days, Saturdays and Sundays.

**Haigerloch**
*Atom Museum*
Open: May to September daily
10am-12noon and 2-5pm, March,
April, October and November.
Same times Saturday and Sunday
only.

**Holzmaden**
*Museum Hauff*
Open: daily 9am-12noon and 1-
5pm except Mondays.

**Laichingen**
*Laichinger Tiefenhöhle*
Open: Easter to 15 October daily
9am-6pm.

**Lichtenstein**
*Schloss Lichtenstein*
Open: April to October daily 9am-
12noon and 1-5.30pm. November,

*Opposite: (top) Next to the Blautopf spring in Blaubeuren is the restored smithy; (bottom) The beautifully painted Rathaus at Ulm*

February and March, Saturday and Sunday 9am-12noon and 1-5.30pm.

### Ludwigsburg
*Residenzschloss*
Guided tours April to October daily 9am-12noon and 1-5pm, November to March Monday to Friday at 10.30am and 3pm, Saturday and Sunday at 10.30am, 2pm and 3.30pm.

*Schloss Favorite*
Guided tours Tuesday and Sunday 10am-12noon and 1.30-4pm.

### Marbach
*Schiller-Nationalmuseum*
Open: daily 9am-5pm.

### Nebelhöhle
Open: 15 March to 31 October daily 9am-6pm. ☎ (07128) 605

### Neckarsulm
*Deutsches Zweirad Museum*
Open: daily 9am-12noon and 1.30-5.30pm.

### Neuenstein
*Schloss*
Guided tours lasting 1 hour, mid-March to mid-November 9am-12noon and 1.30-6pm.

### Obermarchtal
*Baroque Monastery Church*
For further information contact:
Gemeindeverwaltung ☎ (07375) 205

### Öhringen
*Weygang Museum*
Open: Tuesday to Sunday 10am-12noon and 2-4pm.

### Rottweil
*Stadtmuseum*
Open: Monday to Thursday and Saturday 9am-12noon and 2-5pm, Friday 9am-12noon, Sunday 10am-12noon.

### Schorndorf
*Gottlieb-Daimler-Geburtshaus* (museum)
Open: Tuesday and Thursday 2-4.30pm
☎ (07181) 66510

### Sigmaringen
*Schloss Sigmaringen*
Open: February to November daily 8.30am-12noon and 1-5pm.

### Tübingen
*Schloss Hohentübingen*
Guided tours April to September, Saturday 5pm, Sunday 11am and 3pm.

### Ulm
*Münster*
Open: daily June to August 8am-6.45pm.

*Ulm Museum*
Open: June to September Tuesday, Wednesday and Friday to Sunday 10am-5pm, Thursday 10am-12noon and 2-8pm, Sunday 10am-1pm and 2-5pm.

### Veste Comburg
(Kloster Comburg)
Open: Tuesday to Saturday 9am-12noon and 1.30-5pm. Sunday 1.30-5pm.
(Entrance fee).

**Wackershofen**
*Hohenloher Freilandmuseum*
Schwäbisch Hall
Open: April, May and October
daily 10am-5.30pm. June, July,
August & September daily 9am-
6pm. Museum is closed Mondays.
☎ (07170) 751363

**Wildpark Josephslust**
4km (2 miles) south of Sigmaringen
in the direction of Krauchenwies
Open: all year from dawn to dusk
☎ (07571) 66510

**Zwiefalten**
*Wimsener Höhle*
Open: 15 January to 20 December
daily 9am-6pm.

# Tourist Information Centres

**Bad Wimpfen**
Rathaus, on the Marktplatz
Open: Monday to Friday 9am-
12noon and 2-4pm. Saturday and
Sunday April to September 10am-
12noon and 2-4pm.
☎ (07063) 7052

**Bad Urach**
Städtische Kurverwaltung
Haus des Gastes
Bei den Thermen 4
Open: Monday to Friday 9-11.45am
and 2-4.45pm. Saturday 9-11.45am
☎ (07125) 1761

**Esslingen**
Kulturamt
Marktplatz 16
Open: Monday to Friday 8am-6pm,
Saturday 9am-12noon.
☎ (0711) 3512 441 or 645

**Heilbronn**
Marktplatz
Open: Monday to Friday 9am-
5.30pm, Saturday 9am-12.30pm.
☎ (07131) 562270

**Schwäbisch Gmünd**
Johannisplatz 3
Open: Monday to Friday 9am-
5.30pm, Saturday 9am-12.30pm,
May to October, also Sunday 10am-
1pm.
☎ (07171) 66244

**Schwäbisch Hall**
Marktplatz
Open: April to September, Monday
to Friday 9am-12noon and 2-6pm.
Saturday and Sunday 10am-2pm,
November to March Monday to
Friday 9am-12noon and 2-5pm.
☎ (0791) 751246/751321

**Sigmaringen**
Schwabstrasse 1
Open: Monday to Friday 9am-
12.30pm and 2-5.30pm. Saturday
9am-12noon.
☎ (07571) 106233

**Tübingen**
An der Neckarbrücke
(Eberhardsbrücke)
Open: Monday to Friday 8.30am-
6.30pm, Saturday 8.30am-12.30/
5pm according to season.
☎ (07071) 35011

**Ulm**
Münsterplatz 51
Open: Monday to Friday 9am-6pm,
Saturday 9am-12.30pm.
☎ (0731) 64161

# 5
# *LAKE CONSTANCE AND UPPER SWABIA*

---

The small corner of Germany covered in this chapter is character-ised by a gentle landscape of hills, lakes and moors. Close as it is to the Allgäu and Bavarian Alps, it is easily overlooked while driving through. The attractions of Lake Constance (Bodensee) are obvious but those of Upper Swabia (Oberschwaben) are hidden in the Baroque splendour of its churches and the rural seclusion of its villages.

## Route 12 • Upper Swabia 125km (78 miles)

**Biberach** lies on the Schwäbische Dichterstrasse (Swabian Poet's Road) and on the Oberschwäbische Barockstrasse (Upper Swabian Baroque Road). There is, indeed, a bit of both in this town which came to prosperity in the late Middle Ages, helped by its resourceful merchants and a flourishing cloth industry. One of Biberach's most famous sons is the poet Christoph Martin Wieland (1733-1813). He translated a number of Shakespeare's works and it was he who first brought Shakespeare onto the German stage in 1761, with his translation of *The Tempest*. His small memorial museum is located in the Wielandsgärten.

Biberach's Marktplatz is one of the nicest in the area. Forming a border at one end is the Martinskirche, a Gothic basilica which dates back to the fourteenth century. The interior was changed into the Baroque style between 1745 and 1748. In the Heilig-Geist-Spital (1519) is the Braith-Mali-Museum including, among other things, work by local artists. In June the town celebrates its Schützenfest (Riflemen's Festival) with parades in historical costumes. Just north of the town Schloss Warthausen (sixteenth century) is open.

From Biberach take the B312 (Baroque Road) to **Ochsenhausen**. Here the main attraction is the former Benedictine Kloster (1090)

117

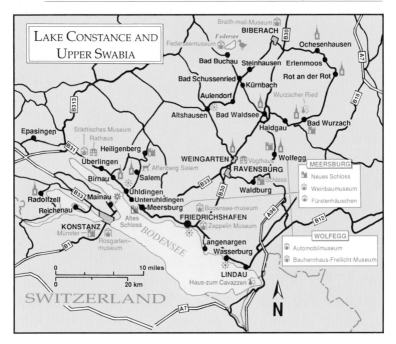

with its Baroque church. According to legend a nunnery once existed on this spot, which was destroyed by invading Hungarians. The fleeing nuns hid their valuables in a field and some hundred years later they were turned up by a farmer ploughing with his ox (*Ochse*). Monks took this as a sign of God and that led to the founding of the present monastery. Worth noting in the church is the Rococo high altar, pulpit (1740) and a huge church organ by J. Gabler, the greatest organ builder of the Baroque. Apart from good walking and cycling in the general area, there is also a narrow gauge railway — the Öchsle-Schmalspur-Museumseisenbahn — that runs between Ochsenhausen and Warthausen.

Continue to Erlenmoos and then turn right off the B312 to get to **Rot an der Rot**. The Baroque monastery church of St Maria and St Verena (1763-86) is another of those churches showing the gradual change from Baroque to classicist style. Particularly impressive is the stucco work by F.X. Feuchtmayer, the frescoes by J. Zick and the high altar by F.X. and S. Feuchtmayer.

Take the B312 south-west from Rot an der Rot to get to **Bad Wurzach**. Baroque and Rococo art is to be found here as well, but to

*Biberach's Marktplatz*

counterbalance art with nature the Wurzacher Ried shall be mentioned first. A 'Ried' is a moor, or marsh, and the **Wurzacher Ried** is the largest intact upland moor in central Europe. It is a protected area with rare plants and stands of birch trees. Mud from this, and other moors in the area, has therapeutic qualities and this fact has enabled Wurzach, Buckau, Schussenried and Waldsee to add Bad (spa) to their names. Some lakes in the Ried area are fine for swimming.

One of the main attractions in town is the Wurzacher Schloss (1723-8) with its magnificent Baroque staircase. Also worth seeing is the parish church of St Verena (1777) and the Kloster Maria Rosengarten with its beautiful staircase (1764) and a Rococo chapel. Every July the town celebrates the Heilig-Blutfest with a horse procession.

Continue west via Haidgau and Haisterkirch to **Bad Waldsee**. The town is situated prettily around two lakes — the Schlosssee and the Stadtsee — with a skyline dominated by the twin towers of the collegiate church of St Peter. The most famous work of art here is the sepulchral slab of Georg I of Waldburg. Some other places of interest are the Baroque Schloss (1745) which can only be viewed from the outside, the Frauenbergkapelle (1471), the Rathaus (1426) and the Kornhaus, opposite the Rathaus, which dates from the fifteenth century and contains a museum.

From Bad Waldsee take the B30 south to **Weingarten**. The town's Baroque basilica is the largest in Germany. It was built between 1715 and 1724 under the direction of a number of respected architects, including Franz Beer and D.G. Frisoni. Nor was money spared in employing the best artists of the time to do the interior; Cosmas Damian Asam, one of the leading figures of the late Baroque, was responsible for the brilliantly detailed and richly coloured ceiling frescoes. Also worth noting is the Baroque organ (1737-50) by J. Gabler and the choir stalls.

Around here religious feeling is not only expressed in ornate church interiors, as the Blutritt demonstrates. This horse procession takes place on the Friday after Ascension Day (Christi Himmelfahrt) and many farmers still keep horses just for this purpose. They also come in such numbers that it has become the largest procession of its type in Germany.

A scenic excursion from Weingarten is east, via Unterankenreute, to **Wolfegg**. There are a number of things to be seen here, including the parish church with its colourful Baroque interior, a car museum — open Sundays — and the excellent Bauernhaus-Freilicht-Museum. On show at this open-air museum are farm dwellings once typical for Upper Swabia and the western Allgäu. There is a museum festival held here on the first Sunday in September. Wolfegg's Renaissance Schloss is only open to public view during concerts, so it is advisable to inquire first at the tourist office. In the general area are some small lakes, some of which are good for swimming.

**Ravensburg** directly south of Weingarten, established itself as an important trading centre in the Middle Ages. The Ravensburger Handelsgesellschaft (1380-1530) was the most important trading company in Southern Germany, until the rise of the House of Fugger in Augsburg. Relics of this illustrious past are still to be seen in the many gates and towers from the fourteenth to sixteenth centuries that characterise the town's skyline. Good views over the old part of town can be had from the Veitsburg (1750). Among the historic buildings of interest are the Vogthaus dating from around 1480 with the town museum, the Renaissance Lederhaus and the Haus der Grossen Ravensburger Handelsgesellschaft (1446). To the east of Ravensburg, in **Waldburg**, is an interesting Schloss (1525) — now a museum — as well as some pretty old farm houses. To join Route 13 take the B33 south-west to Meersburg (car ferry link to Konstanz).

Return to Weingarten, but this time take the B32 north to **Altshausen**. The Teutonic Order of Knights left their mark here in the form of a Baroque Schloss and its attached church from the fifteenth century, later redone in Baroque manner. The most attractive aspect of the Schloss is the gate-house (1731).

Turn east off the B32 to go via Ebersbach to **Aulendorf**. As reminders that the town was once an important railway junction are a full-sized steam engine and a miniature steam railway. Swimming is possible in the Steegersee and the Schloss and parish church of St Martin are of interest. Continue north via Otterswang.

**Bad Schussenried** has as its major attraction a former Premonstratensian abbey which was founded in 1183. However from that time virtually nothing has remained and the impressive Bibliotheksaal (library hall) was only built around 1760. The abbey church contains elaborate stucco work by Johannes Zick (dating around 1740) and the incredibly intricate carvings of the choir stalls from 1718 should not be overlooked. In nearby Kürnbach there is an open-air museum with farm buildings which date from as far back as the sixteenth century.

The **Federsee**, a few kilometres north of Bad Schussenried, is a lake surrounded by marshlands. The whole area is protected and forms the largest nature reserve in south-west Germany. Bird-watchers should bring their binoculars as there are some 250 species of birds to be observed here. A narrow, raised wooden walkway leads over the marsh and ends at an observation platform from where boats can be hired. At the start of the walkway the Federseemuseum has as its central theme the prehistoric settlement of the area. The church of St Cornelius and St Cyprian in **Bad Buchau**, at the edge of the reserve, has an interior in classical style from 1774 to 1776 — something unique in the Baroque stronghold of Upper Swabia.

From Bad Schussenried continue to **Steinhausen**. The pilgrimage church of St Peter and Paul (1727-33) has been described by some as 'the most beautiful village church in the world'. In fact the church really is a fine example of Baroque art and architecture and is a tribute to the genius of Dominikus and Johann Baptist Zimmermann. It is above all the remarkable harmony achieved in the brothers execution of the interior decoration that gives the church much of its unique appeal. Continue back to Biberach.

# Route 13 • Lake Constance 95km (59 miles)

Most of Bodensee is divided between Germany and Switzerland, with Austria controlling a small portion of its south-eastern shore. It is sometimes given the rather exaggerated title of Schwäbisches Meer (Swabian Sea). A total area of 538sq km (335sq miles) is however, big by German standards, even though North Americans might smile when they compare it to their Great Lakes. Unique to the lake are some excellent wines — in the area of Meersburg and Hagnau — and tasty fish dishes of Blaufelchen (powan) or Kretzer (perch).

Close to the Swiss border **Konstanz** is the largest town on the lake. In the Middle Ages the town grew rich through trade as its geographical situation was ideal and even today there is still much to give evidence of this early prosperity. An interesting fact on the side is that one of the town's most famous sons was Count (Graf) Ferdinand von Zeppelin. It was he who designed the famous airships later named after him.

The harbour in Konstanz is not, perhaps, as picturesque as that in Lindau, at the lake's other end, but it is still a good place to form first impressions — especially for those coming by train as it is near the station. On the lake front is the old Kaufhaus or Konzil (1388), a large building that was formerly used as a storage house. Boats doing excursions on the lake leave from near here. To get to the Altstadt go through the subway passage next to the station, at the end of which is a tourist office.

The Münster Unserer Lieben Frau is the town's most important church. Parts of the basilica date back to the tenth century but the overall impression is that of a medieval church. Of particular interest are some finely carved doors (1470) and the Heiliges Grab, a sandstone tomb in the Mauritiuskapelle which dates from around 1280. A small charge is asked for the steep climb up the tower, but clear views over the lake make it worthwhile.

Most of the other places of interest in Konstanz lie within or near the pedestrian zone and can be reached in the course of a pleasant stroll. The Dreifaltigkeitskirche, in the Rosgartenstrasse, is a Gothic basilica famous for its cycle of wall frescoes (fourteenth century). Nearby in the Rosgartenmuseum are collections dealing with prehistory and medieval art. Some of the town's most attractive buildings include the Wohnturm zum goldenen Löwen (1450), in the Hohenhausgasse, and the Rathaus (1594), in the Kanzleistrasse. Concerts take place in the pretty Rathaus courtyard during summer.

There are a number of places outside Konstanz that are worth visiting and the island of **Mainau** is one of the most interesting. It is also called the Blumeninsel (Island of Flowers) because it was turned into one large flower garden by Grand Duke Friedrich I of Baden, in the nineteenth century. Apart from the multitude of exotic flowers there is also a Schloss and church to be seen. A fee is charged for entering the gardens and the island is reached over a footbridge, near

*The Baroque interior of the Klosterkirche in Weingarten*

*Part of the finely carved doorway of the Münster Unserer Lieben Frau in Konstanz*

the large car park on the mainland. There are also boat connections from Konstanz.

The island of **Reichenau** can be driven to over a tree-lined causeway and is famed for its vegetables rather than its flowers. The main interest here lies in the island's three Romanesque churches: in Oberzell St George's Church has outstanding frescoes from the tenth century; in Mittelzell the minster has a valuable collection of reliquary shrines and in Niederzell St Peter and Paul's Church contains Romanesque frescoes, only discovered in 1900.

Just west of Konstanz is an area of marshy land known as the **Wollmatinger Ried**. It is the habitat of many species of birds and rare plants. As the Ried stands under strict protection it is only possible to visit it as part of a guided tour. Inquire at the tourist information in Konstanz for more details.

From Konstanz this route now continues around the lake via Radolfzell. Those who prefer can, however, take a car ferry directly across to Meersburg in order to save a bit of time. **Radolfzell** is reached directly on the B33 and is mainly interesting for the Liebfrauenmünster (1436-1550) in the Marktplatz. A colourful tradition is the procession of decorated boats that crosses the Zeller See from Moos to Radolfzell on the Monday after the third Sunday in July. Continue north on the B34 to Espasingen and shortly afterwards join the B31, to get to Überlingen on the shores of the Überlinger See which is an arm of Bodensee.

**Überlingen's** main attraction is the Nikolausmünster (1350-1563), a late Gothic basilica. Inside is a huge, brilliantly carved high altar by Jörg Zürn. He was born in 1583, in nearby Bad Waldsee, and worked 6 years on the altar, together with his father and two brothers. Some 10m (33ft) high it is a masterpiece of German Renaissance sculpture. The carvings in the Rathaussaal of the old Rathaus (1490) by Jakob Ruess are also of exceptional quality. Other sights include the Franziskanerkirche (1753-60), which was remodelled in Rococo style and contains an altar by J.A. Feuchtmayer. In the Städtisches Museum is a fascinating collection of dolls houses, of interest to adults and children alike. For those who just want to stretch their legs, some 5km (3 miles) of lake promenade should provide room enough.

From Überlingen the B31 now climbs the steep slopes behind town and after a few kilometres it passes close to the church of **Birnau**. The church occupies an excellent vantage point above the lake and this fact in itself makes the trip worthwhile. But apart from that Birnau also happens to be one of the most beautiful Baroque churches in all Southern Germany. It was built between 1746 and 1750 and some of the most famous artists of the time took part in its decoration.

The B31 now returns to the lake at **Uhldingen**. In **Unteruhldingen** are the famous Pfahlbaudörfer. They are reconstructions of two prehistoric villages raised on stilts above the waters of the lake. One village is made up of Stone Age dwellings, the other of Bronze Age dwellings. An attached museum offers information about the prehistoric cultures that once lived around the shores of Bodensee.

A pleasant detour from the lake is to take the road via **Salem** to Heiligenberg. Kloster Salem is a former Cistercian monastery that now houses an exclusive boarding-school. It is only possible to see the lavishly decorated interior of the Kloster in the course of one of the guided tours that take place every hour, April to October. The last 8km (5 miles) of the Prälatenweg (Prelate's Way) continue from the Kloster down to Birnau. This long-distance walking path (it can also be driven along here) goes past the Affenberg Salem, near Mendlishausen. The Affenberg is a breeding station for endangered Barbary apes. Over 200 of these animals, which are found in north Africa and on the island of Gibraltar, are allowed to wander in relative freedom within a large wooded enclosure. Visitors can walk freely among the apes and are given specially prepared food with which to feed them (open daily from 15 March to 1 November). The Renaissance Schloss in **Heiligenberg** contains a very impressive Rittersaal (1562-84) with an ornately carved ceiling. It gives an idea of the magnitude of the task when it is realised that it took the carver Jörg Schwarzenberger about 22 years to complete this masterpiece.

Continue along the lake shore from Uhldingen (not on the B31) to **Meersburg**. With a history spanning more than 1,000 years Meersburg still presents a beautiful medieval townscape of half-timbered houses, narrow winding streets and towers. The vineyards which climb the steep lake shore near town are known for their Weissherbst, a kind of rosé wine.

Meersburg's Altes Schloss is a picturesque castle overlooking the lake. It originates, for the most part, from the fifteenth and sixteenth centuries. A famous German poetess, Annette von Droste-Hülshoff, lived here for many years and eventually died in the castle in 1848. Although the castle is in private hands (it is the oldest castle in Germany that is still lived in) there are quite a few rooms open to the public. Below the bridge crossing to the castle is the Schlossmühle (Castle Mill) with its large water-wheel. Just across from the Altes Schloss is the Neues Schloss (1741-50). It was built to plans by the great architect Balthasar Neumann and a number of rooms are open to view. Also of interest is the Weinbaumuseum (Wine Museum), the

*Mainau — the Island of Flowers*

*The beautiful medieval town of Meersburg*

Fürstenhäuschen (dating from around 1640) which was used by the poet Droste-Hülshoff as a place to write in summer, and the Grethhaus, a former granary on the lake front dating around 1500.

**Friedrichshafen** is the second largest town on the lake and though it cannot compare with the pretty townscape of Meersburg there are, nevertheless, some places of interest that justify a short stop. Close to the lake the Schlosskirche (1695-1701) is worth seeing for the fine stucco work produced by artists of the famous Wessobrunn school. Unfortunately the Schloss itself, and the park, are not open to the public. On the 2 July 1900 the first dirigible became air-borne in the nearby Manzeller Bucht (bay). This fact is commemorated in the Zeppelin Museum (housed in the modern Rathaus) which has models of these famous airships. Also here is the Bodenseemuseum with its important art collection.

Continue on the B31 for a few kilometres and then turn right, towards the lake, in the direction of **Langenargen**. The Montfort-Schloss (1861-4) was built in Moorish style and together with the lake as a background, it makes an unusually exotic motif for photographers. Also of interest is Germany's oldest suspension-bridge (1890). It crosses the Argen river, on the old road to Lindau. Today it can only be used by pedestrians and cyclists.

Return to the B31 and then, shortly before Lindau, turn right to the lake again, in order to come to the village of **Wasserburg**. The most picturesque aspect of this lake resort is the small peninsula with the Georgskirche from the fifteenth century and the former Fuggerschloss, now a hotel, from the thirteenth century. Nearby in Reutenen is a chapel from 1693, known in local dialect as the Gfrörenen-Kapelle. It recalls an unusual phenomenon known as the 'Seefrörene': about twice in every century Bodensee freezes completely over, the last time being in 1963.

The island town of old **Lindau** is placed in a picture-postcard landscape; on clear days the lake and the Alps combine to form a breathtaking backdrop, to the slim silhouette of the light-house and the marble Bavarian lion that flank the narrow harbour entrance. Lindau is, in fact, Bavaria's main outpost on Lake Constance, as most of the rest of the lake belongs to Baden-Württemberg. For those with cars it is best to park at the large car park (Seeparkplatz) on the island (clearly signposted) as the town centre is largely closed to traffic. Those travelling by train are delivered close to the harbour.

Lindau's harbour promenade is marked by the distinctive tower of the old light-house (Mangturm). There is, of course, plenty to see; the beautiful frescoes on the outside of the Altes Rathaus (1422-36), the Peterskirche from the tenth century, with frescoes attributed to Hans Holbein the Elder, or the Haus zum Cavazzen, with its museum on local history. In any case Lindau makes a fitting end to this route and, with the Alps already in sight, a good introduction to the next chapter — continue north on the B12/18 to join Route 14 at Wangen.

# *Additional Information*

## *Places of Interest*

**Aulendorf**
*Miniature Steam Railway*
Further information: Schwäbischer Eisenbahnverein; c/- Dieter Riehlein, Weisshauptstrasse 22, D-7950 Biberach 1, ☎ (07351) 22510 or contact Verkehrsamt above.

*Schloss*
Open: because of restoration work no times were available at the time of writing. For further information contact: Verkehrsamt ☎ (07525) 415

**Bad Waldsee**
*Städtisches Museum*
(Municipal Museum)
Kornhaus
Open: May to September, Saturdays and Sundays 9.30-11.30am.

**Bad Wurzach**
*Wurzacher Schloss*
Open: the schloss is lived in (boarding-school) but the Baroque staircase and Schlosskirche are open during the day. Guided tours can be arranged.
For further information contact: Städtische Kurverwaltung
☎ (07564) 302150

**Biberach**
*Braith-Mali-Museum*
Heilig-Geist Spital

Open: daily, except Mondays 10am-12noon and 2-5pm.

*Wieland-Schauraum* (museum)
Open: Saturday and Sunday 10am-12noon. From October to March also 2-5pm and Wednesdays 10am-12noon and 2-6pm.

**Federsee**
*Federseemuseum*
Naturschutzgebiet Federsee
Open: 1 April to 15 October, daily 9-11.30am and 1.30-5pm. 1 November to 31 March, Wednesdays 2-5pm and Sundays 1-4pm.
☎ (07582) 8350

**Friedrichshafen**
*Zeppelin and Bodensee-Museum*
Kirchplatz
Open: daily, except Mondays 10am-12noon and 2-5pm. Wednesdays 10am-12noon and 2-7pm. May to October daily 10am-5pm. Wednesdays 10am-7pm.

**Heiligenberg**
*Schloss Heiligenberg*
Open: Easter to October. Restaurant. ☎ (07554) 246

**Konstanz**
*Münster* (tower)
Open: Monday to Saturday 10am-5pm. Sunday 1-5pm.

*Lindau's harbour is marked by the tower of the old lighthouse*

*Enjoying the holiday atmosphere at Meersburg's lake-side café*

*Rosgartenmuseum*
Open: Tuesday to Sunday 10am-5pm.

## Langenargen
*Schloss Montfort*
Open: contact Verkehrsamt for further information.
☎ (07543) 30292

## Lindau
*Haus zum Cavazzen*
Open: Tuesday to Saturday 9am-12noon and 2-5pm, Sunday 10am-12noon.

## Meersburg
*Altes Schloss*
Open: March to September daily 9am-6pm, November to February 10am-5pm.

*Fürstenhäuschen with Droste-Hülshoff-Museum*
Stettener Strasse
Open: April to September, daily 10am-12noon and 2-6pm. Sundays and public holidays 2-6pm.

*Neues Schloss*
Open: April to October, daily 10am-1pm and 2-6pm.
(Entrance fee).

*Weinbaumuseum*
Vorburggasse 11
Open: April to September, Tuesday, Friday and Sunday 2-5pm.

## Ravensburg
*Vogthaus*
Städtisches Museum
Open: Tuesday to Saturday 3-5pm. In July/August also Mondays 10am-12noon, Sundays 10am-12noon and 3-5pm.

## Überlingen
*Heimatmuseum mit Puppenstuben-Sammlung* (Städtisches Museum)
Open: Tuesday to Saturday 9am-12.30pm and 2-5pm. Sundays (only in April to October) 10am-3pm.

*Rathaus*
Open: Monday to Friday 9am-12noon and 2.30-5pm. Saturday 9am-12noon.

## Unteruhldingen
*Freilicht-Museum Deutsches Vorzeit-Pfahlbaumuseum*
Seepromenade 6
Open: April to October 8am-6pm.
☎ (07556) 8543

## Waldburg
*Schloss*
Open: throughout the year. Further information from Bürgermeisteramt
☎ (07529) 1234 and 1235

## Warthausen
*Schloss Warthausen*
Open: July to September daily 2-6pm, Sundays and public holidays 2-5pm.

## Wolfegg
*Automobilmuseum*
(next to the Schloss)
Open: April to October 9am-12noon and 1-6pm. Winter only Sundays 9am-5pm.
☎ (07527) 6294

*Bauernhaus-Freilicht-Museum*
Fischergasse 29
Open: April to October, Tuesday to Saturday 10am-12noon and 2-5pm. Sundays 10am-5pm.
☎ (07527) 6300

*Schloss Wolfegg*
Open: can only be visited in conjunction with the Internationale Festspiele Baden-Württemberg (music festival at the end of September). Further information from Verkehrsamt, Rötenbacher Strasse 13 ☎ (07527) 5200

## Tourist Information Centres

**Bad Schussenried**
Städtische Kurverwaltung
Bahnhofstrasse 10
☎ (07583) 40133 or 40134

**Bad Waldsee**
Städtische Kurverwaltung
☎ (07524) 10378

**Bad Wurzach**
Städtische Kurverwaltung
☎ (07564) 302150

**Biberach**
Städtische Fremdenverkehrsstelle
Theaterstrasse 6. ☎ (07351) 51436

**Friedrichshafen**
Tourist-Information
Friedrichstrasse 18. ☎ (07541) 21729

**Heiligenberg**
Kurverwaltung im Rathaus
☎ (07554) 246 and 8446

**Konstanz**
Bahnhofsplatz 13
Open: Monday to Friday 8.45am-6pm. Saturday 10am-1pm and 4-6pm. Sunday 4-6pm.
☎ (07531) 284376

**Langenargen**
Verkehrsamt
☎ (07543) 30292

**Lindau**
Verkehrsverein Am Bahnhofsplatz
Open: Monday to Saturday 8am-12noon and 2-6pm, Saturday 9am-12.30pm. ☎ (08382) 26000

**Meersburg**
Schlossplatz
Open: Monday to Friday 8am-12noon and 1.30-5pm, Saturday 10am-12noon. ☎ (07532) 82383

**Ochsenhausen**
Städtisches Verkehrsamt
☎ (07352) 201-11

**Ravensburg**
Kultur- und Verkehrsamt der Stadt Ravensburg
☎ (0751) 82324 and 82326

**Reichenau**
Verkehrsbüro Reichenau
Ergat 5
☎ (07534) 276

**Salem**
Bürgermeisteramt
☎ (07553) 82312

**Überlingen**
Städtische Kurverwaltung
Landungsplatz 7
☎ (07551) 87291 and 4041

**Wasserburg**
Fremdenverkehrsamt
☎ (08382) 5582

**Weingarten**
Kultur- und Verkehrsamt
Rathaus
☎ (0751) 125

**Wolfegg**
Verkehrsamt
☎ (07527) 5200

# 6
# *ALLGÄU*
# *AND BAVARIAN ALPS*

As much as there is to see of historical interest in the Allgäu and Bavarian Alps it is the outstanding natural scenery that draws most people to the region. In the whole alpine area the classic forms of recreation are walking and skiing. Virtually every place described here offers usually both of these activities, along with many others. Though it might seem obvious, it should nevertheless be mentioned that walking at higher altitudes requires an awareness of the degree of difficulty and proper clothing. Even in summer a rain-coat and warm pullover, along with solid footwear, are prerequisites. A good walking map (*Kompass Wanderkarten* are not a bad choice) is useful for finding the quickest way back if the weather gets bad.

## Route 14 • Allgäu 185km (115 miles)
Onion-domes on the towers of the churches and cows with bells around their necks are all characteristics of the Alps, however they seem to be particularly numerous in the green valleys of the Allgäu. This beautiful region, which is mainly within the boundaries of Bavaria, does not form a distinct geographic entity, but its inhabitants have a distinctive dialect and customs which are more akin to those of Baden-Württemberg's Swabians than to those of Bavarians.

**Wangen im Allgäu** is the main town in that small part of the Allgäu that belongs to Baden-Württemberg. Part of the town's present prosperity is linked to the tasty Emmentaler cheeses that are exported all over the world. In the Eselmühle is a cheese museum, for those interested, otherwise the more direct approach is to simply try *Kässpätzle*, a baked cheese dish, in a local restaurant. Inquire at the tourist office about the possibility of visiting the Allgäuer Emmentalerwerke cheese factory.

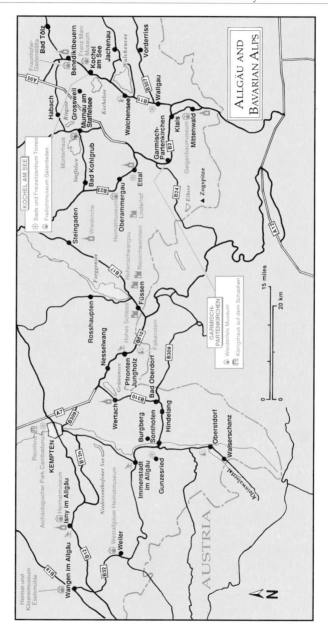

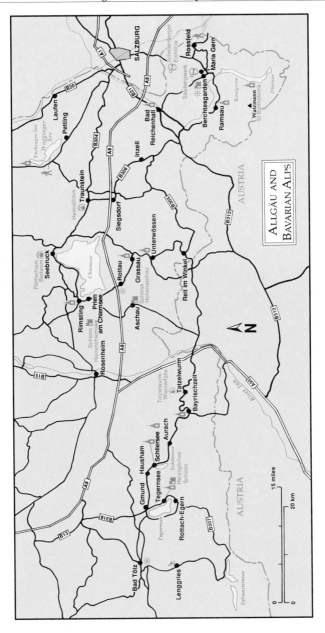

Wangen's well preserved Altstadt is a pleasant place to stroll around and work up an appetitie. A couple of the most picturesque streets are the Paradiesstrasse with its Martins Gate and the Herrenstrasse with its Liebfrauen Gate. On top of this there are some lakes in the general area good for swimming and the town's carnival celebrations in February belong to the most colourful in Germany.

Continue east on the B12 but first go south on the B32 to **Isny im Allgäu**. This town has as an attractive backdrop the Adelegg Ranges, which have also enabled it to develop as a winter sports resort. Skis can be hired in town and the Schwarzer Grat (1,118m 3,667ft) near Grossholzleute is a favourite goal for skiers. You can swim in the nearby Hengelesweiher (a small lake).

Isny has, like Wangen, been able to preserve a good bit of its medieval appearance, including large parts of the medieval town walls. Of the churches the most interesting are the Nikolaikirche with its medieval library, the St Georgs-Kirche with its beautiful high altar and Rococo decoration, and the Baroque Josefskapelle which is renowned for the excellent echoes that can be produced inside! Also of note is the Rathaus dating around 1685 and the Heimatmuseum (local museum) in the Wasserturm.

Continue on the B12, past the ski resort of Wengen, to **Kempten**. The so-called 'capital' of the Allgäu is prettily situated on both banks of the Iller river. History goes back a long way here and this spot was first settled by the Celts and then the Romans. In the year AD752 Christianity made its presence felt in the form of a Benedictine abbey. Centuries later, after the spread of the teachings of Martin Luther, the locals showed that tolerance was not necessarily one of the Christian virtues that they had mastered. For a considerable period of time Kempten was divided by more than just a river; religious differences divided the townsfolk and it split into a Catholic quarter (Bischofsstadt) and a Protestant quarter (Reichsstadt). As late as 1848 there was even serious speculation as to whether there should be a separate railway station for each faith!

An insight into Kempten's early history can be gained at the Archäologischer Park Cambodunum, where the temple district of an ancient Roman town has been largely unearthed. Worth seeing in the Bischofsstadt is the Baroque church of St Lorenz (1652-74) and the immense Residenz (1651-74) of the once powerful prince-abbots. In the Reichsstadt the St Mang-Kirche (1426-8), numerous old houses and Rathaus (1474) are of interest. The Rathaus fountain (1601) is said to be one of the most beautiful Renaissance fountains in Germany.

An excursion south of Kempten can be made on the B19 to the

Niedersonthofener See. In some summers the lake can get as warm as 26 °C and is therefore very popular for swimming. There are also a couple of camping grounds close to the lake.

The main route continues from Kempten on the B309, then after Weissbach on the B310 to **Füssen**. Surrounded as it is by several lakes, and with the Alps at its back door, this town on the Lech river cannot help but be attractive. It is also no surprise that two of Germany's most famous tourist roads include Füssen on their itineraries: the Romantic Road (Romantische Strasse) ends here and the Alpine Road (Alpenstrasse) passes through.

Füssen's Hohes Schloss hunches on a hill above the Altstadt and seems to have been built with more practical things in mind than its romantically placed neighbour, Schloss Neuschwanstein, a few kilometres away. It was built in 1322 by the prince-bishops of Augsburg, but has been changed many times over the centuries. A collection of paintings that form part of the Bavarian State Collection and some rooms — an attractive Rittersaal — can be seen within. Just below the Schloss, the Baroque church of St Mang (1701-17) is marked by its beautiful dome. Of interest here is, above all, the Romanesque crypt with its nearly 1,000-year-old fresco of the saints Magnus and Gallus. Next door, in the St Anna-Kapelle, are some more famous frescoes, this time from the sixteenth century, which depict the Füssener Totentanz (danse macabre). Also in the vicinity is Kloster St Mang (1703-27), a former Benedictine monastery with a number of rooms open to view in Baroque and Rococo styles. A photogenic church worth searching out is the small Baroque Spitalkirche (1749). The front is completely covered with the typical frescoes that are known here as Lüftlmalerei.

The Forggensee, on Füssen's doorstep, is a large reservoir formed by a dam near Rosshaupten on the Lech river. This, and several other lakes in the area, have facilities for various water sports. Passenger vessels sail between Füssen and the resort of Rosshaupten during the summer season. For those who prefer walking there is ample opportunity in Bavaria's largest nature reserve, the Naturschutzgebiet Ammergebirge, which stretches right across to Garmisch-Partenkirchen. Recommended walking maps are *Kompass Wanderkarten Füssen-Ausserfern*, 1:50,000; *Wettersteingebirge*, 1:50,000. Both show cycling paths (Radwanderwege) as well.

A must when in Füssen is to go to **Schwangau**. In the mountains around this small town are two of the most famous castles in all Germany. King Ludwig II, Bavaria's 'Mad King', started the building of Schloss Neuschwanstein in 1869. Although it was never fully

*Opposite: Both cultivated and wild flowers provide much summer colour*

completed, due to the king's tragic drowning in 1886, it has become the romantic archetype of a medieval castle. Despite long queues the magnificently decorated castle interior is also worth seeing. Good photos of the castle can be had from the Marienbrücke, a bridge just to the south. Nearby, Schloss Hohenschwangau is beautifully situated above the Alpsee and the Schwansee. It was built by King Ludwig's father, King Maximilian II, between 1833 and 1837. This Schloss is only a 5 minutes walk from the village of Hohenschwangau.

Near Schwangau the Tegelberg-Kabinenbahn (cable railway), goes up to a panoramic restaurant on the Tegelberg (1,720m, 5,641ft). There is also an international hang-gliding centre here. In Schwangau itself the pilgrimage church of St Coloman (1673) is worth a look.

A pleasant excursion from Füssen is to take the B17 north to **Steingaden**. In town the Premonstratensian monastery church of John the Baptist (1176) is the main attraction. The Wieskirche (1746-54), a few kilometres outside of town, to the south-east, is considered to be the finest example of Rococo in Bavaria. It was planned by the Wessobrunn architect Dominikus Zimmermann and his brother Johann Baptist Zimmermann was largely responsible for the lavish interior.

To join Route 15a take the road east of Steingaden via Wildsteig, then go south on the B23 via Oberammergau to Garmisch-Partenkirchen — this route follows the Alpenstrasse. An alternative is to go south into Austria, via Reutte and Ehrwald, to Garmisch.

This route continues back along the B310, following the Alpenstrasse virtually all the way back to Wangen, to where it meets the B309 at Pfronten-Weissbach. The 'town' of **Pfronten** is actually an amalgamation of thirteen villages with the centre being at Ried. Most people come here for the skiing or to do one of the many spectacular mountain walks. Of all the chapels and churches in the area, it is perhaps the parish church of St Nikolaus (1687) in Berg that is most interesting.

From Meilingen, just across the railway lines from Ried, there is a well defined path that leads up to the castle ruins of **Falkenstein**. This is the most highly situated castle in Germany (hotel and restaurant) at 1,277m (4,190ft) and naturally the views are excellent. Ludwig II would have liked to have built a second Neuschwanstein here, but his untimely death halted building, which was already well

under way. A bit further south of Ried, near Steinach, there is the Breitenbergbahn, a cable railway that goes up the Breitenberg (1,838m 6,028ft). The Hochalp chair-lift continues from the end-station of the cable railway to reach an altitude of 1,730m (5,674ft). In summer the Hochalp is an ideal starting point for mountain walks. The Ostlerhütte (a mountain hut) can be reached from the chair-lift's upper station in about 35 minutes.

Continue back to Nesselwang on the B309 and then turn south-west towards **Wertach**, at the southern end of the Grüntensee. The Sebastian-Kapelle (1763) here is somewhat reminiscent of the Wieskirche near Steingaden. There is also an Alpine dairy (Sennerei) and a 350-year-old smithy (Hammerschmiede) that may be visited. A local speciality to try is Weisslacker, a type of cheese 'discovered' here in 1874. Also to be recommended is a trip south to the Wertacher Hörnle (1,685m 5,528ft), at the height of summer, to see the alpine roses in bloom — accessible by bus as far as Königsträsschen. Skiing is possible on the nearby Reuterwanne (1,541m 5,054ft).

A short distance south and just off the B310 is the enclave of **Jungholz**. This 8sq km (5sq miles) morsel of Austria is only accessible by road from Germany. There are no customs formalities and everything is paid in German currency. Camping is possible all year round here and the ski season lasts right into spring. A beautiful walk goes from Jungholz along the Vils valley to Pfronten and takes about 2 hours.

Continue south on the B310 to Oberjoch. From here the road winds its way down to **Hindelang**, a popular town resort. Apart from a painting by Hans Holbein the Elder in a church in nearby Bad Oberdorf, the main attractions lie in the countryside. Especially scenic is the Bärgündele valley near Giebel-Haus to the south. The valley can be reached via Hinterstein, after which it is necessary to take either a bus or to go on foot (about 2 hours) as the road is closed to private vehicles.

Continue west on the B308 to **Sonthofen**. This town lacks the charm of most other resorts in the region, but it does have the advantage of being central to a number of interesting places. A pretty ravine known as the Starzlachklamm can be reached via Burgberg, a village to the north. The Grünten (1,738m 5,700ft), which rises behind the village, is quite popular among skiers. Unfortunately the many ski-lifts on the northern slopes have a defacing effect in summer.

**Gunzesried** to the west of Sonthofen is just one of many alpine villages that celebrates the Viehscheid. This festival takes place in autumn, but only if the cowherds manage to pass the summer in the mountains without serious mishap. If this is the case the leading animal is colourfully decorated and on a prearranged day the cows are herded down to the cowherd's village where the actual Viehscheid — the separation of the animals from the collective herd — takes place. This event is always accompanied by lots of beer and music. For exact dates contact the local tourist offices.

Directly south of Sonthofen is the very popular resort of **Oberstdorf**. With several peaks over 2,000m (6,560ft) nearby, it almost goes without saying that the scenery is spectacular and that the emphasis here is on the outdoors. The Nebelhornbahn provides easy access to the 2,224m (7,294ft) high peak of the Nebelhorn. Not to be missed is a walk through the spectacular ravine of the Breitachklamm.

A few kilometres south again and the B19 enters the Kleinwalsertal at **Walserschanz**. Like Jungholz this valley is another Austrian enclave, only accessible by road from Germany. German currency is used for everything, even to buy Austrian stamps from the Austrian post offices. Another peculiarity here is that the locals have to pay customs for goods coming from their own country! But apart from these unusual circumstances the valley is also an excellent place for walking and skiing.

The main route continues north-west from Sonthofen to **Immenstadt im Allgäu**. In the 600 years or so of its history the town has been the victim of a number of devastating fires, the last being in 1844 which destroyed much of historical interest. However there are still a few historic places left such as Schloss Königsegg (1550-1620), the Rathaus (1640), and the parish church. The surrounding area offers outstanding cross-country skiing.

An amusing event that takes place here, after the cows have been driven down from the alpine pastures in September, is the election of the Bartkönig (Beard King). It opens to the fanfare of a trio of alpine horns in the Hofgarten. The cowherdsman who has managed to grow the most impressive beard during his sojourn in the mountains is awarded a cow-bell as first prize.

From Immenstadt the B308 continues on past Oberstaufen and then to **Weiler-Simmerberg**, where the Westallgäuer Heimat-museum in Weiler is of interest with its exhibits on regional history (closed Mondays and Fridays). Shortly after Weiler this route leaves the B308 — the Alpenstrasse continues as the B308 to its official starting point in Lindau to follow the B32 back to Wangen.

*The emphasis around Oberstdorf is on the outdoors as the Alps nearby are excellent for walking*

*The easiest way to climb the Zugspitze is by mountain railway*

*The craggy peaks of the Karwendel tower above Mittenwald*

*Garmisch-Partenkirchen*

# Central Bavarian Alps
## ROUTE 15A • THE ALPS AROUND GARMISCH-PARTEN-KIRCHEN 116KM (72 MILES)

**Garmisch-Partenkirchen** is one of the largest of Bavaria's winter resorts. The double name comes from the fact that two neighbouring towns were joined for the Winter Olympics held here in 1936. In Garmisch the Gothic church of St Martin (1456-1520) has important wall frescoes, including a huge figure of St Christopher from the thirteenth century and scenes of the Passion from the fifteenth century. The new parish church of St Martin (1730-34) was built in Baroque style and contains impressive ceiling frescoes by Matthäus Günther. The pilgrimage church of St Anton (1704), in Partenkirchen, has an outstanding ceiling fresco (1739) by Johann Holzer. Also in this part of town is the Werdenfels Museum with exhibits on the history and culture of the region.

The great scenic attraction in the vicinity of Garmisch-Partenkirchen is Germany's highest mountain, the Zugspitze (2,963m 9,721ft). A cog-wheel railway goes from town up to Hotel Schneefernerhaus (2,650m 8,692ft). From here a cable railway goes up to the summit. An alternative is to start from a pretty lake known as the Eibsee and go direct to the summit with the cable railway — the train can also be joined here. Both alternatives are, however, not exactly cheap and those with the necessary stamina could save money by walking to the top. The safest route is to go through the Reintal and then via Schneefernerhaus. The other routes through the Höllental and via the Wiener-Neustädter huts are best left to those with mountaineering experience. The Höllentalklamm and the Partnachklamm (both gorges) are highly recommended excursions in themselves.

Continue east on the B2 to **Klais**. From the village a path leads via Schloss Elmau (private) to the Königshaus auf dem Schachen (1872). This was once a hunting lodge belonging to Ludwig II and it takes from 3-4 hours to walk there.

From Klais take the road south to **Mittenwald**. This town is nestled below the craggy peaks of the Karwendel. The local craftsmen have long been famed for their beautifully made violins and the Geigenbaumuseum deals with this highly skilled craft. Some of Bavaria's best Lüftlmalerei is also to be found here. This term is used to describe the exterior wall frescoes decorating houses and churches in the Alpine region, especially those from the eighteenth century. The parish church of St Peter and Paul (1734-40) has good examples of Lüftlmalerei on its tower. The Alpine peaks can be scaled with the help of a cable railway that goes up to the Karwendelspitze and a chair-lift up the Kranzberg.

Return north to **Wallgau** on the B11. Of interest here is the Baroque St Jakobskirche from the seventeenth century and also the good Lüftlmalerei on the houses. Note in particular the frescoes from 1763 on Gasthof Post (1621). Near the end of town the Alpenstrasse turns east to follow a toll road along the very scenic Isar valley to Vorderriss. Those who wish could join Route 15b by continuing on this road to the far end of the Sylvensteinsee.

Further up the B11 is the **Walchensee**, the biggest of Germany's mountain lakes. From the small town of the same name a chair-lift goes up the Herzogsstand (1,600m 5,249ft). At the top is a fantastic panorama of lakes and mountains. A toll road at the south end of the lake curves its way to the village of Jachenau. The scenic drive is worth it in itself, but there is also the extremely old church of St Nikolaus (1291) to be seen.

From Walchensee the B11 climbs up the Kesselberg (858m 2,815ft) and then descends in a series of sharply twisting bends to the Kochelsee, which is a couple of hundred metres lower than the Walchensee. **Kochel am See** has a museum dedicated to the painter Franz Marc, who lived here for a while and is famed as one of the founders on the Blaue Reiter (Blue Rider) school. Directly on the shores of the lake is the Bade und Freizeitzentrum Trimini — a kind of aquatic amusement park. West of Kochel, near Grossweil, is the Freilichtmuseum Glentleiten, which specialises in traditional crafts and has a large number of buildings once typical for Upper Bavaria.

Continue north on the B11 to reach **Benediktbeuern**. The former Benedictine Kloster was founded around AD740 and is one of the oldest monasteries in Upper Bavaria. It was here that the songs of the *Carmina Burana* were written down in the thirteenth century. In 1936 Carl Orff brought them to a wider public with his famous musical setting. After secularisation in 1803 parts of the Kloster were used as a glassworks by Josef von Fraunhofer, who was able to initiate a breakthrough in the production of optical glass. The Fraunhofer-Gedenkstätte is a museum which preserves the old glassworks. Also of interest is the early Baroque monastery church, which was worked on by a number of important artists. The start of Route 15b can be joined by following the B11 north and then turning east on the B472 to Bad Tölz.

Continue towards Bichl and then take the B472 west. At Habach leave the B472 and turn south to Hofheim, near the Riegsee. From here continue to **Murnau am Staffelsee**, where the neo-Baroque

*The painted façade of this building in Oberammergau depicts the story of*
Hansel & Gretel

*The Rococo Schloss Linderhof*

house fronts along the Marktstrasse and the Baroque Nikolauskirche (1717-34) draw one's attention. In the Münterhaus is another museum devoted to artists of the Blaue Reiter school, in particular Gabriele Münter and Wassily Kandinsky, who lived here.

The B2 returns directly south to Garmisch but it is more interesting to follow the Alte Salzstrasse (Old Salt Road) west to Bad Kohlgrub. From here a cable railway (Hörnle Schwebebahn) goes up the Hörnle (1,400m 4,593ft). Continue to join the B23 and follow this road south to Oberammergau.

**Oberammergau** is internationally famous for the Passionsspiele (Passion Plays) which are performed here between May and September in 10 year cycles — the next performances will be in the year 2,000. Apart from this major attraction the town, which always seems crowded in summer, has a number of other things of interest to fill in the long gap between. What immediately comes to notice is the colourful Lüftlmalerei that graces many of the house fronts, with the Geroldhaus (1778) and the Pilatushaus (1784) providing especially good examples. It is also hard not to notice all the souvenir shops selling wood-carvings. The town has, in fact, a long tradition of

wood-carving and in the Heimatmuseum there are some very good specimens. A cable railway ascends the heights of the Laber (1,688m 5,538ft) from the eastern edge of town.

To the south-west of Oberammergau is Schloss Linderhof (1869-78), another of the famous Schlösser built for King Ludwig II. It is an exceptionally pretty Rococo palace, inspired by one of the palaces in Versailles. In the spacious park are a number of very decorative fountains which are turned on at hourly intervals. Like Schloss Neuschwanstein it is one of those 'musts' for visitors to this part of Bavaria.

Return to the B23 and a short distance further south is the village of **Ettal**. Overriding everything else is the large Benedictine Kloster, founded in 1330. The greater part of the old monastery was torn down during the time of secularisation, so that most of the complex dates from the nineteenth and twentieth centuries. Of central interest is the monastery church of St Marien (1745), a largely Baroque building with a huge ceiling fresco (1751) by Johann Zeiller. As many of the best artists of the time worked on the church interior it is not surprising that it ranks as one of the most important creations of Rococo art in Germany. Continue on the B23 which soon joins the B2 back to Garmisch.

## ROUTE 15B • THE ALPS AROUND BAD TÖLZ
### 96KM (60 MILES)

**Bad Tölz** is another of Germany's many spa towns. It is divided into a spa quarter (iodine springs) on the left bank of the Isar river, and an Altstadt on the right bank. In the Altstadt the Marktstrasse is particularly attractive with its nicely painted old houses. Of the churches in town the late Gothic church of Maria Himmelfahrt (1453-66) and the Baroque church of Mariahilf (1735-7) are of interest. On the Kalvarienberg is the Baroque Kalvarienbergkirche (1723-32) and next to it the Leonhardskapelle. This chapel is the goal of a famous annual procession known as the Leonhardifahrt on the 6 December. It is the largest of the many celebrations in the name of St Leonhard — the patron saint of farm animals — in Bavaria. Not far from town there is a chair-lift that ascends the Blomberg (1,237m 4,058ft).

Continue south on the B13 to **Lenggries**. Among the many facilities offered by this winter sports resort is a cable railway (Brauneckkabinenbahn) and several chair-lifts to cater for the swarms of skiers during the ski season. Lenggries is also a good base for walks or drives in the spectacular landscape of the Vorderriss. Of interest in town is the Baroque parish church of St Jakob (1722).

Follow the B13 south until it joins the B307 near the **Sylven-steinsee**. This beautiful lake was formed after a dam was completed on the Isar river in 1959. Continue east on the B307 (Alpenstrasse) which briefly enters Austria before climbing steeply to the Kaiserwacht, an old border station. Note that this stretch of road can only be used by cars with caravans if travelling in a northerly direction (i.e. cars with caravans cannot travel in the opposite direction). From the Kaiserwacht the gradient is no longer so steep to the Achen pass (941m 3,086ft), shortly after which is the pretty village of Glashütte. The road now follows the steadily widening Weissach valley down to Rottach-Egern on the Tegernsee.

Although the shores of the **Tegernsee** (lake) are somewhat spoiled by being heavily built-up, the lake is nevertheless situated in one of the prettiest areas of the entire Alps. It is a favourite playground for the rich and famous and those with the money could stay at luxurious hotels like Bachmair am See or Überfahrt, both in Rottach-Egern. Near the town a cable railway (Wallberg-Gondelbahn) ascends the Wallberg (1,722m 5,650ft). At the Greifvogelpark there are demonstrations of falconry.

In **Tegernsee** a bit further north, there is a Benedictine abbey, which was established here in AD746 and rapidly became one of the most important abbeys in southern Bavaria. After secularisation in 1803 a great part of the old abbey was torn down. What was left was turned into a summer residence for King Maximilian I. In the former abbey church of St Quirin are some impressive frescoes by Hans Georg Asam. The Schloss houses the atmospheric Bräustüberl, where guests can enjoy frothing beer fresh from the ducal brewery. In summer a steam train runs between Tegernsee and Schaftlach.

From Gmund, at the north end of the lake, it is no longer far back to Bad Tölz. However this route continues east along the Alpenstrasse — the turn-off is shortly before town — towards **Hausham**, a former coal-mining town. From here take the B307 south to the neighbouring town of **Schliersee**, on the lake of the same name. A very scenic alternative way of getting to Schliersee would be to take the toll road south-east of Rottach-Egern, through the Weisse and Rote Valepp valleys.

Locals still refer to the Schliersee as the Bauernsee (Farmer's Lake) and that name pretty much captures the peaceful rural character of this lake. Worth seeing in town is the former collegiate church (1712-14) with interior decoration by J.B. Zimmermann and the Weinbergkapelle St Georg. Good overall views can be had from the Schliersberg (1,258m 4,127ft) which can be ascended on foot or with a small cable railway. However it only goes part way to the top. At Fischhausen on the southern end of the lake is the interesting St Leonhards-Kirche (1670).

Continue south on the B307 to **Aurach**. Of interest here is the superb Lüftlmalerei on the Jodlbauerhof. Shortly before Bayrischzell, near Osterhofen, is the starting point of the cable railway up the Wendelstein (1,838m 6,030ft). There is also a rack railway which runs up the mountain from Brannenburg in the Inn valley and it is a great experience to go up with the one railway and down with the other — buses run between the two. The ride to the top is rewarded with  tremendous views over the Inn, Leitzach and Mangfall valleys. At the top is a restaurant (caves nearby) and there is also a 2km (1 mile) trail which circles the summit.

**Bayrischzell** with its pretty Baroque church of St Margaretha is a pleasant holiday resort at the foot of the Sudelfeld, one of the best ski  regions in the entire Bavarian Alps. From here the B307 continues to Tatzelwurm, an historic inn, close to which are the Tatzelwurm-Wasserfälle (waterfalls). Tatzelwurm marks the end of the B307 and the end of this route.

To continue to the start of Route 19 (Chapter 7) at Rosenheim or Route 16 at Prien am Chiemsee follow the road east to Auerbach and then go north along the Inn valley, parallel to the A93 motorway, to Degerndorf, near Brannenburg. There is also a toll road near Tatzelwurm that goes directly north to Degerndorf. To get to Rosenheim from here join the B15 just north of town and go via Raubling. The simplest way to Prien is to join the A93 at Degerndorf — the same route as the Alpenstrasse — and then follow the A8 east to Bernau. The Alpenstrasse now goes south on the B305 towards Berchtesgaden, but Prien is reached by leaving the motorway on the road going north.

# Route 16 • Chiemsee and Chiemgau Alps
## 175km (109 miles)

**Prien am Chiemsee** is the largest town on the Chiemsee and a starting point for various boat trips around the lake. The main reason for coming here is to visit the fourth and last of the famous palaces built for King Ludwig II. The piers at Stock can be reached in novel fashion from the railway station in Prien by taking a ride on *Feuriger Elias* (Fiery Elias), a little steam train built in 1887. There is also a large car park at Stock. In summer boats cross several times daily to the Herren (Men's) and Frauen (Women's) islands.

*Alpine meadows
near Tegernsee*

*The passenger ferry
on the Chiemsee*

King Ludwig's palace, Schloss Herrenchiemsee, is situated on the Herreninsel. From where the boats dock it is about a 15 minute walk, or there are horse-drawn wagons which go right to the palace. It was modelled on Versailles, as Ludwig II was a great admirer of Louis XIV, but was never finished owing to lack of funds and Ludwig's sudden death. Of particular interest is the Spiegelsaal (Hall of Mirrors) and in the south wing the King Ludwig II Museum, which gives a good overview of this fascinating man's life. Also on the island is the Altes Schloss now used as a hotel-restaurant and the Gothic church of St Maria (1446).

On the much smaller Fraueninsel is the Benedictine convent church of St Maria. The core of the present church is Romanesque and dates back to the eleventh century. In contrast to the Herreninsel, with its show of royal splendour, the character of this island is very much determined by the small community of nuns and fishermen who still live here. There is a bathing beach on the Fraueninsel and also boats for hire.

An excursion can be made south of Prien via Bernau to **Aschau**. The main attraction here is Schloss Hohenaschau (twelfth century). It is one of the largest castles in Upper Bavaria and though it dates from medieval times almost the entire interior has been redone in Baroque style. The nearby Kampenwand (1,640m 5,380ft) can be ascended by cable railway as far as the Kampenwandhaus, but there are also numerous footpaths of varying degrees of difficulty that could be used.

The main route continues around the lake shore to **Rimsting**, where the Nikolauskirche contains three magnificent Baroque altars. Several small lakes lie to the north of here and a few are suitable for swimming. The general area also makes for nice walking and there is a pleasant trail around the Hartsee.

Continue through Gstadt and Gollenshausen to **Seebruck**. A record of the town's earliest history is kept in the museum Römerhaus Bedaium, which exhibits finds from the excavations of a Roman settlement. From here the route continues to Traunstein.

**Traunstein** is the Chiemgau's most important town. Some severe fires over the centuries laid much of it waste, but the churches of St Oswald and St Rupert have managed to survive. A nice part of town is around the Stadtplatz, and the Heimathaus (formerly a tavern) has excellent exhibits on local history and the old salt trade. In nearby Ettendorf the church of St Veit and St Anna (1470) is the goal of a colourful horse-back procession known as the Georgiritt. It takes place annually on Easter Monday.

North-east of Traunstein is a very pretty area with several lakes, the largest of which are the Tachinger See and **Waginger See**. A pleasant aspect of the latter is that it is relatively peaceful due to the fact that no motor-boats are allowed. At the lake's southern end, near Petting, there is good walking in the beautiful scenery of the Schönramer Filz nature reserve. At the north end of the **Tachinger See** the small church of St Coloman is worth a look. East of these lakes the pretty town of **Laufen** is located north of the Abtsdorfer See, next to the Austrian border. The most significant architectural monument here is the church of Maria Himmelfahrt (1330). As a matter of interest the Christmas carol *Silent Night* was composed in the town of Oberndorf, just across the border.

Continue south from Traunstein on the B306 to **Siegsdorf**. In 1985 a complete mammoth skeleton was found near here. A museum is being built to house the skeleton and it should be finished by 1991. Follow the B306 to Inzell and then the B305 to Unterjettenberg. Now take the B21 east past the Saalachsee to Bad Reichenhall.

The salt springs at **Bad Reichenhall** have made it one of Germany's most important spa towns. One of the main historic attractions is the minster of St Zeno (1136-1228), as it is the largest Romanesque basilica in Upper Bavaria. Note particularly the Romanesque portal and cloister. Alte Saline is the name given to the surprisingly attractive building of the old salt-works (dating around 1850), where guided tours take place throughout the year. A cable railway ascends the nearby Predigtstuhl (1,515m 5,299ft) and bathing is possible in the Thumsee.

From Bad Reichenhall the route follows the B20 south to **Berchtesgaden**. Hitler quite liked this exceptionally beautiful part of the Alps himself and did his bit for the tourist boom by leaving behind a few buildings from the time of the Third Reich. On the Obersalzberg (cable railway to the top) is what remains of a fortress blown-up in 1952. Special buses run to the Kehlsteinhaus (excellent views) which is also referred to as Hitler's tea-house.

The old town centre around the collegiate church and Schloss is now a pleasant pedestrian zone. The Schloss was originally an Augustinian Kloster (1100) but then in 1818, it became a summer residence for the Bavarian kings. In the Schloss museum is an important art collection. The collegiate church of St Peter and St Johannes was originally Romanesque but was later remodelled in the Gothic style. A good place to visit on a rainy day is the Salzbergwerk (Salt Mine), where one of the old tunnels can be entered by sliding down a chute.

*Schloss Herrenchiemsee, modelled on the Palace of Versailles*

*An ornate fountain in the garden at Schloss Herrenchiemsee*

There is a great deal to see in the general area of Berchtesgaden and one of the nicest scenic drives is along a toll road known as the Rossfeld-Ringstrasse. It goes over the highest mountain pass in Germany at 1,550m (5,084ft) and offers fantastic views over the Berchtesgaden Alps and Salzburger Land. At **Rossfeld** there is a Gasthaus and from here there are good walking opportunities. In a beautiful valley, just north of Berchtesgaden, is the very picturesque church of Maria Gern (1709-24) and further north on the B305 are the Schellenberger Eishöhle, Germany's largest ice caverns.

The **Nationalpark Berchtesgaden**, to the south of Berchtesgaden, is thankfully without roads and the only means of public transport, apart from feet along mountain paths, are the electrically powered boats that ply the waters of the idyllic Königssee. There is no doubt that the highlight of such a trip is the exceedingly beautiful ensemble of St Bartholomä (1697) with the Watzmann (2,713m 8,901ft) in the background. Next to the church is a Gasthof and walks in the area — for instance to a romantic little lake called the Obersee — are thoroughly recommended. People who choose to walk along the shores of the lake should get hold of a boat time-table in Dorf Königssee as the boats will stop and pick them up at points provided with a jetty. It should also be mentioned that the Viehscheid here in autumn is particularly interesting, as the cows have to be ferried across the lake, after having been brought down from their Alpine pastures. The recommended map for this National Park and the general area is: *Kompass Wanderkarte Berchtesgadener Land — Chiemgauer Alpen 1:50,000*.

From Berchtesgaden take the B305 south-west to **Ramsau** — the village lies a little off the main road. The most famous sight here is the picture-postcard scene of the small pilgrimage church of St Fabian and St Sebastian, with the Alps in the background, and the Ramsauer Ache stream in the foreground. A good walk from near here is to go along the Wimbachklamm to the Wimbachgries-Hütte.

The B305 climbs up from Ramsau, over the Schwarzbachwacht Saddle (868m 2,848ft), and through grandiose mountain scenery that is typical for virtually the rest of this route. After descending again to Unterjettenberg continue on past Weissbach, keeping to the B305, following it west past the popular tourist resort of Ruhpolding. To the south is the nature reserve of the Chiemgauer Alpen, one of the most untouched regions in the Alps. The B305 cuts through the reserve's western corner, passing several pretty lakes on the way, to the mountain resort of Reit im Winkel. From here continue north through Oberwössen to Unterwössen.

In **Unterwössen** the parish church is worth a look because of an interesting ceiling fresco that depicts the Battle of Oran in 1732. Every year on Ascension Day there is a large procession in traditional costumes to the Marienkirche in nearby Raiten.

Continue through Marquartstein to **Grassau**. In the parish church of St Maria Himmelfahrt are some highly original ceiling frescoes. A little further on the village of **Rottau** is noted for its impressive farm houses and the masses of flowers that decorate balconies in summer. From here it is no longer far to Bernau and then back to the starting point of this route at Prien.

# Additional Information

## Places of Interest

**Aschau**
*Schloss Hohenaschau*
Open: guided tours May to September, Tuesday and Friday 9.30-11.30am.

**Benediktbeuren**
*Fraunhofer-Gedenkstätte*
Open: daily 9am-6pm
☎ (08857) 248

**Berchtesgaden**
*Schloss*
Open: October to April, Monday to Friday 10am-1pm and 2-5pm. May to September, Sunday to Friday 10am-1pm and 2-5pm.

*Salzbergwerk*
Open: 1 May to 15 October daily 8am-5pm, 16 October to 30 April, Monday to Friday 1-4pm.

**Füssen**
*Hohes Schloss*
Open: 1 May to end October daily 10am-12noon and 2-4pm. Sundays 10am-12noon. December to end April Thursdays 2-4pm. November closed. (Entrance fee).

**Garmisch-Partenkirchen**
*Werdenfels Museum*
Ludwigstrasse
Open: daily, except Mondays.

*Königshaus auf dem Schachen
(Jagdschloss Schachen)*
Open: guided tours twice daily 1 April to 30 September 11am and 2pm. Closed from 1 October to 31 March.
☎ (08821) 1800

**Isny im Allgäu**
*Heimatmuseum*
Wasserturm
Open: April to September, Wednesday and Saturday 9.30am and 10.45am, Sunday 10.30am (guided tour).

**Kempten**
*Archäologischer Park (APC)*
Cambodunum
Cambodunumweg
Open: May to October daily 10am-5pm, except Monday, November to April daily 10am-4.30pm, except Monday. January and February closed.
☎ (0831) 79731 or 17189

*Residenz*
Open: the Fürstensaal can be seen
in the course of a guided tour of
town (Stadtführung) every
Saturday at 11am.

**Kochel am See**
*Franz Marc Museum*
Herzogstandweg 43
Open: Tuesday to Sunday 2-6pm.
☎ (08851) 338 or 7114

*Bade und Freizeitzentrum Trimini*
Seeweg 2
☎ (08851) 5300

*Freilichtmuseum Glentleiten*
(near Grossweil)
Open: April to October 9am-6pm.
November only Saturday/Sunday
10am-5pm. Closed Mondays.
☎ (08841) 1098 or 1095

**Linderhof**
*Schloss Linderhof*
Open: April to end September
daily 9am-12.15pm and 12.45-
5.30pm. October to end March
daily 10am-12.15pm and 12.45-
4pm. Fountains play 9am-5pm
every hour on the hour.

**Marktschellenberg**
*Schellenberger Eishöhle* (Ice Caves)
On the Untersberg
Open: June until mid-October.
Admission charge. Guided tour
lasts 1 hour. Refreshments at the
Toni-Lenz Hutte, near cave
entrance. The climb up to the cave
takes about 3 hours.

**Mittenwald**
*Geigenbaumuseum*
Ballenhausgasse
Open: May to October, Monday to
Friday 10-11.45am and 2-4.45pm.

**Murnau am Staffelsee**
*Münterhaus*
Kottmüllerallee 6
Open: Wednesday, Saturday &
Sunday 4-6pm
☎ (08841) 9305

**Nationalpark Berchtesgaden**
Nationalparkverwaltung
Doktorberg 6
Open: 1 May to 30 September
10am-12noon and 2-5pm.
☎ (08652) 61068 or the
Informationsstelle at Königssee
☎ (08652) 62222 (For information
about the national park).

**Oberammergau**
*Heimatmuseum*
Dorfstrasse
☎ (08822) 182

**Prien am Chiemsee**
*Schloss Herrenchiemsee and King
Ludwig II Museum*
Open: April to end September
daily 9am-5pm. October to end
March daily 10am-4pm.

**Schwangau**
*Schloss Neuschwanstein*
*Schloss Hohenschwangau*
Open: April to end September
daily 8.30am-5.30pm. October to
end March daily 10am-4pm.

**Seebruck**
*Römerhaus Bedaium*
Open: Tuesday to Saturday 10am-
12noon and 3-5pm.
Sundays 3-5pm.
☎ (08667) 7133

**Siegsdorf**
The Naturkundemuseum for the
mammoth skeleton has still not
been finished. For further informa-

tion contact: Verkehrsamt Siegsdorf
Rathausplatz 2, D-8227 Siegsdorf
☎ (08662) 7993

**Tegernsee**
*Herzogliches Schloss*
☎ (08022) 1801-40-41

**Traunstein**
*Heimathaus*
Stadtplatz 2-3
Open: (only in the course of a
guided tour) May to June and 1
September to 15 October weekly
2pm and 3.30pm, Sundays and
public holidays 10am. 1 July to 31
August, Thursdays 9am-12noon, 2-
5pm without guided tour, Sundays
and public holidays 10am.
☎ Museum 0861 65258
☎ Städtisches Verkehrsamt 0861
65273

**Wangen im Allgäu**
*Heimat- und Käsereimuseum
Eselsmühle (Cheese Museum)*
Open: Tuesday, Wednesday, Friday
3-6pm. Wednesday, Sunday 10am-
12noon and by prior arrangement. 1
November to 31 March guided tour
every Tuesday at 3.30pm.
☎ (07522) 74-242

**Wertach**
*Sennerei*
Open: visited in the course of a
guided tour which usually takes
place on Tuesdays around 4pm or
4.30pm — it depends on the time of
the year. For precise details enquire
at the Verkehrsamt (☎ 08365 266).
Meeting point is at the Sennerei
'Unterer Markt' opposite
Verkehrsamt.

*Hammerschmiede*
Open: can be visited in the course of
a guided tour. From March to May

Thursdays at 4pm or 4.30pm. June
to October Mondays at 4.30pm. As
times vary it is best to enquire at
Verkehrsamt. Meeting point is at St
Sebastianskapelle.

## Tourist Information Centres

**Bad Reichenhall**
Kur- und Verkehrsverein
Im Hauptbahnhof-Nebenbau
☎ (08651) 3003

**Bad Tölz**
Städtische Kurverwaltung
Ludwigstrasse 11
Open: Monday to Friday 9am-
12noon and 2-5.30pm. Saturday
9am-12noon and Sunday (June to
September) 10am-12noon.
☎ (08041) 70071

**Bayrischzell**
Kuramt. ☎ (08023) 648

**Benediktbeuern**
Verkehrsamt, Prälatenstrasse 5
☎ (08857) 248

**Berchtesgaden**
Königsseer Strasse
Open: Monday to Friday 8.30am-
5.30pm.

**Ettal**
Gemeindeverwaltung
Ammergauer Strasse 8
☎ (08822) 534

**Füssen**
Kurverwaltung
Augsburger-Tor-Platz 1
☎ (08362) 7077-78

**Garmisch-Partenkirchen**
Verkehrsamt (Garmisch)
Bahnhofstrasse
Open: Monday to Saturday 8am-
6pm, Sunday 10am-12noon.
☎ (08821) 1800

**Gunzesried**
Verkehrsamt Blaichach-
Gunzesrieder Tal. ☎ (08321) 3911

**Hindelang**
Kurverwaltung. ☎ (08324) 892-0

**Immenstadt**
Gästeamt, Marienplatz 3
☎ (08323) 80481

Gästeamt Bühl am Alpsee
☎ 80483

**Isny im Allgäu**
Kurverwaltung, Untere Graben-
strasse 18. ☎ (07562) 70110

**Jungholz**
Verkehrsamt. ☎ (08365) 8120

**Kempten**
Verkehrsamt, Rathausplatz 29
☎ (0831) 2525237
or
Amtliches Allgäuer Reisebüro
☎ 25388-0

**Kleinwalsertal**
Hirschegg
Zentrales Verkehrsamt im
Walserhaus (Room Reservations)
☎ (08329) 5114 and 5115

**Mittenwald**
Dammkarrstrasse 3
Open: Monday to Saturday 9am-
5pm. ☎ (08823) 1051

**Oberammergau**
Verkehrsbüro
Eugen-Papst-Strasse 9a
☎ (08822) 4921

**Oberstdorf**
Kurverwaltung und Verkehrsamt
Marktplatz 7, ☎ (08322) 700-0

**Prien am Chiemsee**
Kurverwaltung
Alte Rathausstrasse 11
☎ (08051) 6905-0 and 6905-55 also
2280 and 6950-35

**Pfronten**
Kur- und Verkehrsamt
☎ (08363) 5044 and 5045

**Schliersee**
Kurverwaltung, Bahnhofstrasse
13a. ☎ (08026) 4069

**Schwangau**
Kurverwaltung
Münchener Strasse 2
or from May to September:
Informationsstelle, Hohenschwangau, Bushaltestelle
☎ 81061-63

**Sonthofen**
Verkehrsamt, Rathausplatz 3
☎ (08321) 292

**Steingaden**
Verkehrsamt
Schongauer Strasse 1
Open: July/August Monday to
Saturday 10am-12noon and
Monday to Friday 3-5pm.
☎ (08862) 200 otherwise contact:
Gemeindeverwaltung
Krankenhausstrasse 7
Open: Monday to Friday 7.30am-
12noon, Wednesday 1-6.30pm.
☎ 283

**Tegernsee**
Kuramt in Haus des Gastes
Hauptstrasse 2. ☎ (08022) 180140

**Traunstein**
Städtisches Verkehrsamt
Im Stadtpark. ☎ (0861) 65273

**Wangen**
Gästeamt und Reisebüro
Rathaus. ☎ (07522) 74211
(For information about Allgäuer
Emmentalerwerke in Wangen-
Leupolz).

**Weiler-Simmerberg**
Kur- und Verkehrsamt
☎ (08387) 651

# 7

# *MUNICH AND THE ALPINE PLATEAU*

V oralpenland, the area dealt with in this chapter, covers that part of Upper Bavaria and Bavarian Swabia outside the Alps. There is no doubt that the single most important attraction is Munich, but visitors will discover much more along the routes described; including a few of Germany's largest castles, a medieval fortified town in the middle of a meteorite crater, a monastery as famed for its beer as its church, and a pilgrimage chapel in Altötting, where time seems to have stood still since the Middle Ages.

## Route 17 • Munich and its Lakes
## 164km (102 miles)

Roads radiate from **Munich** (München) like the spokes of a wheel and underline the importance of Bavaria's largest and culturally most interesting city. Because there is so much to see and do it is a good idea to first gather information from one of the two main tourist offices. For those travelling by train the closest is located at the southern exit of the main railway station, in the Bayerstrasse, opposite platform 11. The other is at the Rathaus in the Marienplatz. Try in particular to get information about the excellent regional public transportation system, as many places of interest are easily accessible from Munich.

Munich's cathedral is known as the **Frauenkirche** and its twin towers, capped with copper domes, are visible from afar. It was built in its present form in the fifteenth century and is late Gothic in style. Little remains of the medieval church furnishings, but the stained glass windows of the choir (fourteenth to sixteenth centuries) have been almost completely preserved.

Not far away in the Neuhauser Strasse is the **Michaelskirche**

(1583-97) with its many valuable works of art, including ten altars and some forty terracotta figures. The church as a whole is considered to be one of the supreme achievements of the German Renaissance. Also nearby in the Marienplatz are a couple of other important sights. At the square's northern edge is the **Neues Rathaus** (New Town Hall) from 1867. This building receives a lot of attention not only because of its magnificent façade but also because of the mechanical figures which perform daily in the clock tower. Just beyond the square's eastern edge the much older **Altes Rathaus** (Old Town Hall) dates back to 1470.

It is only a short walk to the south-east of the Marienplatz to reach another two churches. The **Peterskirche** is Munich's oldest church and in its present form it dates back to 1368. Although it has an impressive interior it is the view over old Munich from its tower that many people do not want to miss. Across the road the **Heiliggeistkirche** was completed in 1392 but underwent extensive changes in the eighteenth century. A bit further south is the colourful Viktualienmarkt — an open air food market.

The **Theatinerkirche** (1663) can be reached by following the Weinstrasse and then the Theatinerstrasse north from the Marienplatz. As the first Baroque church to be built in Southern Germany it was to set a whole wave of Baroque church building in motion. No other church in Munich has been able to influence architectural style in Bavaria quite like this one. The **Residenz**, nearby, is a large complex of buildings that grew over several centuries. Eight courtyards link the various buildings, including the famous Brunnenhof with the Wittelsbacher fountain. The **Residenzmuseum** with its fine art collection can be entered from the Max-Joseph-Platz 3.

Follow the Burgstrasse up from the Altes Rathaus to reach the Alter Hof (1255), the first residential palace of the Bavarian dukes. A short distance east is the **Hofbräuhaus**. This establishment was founded as a brewery as far back as 1614, though it lost this function in 1890 when the brewery was shifted to Haidhausen. Today the emphasis is on consumption, rather than production, as the Hofbräuhaus was changed into a huge Gaststätte where visitors can enjoy Bavarian beer to the occasional accompaniment of folk music.

Of Munich's many museums only a few of the more important can be mentioned here. One of the most important art museums in Europe is the **Alte Pinakothek**, with its collection of paintings from the fourteenth to eighteenth centuries. The **Neue Pinakothek** concentrates on paintings from the nineteenth century and contempo-

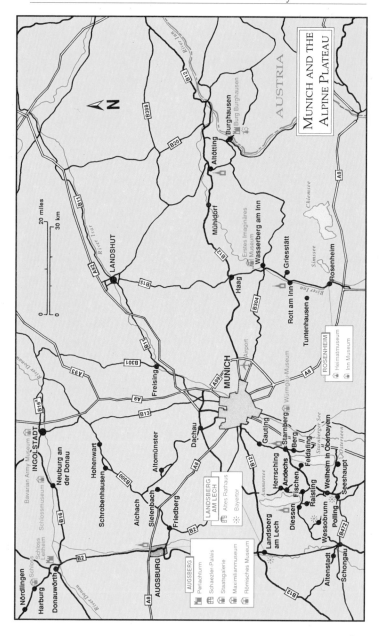

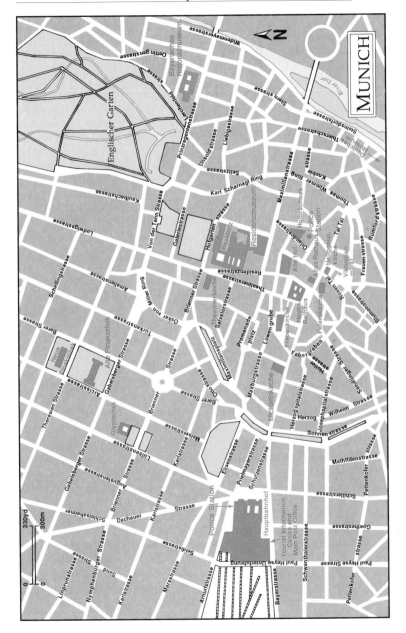

MUNICH

N

River Isar

Englischer Garten

Bayerisches Nationalmuseum

Oettingenstrasse

Lerchenfeld strasse

Prinzregentenstrasse

Widenmayerstrasse

Stern strasse

Steinsdorfstrasse

Liebigstrasse

Unsold strasse

Seitzstrasse

Deutsches Thierschstrasse Museum

Karl Scharnagl Ring

Maximilianstrasse

Thomas Wimmer Ring

Kaulbachstrasse

Residenzmuseum

Knobl strasse

Rumfordstrasse

Von der Tann Strasse

Gabelsbergerstrasse

Ludwigstrasse

Galeriestrasse

Hofgarten strasse

Residenz

Hofbräuhaus

Police

Orlandostrasse

Altes Ratshaus Station

Tal Tal

Oskar von Miller Ring

Brienner strasse

Residenzstrasse

Theatinerkirche

Odeonsplatz

Heiliggeist-kirche

Viktualien-markt

Amalienstrasse

Schellingstrasse

Türkenstrasse

Salvatorstrasse

Theatinerstrasse

Neues Rathaus

Frauenkirche

Peterskirche

Rosen strasse

Frauenstrasse

Blumenstrasse

Barer Strasse

Neue Pinakothek

Alte Pinakothek

Maximiliansplatz

Promenade platz

Löwen grube

Faber graben

Theresien Strasse

Arcisstrasse

Gabelsberger Strasse

Brienner Strasse

Barer Strasse

Maxburgstrasse

Michaelskirche

Hohen strasse

Sendlinger Strasse

Glyptothek

Luisenstrasse

Meiserstrasse

Otto strasse

Brienner Strasse

Herzog spitalstrasse

Herzog

Josephspitalstrasse

Wilhelm Strasse

Sonnen strasse

Gabelsberger Strasse

Augustenstrasse

Karlstrasse

Elisenstrasse

Pfandhausstrasse

Schutzenstrasse

Mathfidenstrasse

Pettenkofer strasse

Schleissheimer Strasse

Brienner Strasse

Dachauer Strasse

Karlstrasse

Strasse

Police Station

Hauptbahnhof

Schillerstrasse

Tourist Information Centre and Main Post Office

Goethestrasse

Seidlstrasse

Paul Heyse Unterführung

Schwanthalerstrasse

Paul Heyse Strasse

Pettenkofer strasse

Linprunstrasse

Nymphenburger Strasse

Sand Strasse

Marsstrasse

Karlstrasse

Arnulfstrasse

Bayerstrasse

330yd
300m

0

0

rary art. Note also the **Glyptothek** (1816-36), with its valuable collection of antiquities from Greece and Rome, the **Bayerisches Nationalmuseum** (Bavarian National Museum) and the **Deutsches Museum**, which specialises in science and technology.

The **Englischer Garten** (English Garden) is somewhat outside the city's old quarter, but it is an excellent place to take a break from all the sight-seeing. The original idea for this huge park came from Sir Benjamin Thompson (Graf von Rumford), an American who lived in Munich in the eighteenth century. Among the park's attractions are a Chinesischer Turm (Chinese Pagoda) and a large beer garden. Also worth seeing outside the city centre is Munich's excellent **Tierpark Hellabrunn** (zoo) and **Schloss Nymphenburg** (1664), one of the most significant Baroque palace complexes in Europe. Further afield, still to the north, is the old bishop's town of **Freising**, where there are several outstanding churches and the world's oldest brewery (1040). In **Dachau**, to the north-west, is a memorial to those who died in the concentration camp, set up here by the Nazis.

Before finally moving on from Munich a few words have to be said about the Oktoberfest. This huge beer festival starts in September and lasts 16 days before staggering to an end on the first Sunday in October. There is no doubt that this is Bavaria's most popular non-religious festival and visitors can be assured that Munich is always packed at this time. For beer connoisseurs there is a good range of characteristic types to choose from. *Pils* is a pale, light type of beer, *Märzen* and *Bock* are strong, dark beers and *Weizen* or *Weissbier* which is made from wheat is usually drunk with a dash of lemon added. Take note that *eine Mass* is about a quart of beer (a huge mug) and *eine Halbe* is a pint — a reasonable quantity for those who want to survive the festival weeks.

**Public Transport in Munich**

Tickets are bought at the blue ticket machines, marked with a white and green 'K' sign. There is a choice between single journey (Einzelfahrkarte) and multiple journey (Mehrfahrtenkarte) tickets. Day tickets (Tageskarten) are obtainable from the Munich Tourist Office, all MVV ticket offices and ticket machines. Before beginning a journey the ticket must first be cancelled. This is done with a cancelling machine (marked by a black and yellow 'E' sign) that is installed at the station barriers or in the streetcars and buses. All tickets are valid for S-Bahn, U-Bahn, streetcars and buses. The automatic ticket machines accept 10 Pfennig coins and all coins of a higher value. It is often possible to use 10 and 20 mark notes as well — change is given.

If you intend to do a lot of travelling about in Munich it is a very good idea to go to a tourist office and pick up some of the detailed pamphlets describing the city's public transportation system.

The town of **Starnberg** at the north end of the Starnberger See can be reached from Munich with the S-Bahn (suburban railway) on line 6. For motorists the simplest route is to follow the A95 south and turn off at the junction 'Dreieck Starnberg', though a prettier route would be to drive via Gauting. In town the parish church of St Joseph (1765)  has a fine Rococo interior and enjoys an elevated position above the lake in pleasant gardens. The Würmgau-Museum is housed in an old  fisherman's cottage from the fifteenth century and deals with local history. To get good views over the lake, which is the second largest in Bavaria after the Chiemsee, walk along the Prinzenweg in the direction of Pöcking. From Starnberg's piers boat trips can be made  to all the important places on the lake.

An excursion to **Berg**, on the lake's eastern shore, is worth it for  those who have been intrigued by the life of King Ludwig II; the man who built Bavaria's most famous castles and palaces. Ludwig, who suffered from a serious mental disorder, was declared incapable of ruling and moved from Schloss Neuschwanstein to Schloss Berg (not  open to the public). Here he was to be treated, but on 13 June 1886 he was to take a fateful stroll with his doctor, from which neither returned. Their bodies were found in the lake and to this day the real circumstances of their deaths have not been satisfactorily explained. A cross marks the place where they were found and in the Schloss park is a neo-Romanesque chapel, erected in memory of Bavaria's most romantic and beloved king.

Continue along the lake shore from Starnberg to **Possenhofen**, Schloss Possenhofen is not open to the public, but a section of the Schloss park provides access to one of the nicest bathing areas on the lake. From the lake shore opposite the neighbouring town of Feldafing it is possible to make a trip on a flat-bottomed wooden boat, known as a *Plätte*, to the Roseninsel (Rose Island). This used to be a favourite haunt of Empress Elisabeth (Sissy) of Austria and her cousin King Ludwig II. Also close to Feldafing is one of Europe's most beautiful golf courses.

Before leaving the Starnberger See there are a couple of other places worth mentioning. At the lake's southern tip is the popular resort of **Seeshaupt**. From here it is possible to reach a very pretty area of small lakes which form part of a nature reserve known as the Osterseen. A marked path goes around the largest lake. There is also a very nice trail running from Seeshaupt, along the Starnberger See, to Bernried. The trail goes through the Bayerischer Nationalpark (Bavarian National Park) with its beautiful stands of oak and beech.

From Feldafing take the road away from the lake, via Traubing and Machtlfing, to **Andechs**, near the shores of the Ammersee. The main attraction here is the Benedictine Kloster with its pilgrimage church of Mariae Verkündigung on the Heiliger Berg (Sacred Mountain). The impressive church interior, which dates back to renovations in the eighteenth century, is largely the work of J.B. Zimmermann from Wessobrunn and is considered one of the finest creations of Bavarian Rococo. Admittedly most people spend more time in the adjacent beer garden (self service) where the monastery's brewery provides good strong beer, along with a *Brotzeit* (snack) that might include the tasty Andechser Käse (cheese).

Continue to the lake shore at **Herrsching**. Boats sail from this pleasant resort to various points on the Ammersee. Just north of here are three pretty little lakes (Pilsensee, Wörthsee and Wesslinger See) that offer ideal bathing conditions as they are among the warmest lakes in Upper Bavaria.

The route now follows the shoreline south to Fischen, from where a detour can be made to the satellite tracking station near Raisting. Go west in the direction of Diessen, but take the turn-off left before town. The tracking station can be visited but the trip is also worth it for the unusual tableau of a tiny country chapel, set in fields, and dwarfed by the huge parabolic antennae of the station in the background. In **Diessen** itself the former collegiate church of Mariae Himmelfahrt (1732-39), with its outstanding interior, is of great interest. On the lake shore is a pavilion which exhibits handicrafts.

From Fischen continue south through Pähl and then join the B2 south to **Weilheim in Oberbayern**. Religious art first began to really flourish here in the sixteenth century, due to the patronage of wealthy monasteries and this allowed the development of a school of artists known as the Weilheimer Schule. Samples of their work can be seen in a number of churches, including the parish church of Mariae Himmelfahrt (1624-31) and the Gothic church of St Salvator and St Sebastian with its fine frescoes (1591).

West of Weilheim, in the village of **Wessobrunn**, was an even more famous school of artists. Fostered by the former Benedictine abbey the school was to produce stucco artists whose work ranks with the very finest of the seventeenth and eighteenth centuries. Some of the most famous artists belonged to the families of Schmuzer, Feuchtmayer, and Zimmermann. The Fürstenbau (1580) is all that remains of the old monastery, but it contains some excellent

*A roofscape view of Munich, the Neues Rathaus and its magnificent façade*

*A sun-dial on the church tower at Andechs*

Wessobrunn art. Note also the stucco work in the parish church of St Johannes (1757-9), at the north end of the monastery courtyard.

Continue south from Weilheim via Polling (interesting Klosterkirche) to join the B472, which is then followed west to **Schongau**. This town is attractively situated on a gently moulded ridge above the Lech river. On a clear day the view south from the town walls can be spectacular. Historically interesting is the Ballenhaus (1515), which has served variously as a storage place for goods (the town once lay on an important trading route between Augsburg and Italy) and as a town hall. The parish church of Mariae Himmelfahrt (church names are not all that hard to remember around here) was partly altered by Dominikus Zimmermann in Rococo style. One of Bavaria's most significant Romanesque churches is the Michaelskirche in nearby Altenstadt. The route now follows the B17 north, which forms part of the Romantische Strasse.

**Landsberg am Lech** is not only a very pretty town but has been the abode of two people who have gone down in history for very different reasons. The great Baroque artist and architect Dominikus Zimmermann lived here and was even mayor between 1749 and 1754. The other historic personality was Adolf Hitler and he did not choose Landsberg as a place to reside of his own free will. He was imprisoned here in 1923 and 1924 after the failed November 'Putsch' and made use of his spare time to jot down *Mein Kampf* (My Struggle).

A good part of Landsberg's fortifications from the thirteenth to fifteenth centuries have been preserved and the Bayertor (1425) is certainly one of Germany's most beautiful town gates. In the Marktplatz is the old Rathaus (there are some nice outdoor cafés around here) with its beautiful stucco façade by D. Zimmermann. Among the churches worth seeing is, above all, the parish church of Mariae Himmelfahrt (1454-88) with its lavish Baroque interior, the Johanneskirche (1750-52) by D. Zimmermann and the Heilig-Kreuz-Kirche (1752-4). Route 18 can be joined by following the B17 (Romantische Strasse) north to Augsburg. Otherwise continue east on the A96 (E54) past the north tip of the Ammersee back to Munich.

# Route 18 • Augsburg and Bavarian Swabia (Bayerisch Schwaben) 191km (119 miles)

**Augsburg** is one of the major attractions along the Romantische Strasse, the third largest city in Bavaria, and the birthplace of the dramatist Bertolt Brecht. The city's history goes back many centuries to the time of the Romans (the name comes from the Emperor

Augustus) but the cultural and economic flowering of the city first began in the fifteenth century. During this period Augsburg became a centre of trade with Italy and the Orient. One of Europe's greatest merchant families, the Fugger, were able to utilise this strategic position and amassed immense wealth and power.

Augsburg's cathedral, the Domkirche St Maria, was originally a Romanesque basilica, but it was altered many times in the following centuries. Among its many valuable works of art are what might be the oldest stained glass windows in the world (twelfth century) and some paintings by Hans Holbein the Elder from the year 1493.

To reach the Ludwigsplatz from the Dom walk along the Hohe Weg and Karolinenstrasse. At the eastern edge of the square is Augsburg's landmark the Perlachturm. This tower was extended between 1614 and 1616 by Elias Holl, the architect responsible for a number of the city's finest buildings, and offers good views over Augsburg. Next to the Perlachturm is the beautifully proportioned Renaissance façade of the Rathaus. It was built by Holl between 1615 and 1620 and stands as his masterpiece.

The broad Maximilianstrasse runs south of the Rathaus and includes several historically interesting places. The Fuggerhaus (1512-15) was built as a palace for the mighty merchant family. Within the building complex the Damenhof (Ladies Courtyard) from 1516 is of interest. Not much further is the Baroque Schaezler-Palais (1765-7), Augsburg's best preserved profane building. Of particular note inside is the Banquet Hall. Accessible via the Schaezler Palais is the Staatsgalerie with its collection of paintings by Southern German masters (fifteenth and sixteenth centuries). At the end of the street, in the Ulrichsplatz, is a magnificent group of buildings formed by the large St Ulrich's Minster (1500) and the smaller Ulrichskirche (1458).

Other places of interest include the St Anna-Kirche (fourteenth century), which lies south-west of the Rathaus, and to the east of the Rathaus the Fuggerei (1516-25). The buildings that comprise the Fuggerei were donated by Jakob Fugger to Augsburg's poor and even today the city's needy can live in the Fuggerei for next to nothing. Near the St Anna-Kirche is the Maximiliansmuseum, which deals with the city's 2,000 years of history and in the Dominikanergasse, in the former Dominican church, is the Römisches (Roman) Museum.

To the west of Augsburg is a large forested area forming the Naturpark Augsburg-Westliche Wälder. Directly south and just outside the city limits is the Augsburger Zoo and the beautiful Botanischer Garten (Botanical Gardens).

This route now continues north-east on the B300 to **Friedberg**. Of greatest interest here is the Baroque pilgrimage church of Unseres Herrn Ruhe from the eighteenth century. Among the famous artists that worked on its lavish interior were Cosmas Damian Asam and Matthäus Günther. Note also the Rathaus from the seventeenth century and a castle which dates back to the thirteenth century.

Further north on the B300 **Aichach** is a pleasant little place where there are still a couple of gates from the wall that once encircled the town. South-west of here, near **Sielenbach**, is the pilgrimage church of Maria Birnbaum (1661-8) with its almost Russian-looking Baroque exterior. Only a little further east in **Altomünster** is Germany's only Bridgettine monastery (Birgittinenkloster). The order was founded by St Bridget of Sweden (1303-73) around 1346 and it was open to both men and women. The Klosterkirche with its beautiful tower was built around 1770 by Johann Georg Fischer and is considered one of Bavaria's most important Rococo churches.

The route continues on the B300 to **Schrobenhausen**. This town lies in the middle of asparagus country — the harvest is roughly from May to June — and those who want to work up an appetite could do so by visiting the parish church of St Jakob (1425-80), or by viewing the remnants of the town walls (fifteenth century). A few kilometres further the small town of **Hohenwart** is already in the middle of hops country. A nice shady beer garden to seek out is by the old Benedictine nunnery on the Klosterberg. It is not far to Ingolstadt, which is reached by branching left off the B300 on to the B13.

**Ingolstadt's** town wall (1363-1430) is still largely intact and it proved a formidable enough barrier in the time of the Thirty Years War to prevent the town being laid waste by Gustav Adolf's invading armies. Of the old gates the Kreuztor (1385) is the most impressive. Just behind the Kreuztor is the Liebfrauenmünster (1425-1536), a large brick church that belongs to the most significant achievements of the late Gothic in Bavaria. In the Rococo church of Maria Viktoria (1732-35) is a huge ceiling fresco (1734) by C.D. Asam treating the spread of Christianity as its theme. Also worth a look is the Neues Schloss (1418-32), close to the River Donau, as it houses the Bavarian Army Museum.

From Ingolstadt continue first on the B13 towards Eichstätt (see Chapter 8 for description) but then turn south-west along the B16 to **Neuburg an der Donau**. Crowning this town is a large Renaissance Schloss built between 1530 and 1545. It contains a very picturesque courtyard, a chapel with sixteenth-century frescoes and a museum. Of interest are the historic buildings along the Amaliengasse, the

*The Marktplatz at Landsberg am Lech*

*The castle at Burghausen*

Rathaus (1609), and former Hofkirche (court church) St Maria (1607).

**Donauwörth** is also reached along the B16 and is situated at the spot where the Wörnitz stream joins the Donau river. Most of the sights here are to be found in the Reichsstrasse or its immediate vicinity. The Fuggerhaus (1505) belonged to the merchant family from Augsburg and was built in Renaissance style. Note also the Gothic parish church of Mariae Himmelfahrt (1444-67) with its high tower and the Baroque Heiligkreuzkirche (1717-22) built by Josef Schmuzer of Wessobrunn. Other sights include the Rathaus (1236) and two town gates known as the Riedertor and Räbertor. East of town is the Rococo **Schloss Leitheim** (1751). Details of concerts held here can be obtained at the tourist office in Donauwörth.

A very worthwhile detour from Donauwörth, instead of returning directly to Augsburg, is to go north along the Romantische Strasse (B25) to Harburg and the fortified town of **Nördlingen**. The mighty Schloss at **Harburg** is located majestically above the Wörnitz stream and ranks as one of the biggest and best preserved castles in Southern Germany. The older sections from the twelfth and thirteenth centuries include the keep and inner walls. In the castle is a library and art collection which contains illuminated manuscripts from the eighth to sixteenth centuries and works by Tilman Riemenschneider.

**Nördlingen's** circular fortifications are completely intact and were erected in the fourteenth century. It is possible to walk along the wall but the best overall impression is to be gained by climbing the tower of the St Georgskirche (1427-1505). The view from here is excellent and takes in not only the wall but also the historic houses of the Marktplatz (a Gothic Rathaus from the thirteenth century) which look like beautifully crafted dolls houses far below.

An interesting fact about Nördlingen is that it lies in a depression, known as the 'Rieskessel', that is in fact the result of a meteorite impact some 15 million years ago. Today the 25sq km (15sq mile) crater is the best preserved and most thoroughly studied on earth.

Either continue along the Romantische Strasse (B25) to Dinkelsbühl (see Route 22, Chapter 9) or return to Donauwörth and then follow the B2 back to Augsburg.

# Route 19 • The Inn Valley Between Rosenheim and Altötting

**Rosenheim** is easily reached from Munich on the A8 motorway. The modern town is not so rich in superlatives as some other places along this valley as fires destroyed much of historical interest, but it nevertheless makes a good place to start exploring what was one of the most important medieval trading routes in Central Europe.

The houses in the Max-Joseph-Platz belong to the few which still testify to Rosenheim's importance as a market town in the Middle Ages. The square is generously laid out and this characteristic, along with the shady arcaded passages, is typical of the old Inn-Salzach style. There are also several churches of interest and there is a Heimatmuseum housed in the Mittertor, a fourteenth century town gate. The Inn-Museum has exhibits dealing with the history of transportation on the Inn river. Just to the east of town is a lake called the Simssee, with camping sites at its north end.

Continue up the B15 to **Rott am Inn**. The former monastery church of St Marinus and Anianus (1759-67) was built to plans by J.M. Fischer, one of the greatest archtiects of his time. Some of the best artists of the time also took part in the interior decoration of this outwardly rather plain church, making it one of the most important achievements of the late Baroque. Those with time could also visit the church of Mariae Himmelfahrt to the south-west in Tuntenhausen or the Dominican church of St Peter and Paul to the north-east, near Griesstätt. ❱

Further north **Wasserburg am Inn** lies east of the B15 on the B304. The Altstadt is almost completely encircled by a bend in the river and can be entered through the massive Brucktor (Bridge Gate) from 1374. There is quite a bit more to see of the typical Inn-Salzach style here than in Rosenheim, especially in the Marienplatz. Of particular interest is the Kernhaus with its stucco front (1740) by J.B. Zimmermann and the late Gothic Rathaus. Near the Brucktor is the Erstes Imaginäres Museum (First Imaginary Museum) with replicas of over 400 famous works of art. Adding to the general picture of an old Inn town is the Burg and a few noteworthy churches.

Return to the B15 then continue north to **Haag**, where a large tower is all that is left of a once massive medieval castle. Take the B12 north-east to **Mühldorf**, another typical Inn town. Note especially the elongated market-place, lined with brightly painted houses, some of which date back to the fifteenth and sixteenth centuries.

A few kilometres away the town of **Altötting** is the most important place of pilgrimage in Bavaria. Opposite the large parish church of St Philipp and Jakob (1499-1511) is the town's main attraction and focal point of all the pilgrimages; a small eighth century chapel known as the Gnadenkapelle. Centre of attention within the chapel is the Black Madonna, a carved figure from around 1330. The atmosphere inside is quite unique and seems to invoke the superstitious

*Opposite: The rooftops of Nördlingen from the tower of St Georgskirche*

spirit of the Middle Ages rather than our present time. Although Altötting is a fascinating place to visit at any time it would be particularly interesting to come here during the main period of pilgrimage in May and August.

From Altötting continue south-east via Emmerting to **Burghausen** on the Salzach river. The old town is dominated by one of the largest castles in Germany and the best views are from the Austrian side of the river. It was built between the thirteenth and fifteenth centuries and actually consists of what amounts to six separate castles that have been linked together. Highlights of this immense complex are the Fürstenbau with museum and gallery, the Gothic Elisabethkapelle (dating around 1475), and the Hedwigskapelle (dating around 1485).

The Altstadt is directly below the narrow ridge surmounted by the castle, on a thin strip of land next to the river. It is well worth taking a stroll here in order to see some fine examples of building in the Inn-Salzach style. On the other side of the narrow ridge is a small lake called the Wöhrsee, where it is possible to swim. Route 20 (Chapter 8) can be joined at Passau by taking the B20 north and then the B12 east. A fact in passing is that Adolf Hitler was born in the Austrian town of Braunau, directly opposite Simbach am Inn on the B12.

# Additional Information

## Places of Interest in Munich

### Alte Pinakothek
Barer Strasse 27
Open: Tuesday to Sunday 9am-4.30pm, Tuesday and Thursday 7-9pm. Open Whit Monday but otherwise closed on public holidays.

### Bayerisches Nationalmuseum
(Bavarian National Museum)
Prinzregentenstrasse 3
Open: April to September Tuesday to Friday 9.30am-4.30pm, Saturday, Sunday and public holidays 10am-4.30pm, October to March Tuesday to Friday 9am-4pm, Saturday, Sunday and public holidays 9.30am-4.30pm. Entry is free on Sundays and public holidays.

### Deutsches Museum
Museumsinsel 1
Open: daily 9am-5pm but closed on public holidays.

### Englischer Garten
Open: dawn to dusk
Access: On U-Bahn lines 3 and 6 to the stations Universität, Münchner Freiheit and Giselastrasse.

### Frauenkirche
The southern tower (Südturm) of the cathedral can be climbed.
Open: April to October Monday to Saturday 10am-5pm.

### Glyptothek
Königsplatz 3
Open: Tuesday, Wednesday and Friday to Sunday 10am-4.30pm, Thursday 12noon-8.30pm.

### Hofbräuhaus
Am Platzl 9
Open: same hours as other Gaststätten, cafés, etc.

### Michaelskirche
Crypt open: Monday to Friday 10am-1pm and 2-4pm. Saturday 10am-3pm.

### Neue Pinakothek
Barer Strasse 29
Open: Tuesday to Sunday 9am-4.30pm, Tuesday 7-9pm. Open Easter and Whit Mondays, otherwise closed on public holidays. 31 December closes 12noon.

### Neues Rathaus
Marienplatz 8
Carillon and automata display at 11am daily, from May to October also at 12noon, 5pm and 9pm. Rathaus tower open: summer Monday to Friday 8.30am-7pm, Saturday, Sunday and public holidays 10am-7pm. Winter daily 9am-4.30pm.

### Peterskirche
Rindermarkt (near Marienplatz)
The tower known as 'Alter Peter' can be climbed.
Open: Monday to Saturday 9am-4pm, Sundays and public holidays 11am-4pm.

### Residenzmuseum
Entrance at Max-Joseph-Platz
Open: Tuesday to Saturday 10am-4.30pm, Sundays and holidays 10am-1pm. Closed Mondays.

### Schloss Nymphenburg
U-Bahn to Rotkreuzplatz and then tram 12
Open: April to end September daily except Mondays 9am-12.30pm and 1.30-5pm. October to end March daily except Mondays 10am-12.30pm and 1.30-4pm.

### Tierpark Hellabrunn
Siebenbrunner Strasse 6
Open: April to September daily 8am-6pm. October to March daily 9am-5pm. Accessible on bus lines 31, 52, 57.

## Useful Information

### Airport (Flughafen)
Arrival Lounge
Open: Monday to Saturday 8.30am-10pm, Sundays and holidays 1-9pm.

### Airport Information
☎ 921 12127
A bus departs from Hauptbahnhof to the airport daily every 15 minutes from 4.15am-9pm.

### Area Code
☎ 089

### Banks
Hauptbahnhof is open daily 6am-11.30pm.

### Car Rental
*Europcar*
Schwanthalerstrasse 10a
☎ 594723

## Consulates

*America*
Königinstrasse 5
☎ 23011

*Canada*
Maximiliansplatz 9
☎ 558531

*UK*
Amalienstrasse 62
☎ 394015

## Emergencies
Dentist ☎ 7233093
Doctor ☎ 558661
Hospital, Isamingerstrasse 22
☎ 41401
Pharmacist ☎ 594475
Police ☎ 110

## Guided Tours
Outside the Hauptbahnhof at
10am, 11.30am and 2.30pm, May to
October. Winter, 10am and 2.30pm.
The guides speak English.

## Ruffinihaus
Rindermarkt/Pettenbeckstrasse
Open: Monday to Friday 9.30am-
1pm and 2-5pm. Closed on public
holidays.

## Taxis
☎ 21611

## Tourist Information Centre
Hauptbahnhof
Open: Monday to Saturday 8am-
11pm, Sunday 1-9.30pm.
☎ 239 1256/57

Landesfremdenverkehrsverband
Bayern
Prinzregentenstrasse 18 IV
Postfach 221352
8000 Munich 22
☎ (089) 212397-0

# *Other Places of Interest*

## Augsburg
*Augsburger Zoo*
Brehmplatz 1
Open: daily October to March
8.30am-5pm, April to May,
September 8.30am-6pm, June to
August 8.30am-6.30pm.
☎ (0821) 3244993

*Botanischer Garten*
Dr Ziegenspeck-Weg 10
(next to the zoo)
Open: daily 1 January to 31 March
9am-5pm, 1 April to 30 April 9am-
6pm, 1 May to 31 May 9am-8pm, 1
June to 31 August 9am-9pm, 1
September to 30 September 9am-
7pm, 1 October to 31 October 9am-
6pm, 1 November to 31 December
9am-5pm
☎ 324-6040 or 324-6038

*Fuggerhaus (Stadtpalast der Fugger)*
Maximilianstrasse 36
Open: only the Damenhof can be
seen during the day.
(No entry charge).

*Maximiliansmuseum*
Philippine-Welser Strasse 24
Open: Tuesday to Sunday 10am-
4pm.

*Perlachturm*
Open: daily 10am-6pm.

*Römisches Museum*
Dominikanergasse 15
Open: Tuesday to Sunday 10am-
4pm.

*Schaezler-Palais* and *Staatsgalerie*
Open: Tuesday to Sunday 10am-
4pm.

## Burghausen
*Burg Burghausen*
Open: April to end September
daily 9am-12noon and 1-5pm.
October to end March daily except
Mondays 9am-12noon and 1-4pm.

## Donauwörth
*Schloss Leitheim*
Open: 1 May to 15 October,
Tuesday to Sunday 10am-12noon
and 2-5pm. Every week on Friday,
Saturday and Sunday, concerts in
the Rococo Festaal.
☎ (09007) 231

## Harburg
*Schloss* (museum)
Fürstlich Oettingen
Wallerstein'sche
Sammlungen
Open: guided tours 16 March to 31
October Tuesday to Sunday 9-
11.30am and 1.30-5.30pm
(October until 4.30pm).
☎ (09003) 1268 and 1211

## Ingolstadt
*Bavarian Army Museum*
(Bayerisches Armeemuseum)
In the Neues Schloss
Paradeplatz 4
Open: daily, except Mondays
8.45am-4.30pm.
Accompanied children free.
☎ (0841) 1370

## Landsberg am Lech
*Altes Rathaus*
Open: May to October Monday to
Friday 9am-12noon and 2-4pm,
Saturday, Sunday and public
holidays 10am-12noon and 2-5pm.
November to April Monday to
Thursday 9am-12noon and 2-4pm,
Friday 9am-1pm.

*Bayertor*
Open: May to October daily 10am-
12noon and 2-5pm.

## Neuburg an der Donau
*Schlossmuseum*
Open: Tuesday to Sunday 10am-
5pm.

## Rosenheim
*Heimatmuseum*
Ludwigsplatz 26
Open: Tuesday to Friday 9am-
12noon and 2-5pm, Saturday 9am-
12noon, Sunday 10am-12noon.
Closed Mondays and public
holidays.
☎ (08031) 391254

*Inn-Museum*
Innstrasse 74
Open: Friday 9am-12noon,
Saturday/Sunday 10am-4pm
☎ (08031) 305171

## Starnberg
*Würmgau-Museum*
(Heimatmuseum)
Possenhofer Strasse 5
Open: Tuesday to Sunday 10am-
12noon and 2-5pm.
Closed Mondays.
☎ (08151) 7721320

## Wasserburg am Inn
*Erstes Imaginäres Museum*
Open: 1 May to 30 September
Tuesday to Sunday 11am-5pm, 1
October to 30 April Tuesday to
Sunday 1-5pm. Closed Mondays.
☎ (08071) 4358

# Tourist Information Centres

**Altötting**
Verkehrsbüro
Kapellplatz 2a
☎ (08671) 8068

**Andechs**
Rathaus
Andechser Strasse 16
☎ (08152) 3051

**Augsburg**
Bahnhofstrasse 7
Open: Monday to Friday 9am-6pm.
Saturday 9am-1pm.
☎ 36026/7 or (0821) 50207-0

**Berg**
Ratsgasse 1
☎ (08151) 5080

**Diessen**
Mühlstrasse 4a
☎ (08807) 1048

**Donauwörth**
Verkehrsamt
Rathausgasse 1
☎ (0906) 789145

**Harburg**
Stadtverwaltung
☎ (09003) 1011

**Herrsching**
Bahnhofsplatz 2
☎ (08152) 5227

**Ingolstadt**
Verkehrsamt
Hallstrasse 5
☎ (0841) 305417

**Landsberg am Lech**
Fremdenverkehrsamt
Altes Rathaus
Hauptplatz 1

Open: Monday to Friday 8.30am-12noon and 2-5pm. Extended times in May to October Saturday, Sunday and public holidays 10am-12noon and 2-5pm.
☎ (08191) 128245-246-268

**Neuburg an der Donau**
Städtisches Verkehrsbüro
☎ (08431) 55240

**Nördlingen**
Verkehrsamt
Marktplatz 2
☎ (09081) 84116

**Rosenheim**
Verkehrsamt
(In the Stadthalle)
Kufsteiner Strasse 4
☎ (08031) 37080

**Schongau**
Verkehrsverein
Bahnhofstrasse 44
☎ (08861) 7216 and 71444

**Seeshaupt**
Weilheimer Strasse 1-3
☎ (08801) 1071

**Starnberg**
Kirchplatz 3
☎ (08151) 13274

**Wasserburg am Inn**
Verkehrsbüro
(in the Rathaus)
☎ (08071) 1050

**Weilheim in Oberbayern**
Verkehrsverein
Am Marienplatz
☎ (0881) 3009

**Wessobrunn**
Gemeindeverwaltung
☎ (08809) 313

# 8
# EAST BAVARIA

The part of Bavaria dealt with here comprises the administrative districts of Niederbayern (Lower Bavaria) and Oberpfalz (Upper Palatinate). It is a hilly to mountainous region with large stretches of forest. Austria forms a border to the south and the region's entire eastern flank is formed by Czechoslovakia.

## Route 20 • From Passau into the Bavarian Forest 138km (86 miles)

**Passau** is one of the most attractive towns in Germany. The Altstadt is situated on a narrow tongue of land at the confluence of the Donau and Inn rivers and seems, when viewed from one of the hills near town, to be like a great medieval galleon with its bow pointing east to Austria.

A good place to begin a walk around Passau is at the Kleine Exerzierplatz, in front of the Nibelungenhalle (generally good parking). Not far to the south and near the Inn river is the Nikola-Kirche (dating around 1070), which is interesting for its Baroque interior. Continue, however, from the Nibelungenhalle in a northerly direction away from the Inn via the Ludwigsplatz into the Ludwigsstrasse. Along this street reach the Rindermarkt from where, to the right, the Baroque St Paulskirche (seventeenth century) can be seen. Go through the Paulusbogen (thirteenth century), once the north gate of the old fortifications, and turn right through the narrow Luragogasse into the Domplatz (Cathedral Square). There are a number of very attractive buildings here but it is of course the Dom St Stephan that captures most attention. Records trace the cathedral's origins as far back as the eighth century but in the course of history the original church has been changed many times. A highlight of the Baroque interior is the world's largest church organ (1925-8). Organ recitals are held between May and October. For details of concerts inquire at the tourist office in the Nibelungenhalle.

From the cathedral go through the narrow Zengergasse into the Residenzplatz, a square lined with buildings in typical Inn-Salzach  style. The Neue Bischöfliche Residenz (New Bishop's Residency) is a representative Baroque building with a magnificent façade. Especially worth noting inside, apart from the many opulently furnished rooms, is an elaborate Rococo staircase. Follow the Innbrückgasse under the buildings of the old Bishop's Palace to the Innbrücktor (thirteenth century), then continue down to the Inn river. By turning left along the Innkai it is possible to follow the river to the point where it meets the Donau. Otherwise continue to the right. Near the spot where a footbridge (*Innsteg*) crosses the Inn river leave the Innpromenade, go left a short way on the Innstrasse and return via the Augustinergasse to the starting point.

Across the Donau from the Altstadt is Veste Oberhaus (1219), a fortress which now contains a Youth Hostel and museum. From here  there are excellent views over the Dreiflusseck, where Donau, Inn, and Ilz rivers meet. There are also good views from the pilgrimage  church of Mariahilf (1672) across from the Altstadt, on the other side of the Inn. Note that the various boat trips start from the Donau side of the Altstadt near the Dreiflusseck.

From Passau take the B85 north to **Tittling** in the Bavarian Forest. The village is situated in a pleasant hilly area just off the B85 and there are several small lakes in the vicinity suitable for bathing. A few kilometres north-west, near the Dreiburgensee, is a very interesting open-air museum known as the Museumsdorf Bayerischer Wald.  Everything has been arranged to create the impression of a genuine old Bavarian village, rather than a lifeless museum; there is even a fully operational old water-mill and farmyard animals to liven things up.

As is the case at all the places to be mentioned along this route there is also plenty of good walking around Tittling. To the east, in the village of **Fürsteneck**, is a thirteenth-century castle and from here there is beautiful walking along the Ilz valley. The Main-Donau-Weg  long distance path also goes along here. Wanderparkplätze with information boards for walkers are located at Trautmannsdorf, Kriestorf and Schrottenmühle which are all in the Ilz valley.

Continue up the B85 along a scenic stretch of road to **Schönberg** off the B85 to the right. Like Wasserburg the town has an almost Italian feel to it; this is most evident in the pretty Marktplatz with its houses

*A view across the River Inn to Passau's Altstadt*

in the Inn-Salzach style. The church of St Margaretha (1834) is worth a look and there are superb views from the Reinsberger Kurpark. In winter the area is popular for cross-country skiing.

Instead of taking the B85 direct to Regen an interesting alternative is to go east from Schönberg to **Grafenau**. In spite of numerous fires in the past the town has still managed to preserve something of its historical substance. Apart from some houses built in the same Inn-style as those seen in Schönberg, there are a few interesting churches  and a Schnupftabakmuseum (Snuff Museum). Sniffing tobacco was once a popular pastime in the Bavarian Forest along with carving wood and even today, in the village of Perlesreut, there is a tobacco-sniffing competition! However, the most important festival here is the Salzsäumerfest on the first Saturday in August. This festival recalls the time when Grafenau was the main resting point on the old salt road to Bohemia. The arrival of the salt-wagons is re-enacted in historical costumes, after which there is a lively fair.

Stretching along the Czechoslovakian border, north-east of

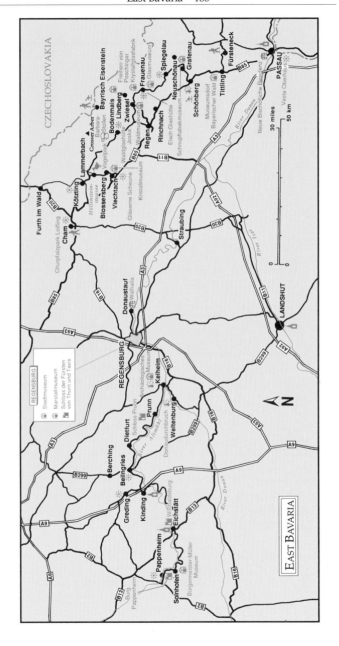

Grafenau, is the **Nationalpark Bayerischer Wald** (Bavarian Forest National Park). It is Germany's oldest National Park (1970) and protects one of the largest regions of relatively undisturbed forest in central Europe, together with the Neighbouring National Park in Czechoslovakia. One of the best places to enter the park is at Neuschönau, north-east of Grafenau. Close to the Nationalparkhaus (Hans-Eisenmann-Haus) which is a park information centre near Neuschönau, are some large enclosures with animals such as wolves and bison that were once found roaming freely in the forests. There are trails of varying length around the enclosures and they would take from 2-6 hours to complete. For further information contact Hans-Eisenmann-Haus, Neuschönau, Böhmstrasse 35, D-8351 Neuschönau ☎ (08558) 1300 or Nationalparkverwaltung, Bayerischer Wald, Freyunger Strasse 2, D-8352 Grafenau ☎ (08552) 2077.

Because this National Park offers such good walking opportunities it is well worth investing in a decent map, at least for longer walks. Some recommended maps are as follows: *Topogragraphische Karte 'Bayerischer Wald' 1:25,000; Kompass Wanderkarte 'Mittlerer Bayerischer Wald' 1:50,000 and Fritsch Wanderkarte 'Rachel-Lusen' (National Park Bayerischer Wald) 1:35,000.* From the railway stations in Freyung, Grafenau and Spiegelau it is possible to catch buses to the Nationalparkhaus.

From Grafenau take the road going in a north-easterly direction to **Spiegelau**, a glass-manufacturing village at the foot of the Rachel (1,452m 4,762ft), the National Park's highest peak. It is possible to visit the glassworks at Hauptstrasse 4 during the week from 9-10.30am.

Continue via Palmberg and Althütte to **Frauenau** in the Naturpark Bayerischer Wald. Sometimes referred to as the 'Glass Heart of the Bavarian Forest' Frauenau is holiday resort and glass-manufacturing centre all in one. The Glasmuseum here has been acclaimed as having the 'most informative exhibition of glass in Europe'. Among the various glassworks that can be visited are the Eich Glashütte and the Freiherr von Poschinger Krystallglasfabrik.

**Zwiesel** is only a few kilometres further on from Frauenau and has an equally beautiful location amidst forested mountains. It is also one of the Bavarian Forest's historic glass-manufacturing towns and has, like Frauenau, developed into an important summer and winter holiday resort. Places of interest include the parish church (1896), Rathaus (1838) with museum, and the Bergkirche (1682) in the Bergstrasse. Just to the north-east of town in **Lindberg** is the  Bauernhausmuseum (Farm-House Museum).

A detour north of Zwiesel can be made to **Bayerisch Eisenstein** near the Czechoslovakian border. This village ski resort makes an  excellent base for walking excursions in the area of the Grosser Arber (1,456m 4,777ft), the highest mountain in the Bavarian Forest. The Arber-Sesselbahn (a chair lift) is open all year round and is reached by taking the road west to Brennes, then the road south towards the Grosser Arbersee. Both the Grosser and Kleiner Arber lakes are  surrounded by magnificent forest and walking trails skirt their shore. There is boat hire on both lakes too.

A road goes south-west from near the Arbersee-Haus (an inn by the Grosser Arbersee) to **Bodenmais**, a town where the tradition of glass-making goes back to the fifteenth century. Worth seeing are the glassworks 'Joska' and the old silver mine known as the Barbara-  Stollen on the Silberberg (955m 3,132ft) outside town. There is a chair-lift going up to the mine, otherwise clearly marked paths can be followed.

The main route continues from Zwiesel on the B11 south to **Regen**. Of interest here is the parish church of St Michael (thirteenth century)  and some attractive old houses, a few of which date back to the seventeenth century. South of town (about an hour on foot) are the castle ruins of Weissenstein (twelfth century) and north-east the pretty Regener See, where there are rowing-boats for hire. The impressive Baroque parish church (1729) in Rinchnach can be visited by going back south a short way on the B85.

From Regen follow the B85 north-west. **Viechtach** is yet another beautifully situated town and there are also boats for hire on the nearby Höllensteinsee. Not far from the railway station is the Ba- roque Rathaus (seventeenth century) and the Kristallmuseum,  which is worth visiting for its collection of locally found rock crystals. By taking the road north-west via Blossersberg it is possible to visit the unique Gläserne Scheune (Glass Barn) at Rauhbühl. Here  the artist Rudolf Schmid has incorporated stained glass windows into the walls of an old hay-barn. The glass murals that have been finished so far depict local legends, and more are to be added.

Those who keep their eyes peeled on the way to the Gläserne Scheune, or when driving in the general area of Kötzting, might see Totenbretter. These wooden boards were once used to carry the deceased to the cemetery. Afterwards they were usually painted with some religious motif or inscribed with verse, before being put up at an appropriate place which was often by a chapel or near the person's favourite spot.

Instead of continuing on the B85 from Viechtach follow the road north to Kötzting. On the way the Vogelpark (Bird Park) at **Lammerbach** could be visited. The most interesting time to come to **Kötzting** is on Whit Monday when the Pfingstritt takes place. This custom goes back to 1412 and involves a colourful procession on horse-back. The parish church of Mariae Himmelfahrt in town is worth noting, as well as the pilgrimage church in nearby Weissenregen with its unique pulpit. Return to the B85 at Miltach, then continue to Cham, the last stop in the Bavarian Forest.

**Cham's** medieval townscape is characterised by remnants of the town walls and an old Schloss that has since been converted into a brewery. By the large car park (Wanderparkplatz Flosshafen) near the Regen river, which flows past town, stands a map with descriptions of the many walks in the general area. A good choice would be the one going to the Vogelschutzgebiet Rötelseeweiher, a small lake where rare birds have been placed under protection. In nearby Chammünster the former Benedictine monastery church is worth closer investigation. Also in the vicinity is an amusement park, the Churpfalzpark Loifling.

By following the B20, which goes off the B85 shortly before Cham, a detour can be made to **Furth im Wald**. The main reason for visiting this town is to see the famous Drachenstich in the month of August. This folk festival goes back over 500 years and involves the spearing of a huge mechanical dragon (Drache). The dragon itself can be viewed between June and September, on Sundays. From Cham take the B85 west and then near Roding, the B16 south-west to join the start of Route 21 at Regensburg.

# Route 21 • From Regensburg into the Altmühl Valley 135km (84 miles)

The Naturpark Altmühltal is one of the largest and most beautiful of the German nature parks. It extends from Kelheim in the east to Wemding in the west, and from Weissenburg in the north to Donauwörth in the south. There is an excellent network of walking and cycling paths throughout the park. In most cases information boards with maps stand at the numerous Wanderparkplätze, or near local tourist offices. Recommended walking maps are *Kompass Wanderkarten Mittleres Altmühltal* and *Unteres Altmühltal*, both 1:50,000.

**Regensburg** is the capital of the Upper Palatinate. A good deal of the city's 2,000 years of history is represented by the magnificent Dom St Peter, one of the most important Gothic cathedrals in

*Visit Frauenau, the 'Glass Heart of the Bavarian Forest'*

*Autumn colours contrast with the white rock face of the Danube Gorge near Kloster Weltenburg*

Southern Germany. You can park nearby in the Alte Kornmarkt. Building began in 1250, using the cathedrals in Troyes, Dijon and Strassburg as models. Other churches of importance include the Basilika St Emmeran with a Rococo interior by the Asam brothers, and the Schottenkirche (Scottish Church) St Jakob. The latter was built by Irish monks in the eleventh century as part of a monastery. In the sixteenth century it was taken over by Scottish Benedictines. The present church dates back to the twelfth century and is considered the most important Romanesque building to be found along the Donau where it is otherwise the Baroque style that sets the tone.

Other witnesses to Regensburg's ancient history are the Porta Praetoria, one of the oldest town gates in Germany and the Steinerne Brücke (Stone Bridge), a masterpiece of medieval engineering. It was built between 1135 and 1146 and for about 800 years was the only bridge over the Donau. The Altes Rathaus dates back to the eleventh century and also houses the tourist office where you can inquire about guided tours in the English language.

There is no shortage of excellent museums in Regensburg but the Stadtmuseum (Municipal Museum) in the Dachauplatz is the most important. Over 100 rooms give a comprehensive coverage of the history, art and culture of East Bavaria. Of especial interest is the  outstanding collection of Roman artefacts. In the Schloss der Fürsten von Thurn und Taxis (Palace of the Princes of Thurn and Taxis) near  the Basilika St Emmeran is the Marstallmuseum (Mews Museum) with a collection of coaches, sledges and calashes. Over 500 years ago this family was instrumental in setting up an international postal network that was to lay the basis for the modern German, Spanish, Austrian and Belgian postal services.

Regensburg has something of a reputation as a 'musical city' and this has a lot to do with the famous Domspatzen, as the boys choir is known. It is possible to hear them singing in the cathedral on Sundays. There are also concerts held in the Minoritenkirche every Wednesday from June to August. Nothing to do with music but no  less entertaining are boat trips on the Donau in summer. An historic place to eat is the Wurstkuchl, near the Steinerne Brücke, which has been serving out sausages and *Sauerkraut* since 1616.

For those whose craving for things historical has not yet been stilled by the city's many churches and museums then a worthwhile excursion is to **Walhalla** (1830-42), near Donaustauf. It is possible to get there by boat from Regensburg. Built by King Ludwig I to honour Germany's great and famous, it is modelled on the Parthenon in Athens. Longer excursions can be made to the historical Lower

Bavarian towns of Straubing, east along the B8, and **Landshut**, south along the B15. St Martin's Minster (1389-1500) in Landshut distinguishes itself by having the tallest brick spire in the world.

From Regensburg the route now continues south on the B16 to **Kelheim**, at the meeting point of the Donau and Altmühl rivers. Already visible from afar the Befreiungshalle (Liberation Hall) is perched high above town on the Michelsberg. It was another idea of King Ludwig I and like Walhalla it was built in neo-classical style. It is possible to drive up to the building and from the top are some magnificent views.

The main scenic attraction near Kelheim is the **Donaudurchbruch** (Danube Gorge) a little further south. In the course of many thousands of years the Donau has cut its way through the soft rock to produce a narrow gorge fringed by spectacular cliffs. During summer the best way to see the gorge is on one of the regular boat trips from Kelheim to Kloster Weltenburg. On the first Saturday in July, during the festival 'Flammende Donau', the gorge is lit up with hundreds of Bengal Lights.

Kloster Weltenburg at the end of the Donaudurchbruch is a major cultural attraction. The monastery church (1716-18) is one of the outstanding achievements of Southern German Baroque architecture and an artistic triumph for the Asam brothers who conceived it. A shady beer garden provides relief from so much brilliance and an opportunity to try the monastery's own brew. By crossing on the small car ferry to Stausacker on the opposite bank it is possible to get the best overall views of the monastery. A good walk to the Kloster starts at Kelheim and goes via the Befreiungshalle along a marked forest path (red rectangle) and takes about $1^1/_2$ hours. Boats can be taken back.

The route continues along the Altmühl river in the direction of Riedenburg, passing on the way some caves. The Tropfsteinhöhle (stalactite cavern) Schulerloch is of particular interest because in 1915 excavations unearthed not only tools belonging to Neanderthal Man, but also skeletons of animals from the Ice Age. There are exhibits of these finds at the cave entrance and also in Kelheim's archaeological museum. Guided tours of the cave are from Easter until October.

Just before **Riedenburg**, atop steeply falling cliffs, is **Schloss Prunn**. The castle was built in the eleventh century and can be visited. Riedenburg's own castle dates back to the twelfth century and houses a falconry museum. Demonstrations of falconry take place daily in summer at 3pm.

Continue along the scenically twisting road, through the small holiday resort of Dietfurth with its five Gothic towers, to the old market town of **Beilngries**. These days tourism does a lot to help the locals get by and there are plenty of facilities for all kinds of recreational activities. It is also quite pleasant to stroll about the narrow streets of the Altstadt, which is still partly encircled by a town wall from the fifteenth century. An important attraction is Schloss Hirschberg (1760-64), a few kilometres north-west of town.

From Beilngries a detour can be made on the B299 to **Berching**. The German predilection for superlatives has given this medieval town the title 'Rothenburg of the Upper Palatinate'; no doubt because of the perfectly preserved town walls. These fortifications were built around 1450 and there are some thirteen towers and four town gates.

Continue along the river, past the small lake at Kratzmühle (good for swimming) to Kinding. From here a detour can be made north to **Greding**, another fortified town with some twenty turrets along its wall that are still lived in. In **Kinding** a fortified church from the fourteenth century is worth seeing.

Pass under the A9 motorway and follow the river to **Eichstätt**. The most significant building in this very pretty town is the cathedral, or Willibaldsdom, as it is called. Dating back to the fourteenth century it is named after an Anglo-Saxon priest who became Eichstätt's first bishop in the eighth century. Especially worth noting is the Mortuarium, the cloister (1420-50) and the stained glass windows (dating around 1500) by Hans Holbein the Elder.

At the south-west edge of town is the Willibaldsburg. It was built in the fourteenth century, though it was greatly extended in the sixteenth and seventeenth centuries. Inside are two museums. The Jura Museum deals with that period in geological history when the Jurassic Sea covered not only this area but also large parts of central Europe. Among the fossil exhibits is a 4m (13ft) long crocodile and a complete skeleton of the reptile-bird archaeopteryx. The other museum deals with prehistoric settlement in the Altmühl valley and also with the time of Roman colonisation. To get the best overall views of the Willibaldsburg drive a short distance out of town on the B13 in the direction of Weissenburg.

For those who want to try their own hand at fossil hunting there is a unique opportunity to do so at a quarry on the Blumenberg, a short distance north-west of Eichstätt. Equipment necessary, like a hammer and chisel, can be hired on the spot — for more details inquire at the tourist office, Domplatz 18, in Eichstätt.

The final stretch of this route keeps close to the river, passing

*Shades of autumn in the Altmühl valley*

through picturesque villages like Dollnstein on the way. Just before **Solnhofen** are the curious looking rock formations known as the Twelve Apostles. In Solnhofen's Rathaus there is an excellent fossil museum.

**Pappenheim** is the last stop on this tour of the Altmühl valley. The town is dominated by its eleventh-century castle and among the other places of interest is Germany's oldest Jewish cemetery (Jüdischer Friedhof) from the twelfth century. To join Route 22 (Chapter 9) continue a little further west along the river and then take the B2 north via the fortified town of Weissenburg to Nürnberg.

# Additional Information

## Places of Interest

**Bodenmais**
*Barbara-Stollen*
Erzbergwerk im Silberberg
(ore mine)
Open: April, May, June daily 10am-4pm. July, August, September daily 9am-5pm. October to first Sunday in November daily 10am-4pm. 25 December to 8 January daily 10am-4pm.

*Waldglashütte Joska*
Near the Postamt (post office)
Open: Monday to Friday 9-11.45am and 1-3.45pm, Saturday 9am-1.45pm. ☎ (09924) 779-0

**Cham**
*Churpfalzpark Loifling*
☎ (07971) 30300
Open: April to October daily 9am-6pm.

**Eichstätt**
*Willibaldsburg*
Jura-Museum and Vor- und Frühgeschichtliches Museum
Burgstrasse
Open: 1 April to 30 September 9am-12noon and 1-5pm, 1 October

to 31 March 10am-12noon and 1-4pm. Closed Monday. Restaurant Tuesday to Sunday.
☎ (08421) 2956

**Frauenau**
*Eisch Glashütte*
Open: tours take place Monday to Thursday 9-11.45am and 1-2.45pm, Friday and Saturday 9-11.45am.
☎ (09926) 189-0

*Freiherr von Poschinger Krystallglasfabrik*
Tours, Monday to Saturday 9.45-11.30am and 12.45-1.30pm.

*Glasmuseum*
Am Museumspark 1
Open: 20 December to 14 May daily 10am-4pm, 15 May to 31 October daily 9am-5pm.

**Grafenau**
*Schnupftabakmuseum*
Open: daily 2-5pm. Closed from 1 November to 15 December.

**Kelheim**
*Archäologisches Museum*
Lederergasse 11
Open: 1 April to 31 October daily 10am-4pm, except Monday.

## Lammerbach
*Vogelpark Viechtach*
Open: 1 April to 31 October daily
9am-6pm.
☎ (09942) 1398

## Lindberg
Near Zwiesel
*Bauernhausmuseum*
Open: Easter Sunday to 31 October
daily 10am-5pm. Otherwise 10am-
4pm. The restaurant has its
Ruhetag (day of rest) on Saturday.
☎ (0992) 1293

## Pappenheim
*Burg Pappenheim*
Open: April to October. Restaurant
Tuesday to Sunday.
☎ (09143) 266

## Passau
*Veste Oberhaus*
Open: 15 March to 31 October,
Tuesday to Sunday 9am-5pm.

*Neue Bischöfliche Residenz*
(with Dom and Diözesanmuseum
accessible from the cathedral)
Open: Monday to Saturday 12.30-
5.30pm, Sunday 12noon-5.30pm.

## Regensburg
*Marstallmuseum*
Guided tours Monday to Friday
2pm, 2.30pm and 3.15pm. Sundays
and holidays 10am, 10.30am and
11.15am.

*Schloss der Fürsten von Thurn und
Taxis*
Emmeramsplatz 5
Open: guided tours Monday to
Friday 2-3.15pm, Sundays and
holidays 10am and 11.15am.

*Stadtmuseum*
Leerer Beutel
Bertholdstrasse 9

Open: Tuesday to Saturday 10am-
4pm, Sunday 10am-1pm.

## Riedenburg
*Schloss Prunn*
Near Riedenburg
Open: daily 9am-6pm, October to
March until 4pm and closed
Monday. Terrace café.
☎ (09442) 1765

*Schloss Rosenburg*
Bayerischer Landes-Jagdfalkenhof
with Burg and Falknereimuseum
Open: Tuesday to Sunday 9am-
5pm. ☎ (09442) 1843

## Solnhofen
*Bürgermeister Müller Museum*
(in the Rathaus)
Bahnhofstrasse 8
Open: until 31 October daily 9am-
12noon and 1-5pm, 1 November to
31 March Monday to Thursday
9am-12noon and 1-5pm, Fridays
9am-12noon. ☎ (09145) 477 and 478

## Tittling
*Museumsdorf Bayerischer Wald*
Open: daily 9am-5pm.

## Viechtach
*Kristallmuseum*
Spitalgasse 5
Open: during the season daily
10am-12noon and 1.30-5pm,
outside the season Tuesday to
Sunday 10am-12noon and 1.30-
4pm. ☎ (09942) 5262

*Gläserne Scheune*
Rauhbühl 3
Open: 1 April to 30 September
daily 10am-5pm, October 10am-
4pm. Children up to the age of 10
accompanied by their parents have
free entry.
☎ (09942) 8147

**Walhalla**
Open: April to September 9am-
6pm.

**Zwiesel**
*Waldmuseum*
Stadtplatz 28
Open: 14 May to 16 October
Monday to Friday 9am-5pm,
Saturday and Sunday 10am-
12noon and 2-4pm. Otherwise
Monday to Friday 10am-12noon
and 2-5pm, Saturday and Sunday
10am-12noon.
☎ (09922) 9640

## Tourist Information Centres

**Bayerisch Eisenstein**
Verkehrsamt
☎ (09925) 327

**Beilngries**
Touristik-Verband Beilngries
Haus des Gastes
Hauptstrasse 14
☎ (08461) 8435 and 214

**Berching**
Stadt und Fremdenverkehrsverein
☎ (08462) 881 and 1260

**Bodenmais**
Kur- und Verkehrsamt
Bahnhofstrasse 56
☎ (09924) 77835 or 77836

**Cham**
Cordonhaus
Propsteistrasse 46
☎ (09971) 4933

**Eichstätt**
Städtisches Fremdenverkehrsbüro
Domplatz 18
☎ (08421) 7977

**Frauenau**
Rathaus
Open: Monday to Friday 8am-
12noon and 1-5pm, Saturday
9-11.30am.
☎ (0992) 6710

**Fürsteneck**
Gemeindeverwaltung
☎ (08555) 632

**Furth im Wald**
Fremdenverkehrsamt
Schlossplatz 1
☎ (09973) 3813

**Grafenau**
Städtisches Verkehrsamt
Rathaus
☎ (08552) 42743

**Greding**
Fremdenverkehrsamt
Rathaus
☎ (08463) 233

**Kelheim**
Verkehrsamt
☎ (09441) 70134

**Kinding**
Verkehrsamt Markt Kinding
Rathaus
☎ (08467) 587 or 588

Fremdenverkehrsverein Kinding
☎ (08467) 372

**Kötzting**
Verkehrsamt
Herrenstrasse 10
☎ (09941) 602150

**Lammerbach**
Kur-und Verkehrsamt Viechtach
Stadtplatz 1
D-8374 Viechtach
Open: from Whitsun to end

September, Monday to Friday 8am-
12noon and 1.30-4.45pm, Saturday
10am-12noon. Otherwise Monday
to Thursday 8am-12noon and 1.30-
4.45pm. Friday 8am-12noon.
☎ (09942) 1661 and 80825

### Landshut
Verkehrsverein, Altstadt 315
☎ (0871) 23031

### Pappenheim
Fremdenverkehrsverein
☎ (09143) 6266 or 511

### Passau
Open: Monday to Friday 9am-6pm,
Saturday 9am-12noon.
☎ (0851) 33421

### Regen
Verkehrsamt
☎ (09921) 2929

### Regensburg
Altes Rathaus
Open: Monday to Friday 8.30am-
6pm, Saturday 9am-4pm, Sunday
9am-12noon. ☎ (0941) 507 2141

### Schönberg
Verkehrsamt
☎ (08554) 821

### Solnhofen
Verkehrsamt
Rathaus
☎ (09145) 477 and 478

### Spiegelau
Verkehrsamt
☎ (08553) 419 or 811

### Straubing
Verkehrsamt
Theresienplatz 20
☎ (09421) 16307

### Tittling
Verkehrsamt
☎ (08504) 2666

### Viechtach
Kur- und Verkehrsamt
☎ (09942) 1661 and 808-25

### Zwiesel
Kurverwaltung
☎ (09922) 9623

## Useful Information

### Naturpark Altmühltal
Canoeists, etc, can use the Altmühl
river between Gunzenhausen and
Dietfurt, a distance of about 150km
(93 miles). As it is a slow flowing
river it is ideal for beginners and
for making leisurely kayak trips.

### Boat Hire
Kanuverleih (canoe hire) WMU
Zum Schiesswasen 7
D-8820 Gunzenhausen
☎ (09831) 2725
or
Auf & Davon
Reiseladen
Alte Poststrasse 9
D-8800 Ansbach
☎ (0981) 17085

Other places hiring out boats are:
Fa. Albot
Bahnhofstrasse 25
D-8830 Treuchtlingen
☎ (09142) 1790

Franken-Boot
G. Egner
Dürerstrasse 18
D-8830 Treuchtlingen
☎ (09142) 4645 or 4444

Gasthof Zum Hollerstein
H. Rottler
Zimmern 32
D-8834 Pappenheim
☎ (09143) 753

Fa. Otto Rehm
Papst-Viktor-Strasse 6
D-8833 Dollnstein
☎ (08422) 278

Campingplatz
D-8079 Kipfenberg
☎ (08465) 588

Campingplatz Kratzmühle
D-8079 Kinding
☎ (08461) 525

Frau Christa Pfaller
Obere Weinbergstrasse 22
D-8432 Beilngries
☎ (08461) 8903

Martin Schäfer
Eichelhofer Strasse 2 or
Ottmaringer Strasse 2
D-8435 Dietfurt-Töging
☎ (08464) 1474

A detailed brochure about boating
on the Altmühl can be obtained
from:
Kreisverkehrsamt Eichstätt
Notre Dame 1
D-8078 Eichstätt
☎ (08421) 70237

**Cycle Hire**
Bahnhof Treuchtlingen
D-8830 Treuchtlingen
☎ (09142) 1041

Bahnhof Solnhofen
D-8838 Solnhofen
☎ (09145) 208

Fa. Otto Rehm
Papst-Viktor-Strasse 6
D-8833 Dollnstein
☎ (08422) 278

Bahnhof Dollnstein
☎ (08422) 261

Bahnhof Eichstätt
D-8078 Eichstätt
☎ (08421) 4409

Campingplatz Kipfenberg
D-8079 Kipfenberg
☎ (08465) 588

Fremdenverkehrsverein
Kipfenberg
☎ (08465) 882

Josef Pröll
Jurastrasse 6
D-8079 Kinding
☎ (08467) 225

Gasthof Gallus
Neumarkter Strasse 25
D-8432 Beilngries
☎ (08461) 247 or 7351

Roswitha Karg
Griesstetter Strasse 25
D-8435 Dietfurt
☎ (08464) 1345

Fremdenverkersdienst Lühmann
Kolpingerstrasse 55
D-8547 Greding
☎ (08463) 763, 459 or 9368

The above list is not exhaustive.
Tourist offices can supply more
information.

# 9
# FRANCONIA

Franconia (Franken) makes up the bulk of northern Bavaria and though a good part of the eastern section has been touched upon in Chapter 1 there is still a great deal left to be seen. With its fortified towns and villages this region seems to have been more faithful to the spirit of the Middle Ages than Upper Bavaria, where the Baroque swept away or changed much of what had come before.

## Route 22 • From Nürnberg to Rothenburg 90km (56 miles)

Nürnberg's (Nuremberg in its anglicised form) Altstadt makes it one ✳ of Germany's most attractive medieval cities. It is enclosed by massive walls, much of which have been preserved. The Altstadt can be divided into two distinct halves separated by the Pegnitz river; the castle or Sebalder half to the north with St Sebaldus and the Lorenzer half to the south with the German National Museum and the church of St Lorenz. The main railway station is just to the south of the Lorenzer Altstadt and is home to the tourist office.

A good place to get a general view over old Nürnberg is from the Burg. The castle complex actually consists of three distinct groups of 🏰 buildings, the oldest of which is the Kaiserburg from the twelfth century. Just below the castle is the Albrecht Dürer house. This half-timbered building was bought by the artist in 1509 and he lived here until his death in 1528. It is now a museum offering an insight into 🏛 how Dürer lived and worked.

Nürnberg's only Baroque church is that of St Egidien, south-east ⛪ of the Burg, otherwise they are all in predominantly Gothic style. Of especial interest in St Sebaldus, directly south of the Burg, is the Sebaldusgrab, a tomb with a housing in bronze by the artist Peter

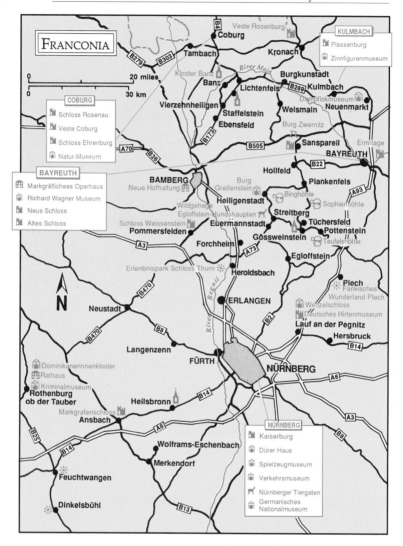

Vischer the Elder (1460-1529) and his sons. Not far from the church
in the Karlstrasse 13 is the Spielzeugmuseum (Toy Museum). The
Frauenkirche (1352-61) further south in the Hauptmarkt has a
beautifully ornate façade. At 12noon the mechanical figures beneath
the church clock put on a performance known as the Männ-

*The Heilig-Geist-Spital restaurant, Nürnberg*

leinlaufen. Opposite the Frauenkirche is one of the city's most impressive fountains, the aptly named Schöner Brunnen, completed towards the end of the fourteenth century. Around St Barbara's Day (4 December) the Hauptmarkt becomes a superb setting for the Christkindlesmarkt, Germany's most famous Christmas Market.

Crossing the river near the Heilig-Geist-Spital, one of the great charitable foundations of the Middle Ages (now a restaurant) it is not far to the Gothic church of St Lorenz (1260-1370). With its twin spires it looks quite similar to St Sebaldus and the older church was in fact used as a model. There is a great deal to see inside this church but one of the most outstanding works of art is the *Englischer Gruss* (Angelic Salutation), a freely suspended group of painted wooden figures created by Veit Stoss around 1517-18. Note also the famous Sakramentshaus (Sacrament-House) by Adam Krafft.

Further south from St Lorenz in the Kornmarkt/Kartäusergasse is the Germanisches Nationalmuseum (German National Museum). This museum is the largest of its type dealing with topics of German cultural history. The extensive art collection includes the work of masters like Dürer, Cranach, and Altdorfer. Just outside the town wall and not far from the railway station is the Verkehrsmuseum (Museum of Transport). East of the city is Nürnberg's zoo, where a miniature railway is an additional attraction for children.

Around Nürnberg there are a number of interesting places worth at least a brief mention. On the B14 going east the town of **Lauf an der Pegnitz** is definitely worth a visit. It is a very pretty old town and the Wenzelschloss with its Wappensaal, a room displaying over 100 coats of arms, is particularly worth noting. A little further on Hersbruck's Hirtenmuseum (Shepherd's Museum) is perhaps unique in Europe. The amusement park Fränkisches Wunderland can be reached on the A9 motorway towards Bayreuth, take the **Plech** exit. Erlebnispark Schloss Thurn, a similar attraction, is reached on the A73 towards Forchheim, exit near **Heroldsbach**.

From Nürnberg the route continues south-west on the B14 to **Heilsbronn**. Apart from some nice half-timbered houses in the Marktplatz the main attraction is the Münster which dates back to the twelfth century. Inside are some beautifully sculpted sarcophagi from the Renaissance and Baroque periods.

A little further on **Ansbach** is renowned as the town of 'Franconian Rococo'. The large Markgrafenschloss (1705-49) does, in fact, have a beautiful Rococo interior and includes an extensive collection of porcelain. East of the palace is the Hofgarten (park) with orangery. The Schwanenritterkapelle inside the St-Gumbertus-Kirche is also of interest for its famous medieval altar. By making a detour south-east on the B13 it is possible to see the fortified villages of Merkendorf and Wolframs-Eschenbach.

Continue along the B14 to **Feuchtwangen** with its pretty Marktplatz and Romanesque parish church, then take the B25 south to **Dinkelsbühl**. This town is, like Feuchtwangen, on the Romantic Road. Among the town's many half-timbered buildings the Deutsches Haus (1440) is especially outstanding. In the Marktplatz the parish church of St Georg (1448-99) is an important representative of the late Gothic style and has an interesting interior. A walk around the town walls takes about an hour and gives a good general impression of some of Dinkelsbühl's most picturesque corners. In mid-July the Kinderzeche festival commemorates the town's narrow escape from destruction by the Swedish army in 1632. According to the story children carried flowers into the enemy camp as a token of peace, thus melting the enemy commander's heart.

Continue back up the B25 to **Rothenburg ob der Tauber**. This impressive medieval town is one of Germany's most famous attractions and also lies along the Romantische Strasse. To get an overall impression of town it is a good idea to walk along the exceptionally well preserved town walls. Starting from the Spitaltor (a town gate) a tour including the Rödertor, Würzburgertor and Klingentor would take a little less than an hour.

Rothenburg's Marktplatz is one of the nicest in Germany and is dominated by the Rathaus, parts of which date back to the thirteenth century. Inside the Grosser Saal and the dungeons are of interest. Climbing the Rathaus tower is well worth it for the fine views over town. Next door the façade of the Ratstrinkstube (Councillor's Tap-Room) is notable for the mechanical figures which put on a daily performance when the clock strikes the hour — from 11am to 3pm and at 9 and 10pm. The performance, known as the Meistertrunk, recalls a legend from the time of the Thirty Years War (1618-48). According to the story after conquering Rothenburg the victorious enemy commander, who was obviously a good sport, said he would spare the town if somebody could drink a jug with $3^1/_4$ litres (over 5 pints) of wine in one draught, without spilling a drop. The mayor came forward and managed this dizzying feat, thus saving the town and no doubt frustrating the enemy.

Some other places of interest worth seeing in the course of a stroll are the parish church of St Jakob (1311-1471) with an outstanding altar by Tilman Riemenschneider, the Kriminalmuseum (Crime Museum) and the former Dominikanerinnenkloster (Dominican Nunnery). The latter contains a museum showing how nuns lived during the Middle Ages. To get back to Nürnberg follow the B25 and B470 north to Neustadt and then the B8 via Langenzenn. Route 3 which also passes through Rothenburg can be followed as described in Chapter 1.

## Route 23 • From Bayreuth into Franconian Switzerland 101km (63 miles)

Franconian Switzerland (Fränkische Schweiz) is by no means an Alpine region, but rather a pretty landscape of modest hills and forest within a rough triangle formed by Bayreuth, Bamberg and Nürnberg. The region is easily reached from all three centres and is particularly attractive for walking or cycling. A recommended walking map is the *Kompass Wanderkarte Fränkische Schweiz 1:50,000*.

**Bayreuth** is a large town that has become almost synonymous with the name of Richard Wagner and the festival of his music that takes place here from 25 July to 28 August. The Festspielhaus (Festival Theatre) is just beyond the north end of town. Another music centre is the Baroque Markgräfliches Opernhaus (Margrave's Opera House) with its magnificent interior. The composer lived in

*Segriner Strasse, Dinkelsbühl*

the Villa Wahnfried and this building, in the Richard-Wagner-Strasse 48, now houses a museum. Other places of interest in town include the Altes Schloss (seventeenth century) and the Neues Schloss (1753-9) with its lavish Rococo interior, town museum and the State Art Collection — mainly paintings from the seventeenth and eighteenth centuries.

About 5km (3 miles) east of town is the famous **Eremitage**, which is comprised of two pleasure seats set in a beautiful English-style park. Of the two Schlösser it is the Neues Schloss (1749-53) with its Rococo Sun Temple that is the most eye-catching. This temple is encrusted with colourful bits of glass and stone and together with the fountains, grottos and mock ruins in the park it could be described as a kind of eighteenth-century Disneyland for aristocrats.

Continue west from Bayreuth along the B22 into the Naturpark Fränkische Schweiz. At **Hollfeld**, note the parish church and

*An evening in Rothenburg ob der Tauber*

Friedhofskapelle (Cemetery Chapel) a detour can be made north to **Sanspareil**, at the foot of Burg Zwernitz. Of interest here are the curious rock formations (Felsengarten) and the ruins of a romantic outdoor theatre, built by Margravine Wilhelmina around the mid-eighteenth century. The Burg is open to the public but closed in winter.

Continue south from Hollfeld along a pretty country road to Plankenfels. From here follow the sign first to Ebermannstadt/ Streitberg but do not turn again until the sign to **Heiligenstadt** can be seen. Just before Heiligenstadt is a turn-off to Burg Greifenstein where there is a museum with a collection of weaponry and a café nearby. From Heiligenstadt follow the road south via Traindorf and Unterleinleiter to Ebermannstadt on the B470.

**Ebermannstadt** is not so interesting in itself, but it is a good starting point for a trip through a very pretty stretch of the Wiesent valley. Before doing so, however, a detour can be made to the **Wildgehege Egloffstein-Hundshaupten**, a few kilometres further south. The enclosure contains an interesting array of native animals such as badgers, foxes and wisent. In the Pfarrwald (Pfarr Woods) near the village of Egloffstein, a bit further on from the Wildgehege, there are still yew trees to be found. In fact there is scarcely another place in Germany where these trees are so numerous. They can reach an age of 2,000 years and were once prized by Germanic tribes for making bows.

From Ebermannstadt continue east on the B470 through the Wiesent valley. **Streitberg** is known for its beer (Streitberger Bitter) and from here the Binghöhle (cave) can be visited. There are over 360 caves so far recorded in Franconian Switzerland and another interesting fact is that the area is rich in fossil remains. Especially common are those of ammonites.

The pilgrimage church Zur Heiligsten Dreifaltigkeit seems rather big for such a small town like **Gössweinstein**, but that makes it all the more impressive. It was built by the great architect Balthasar Neumann between 1730 and 1739. Both the church and the town's Schloss can be seen from an excellent vantage point just behind the church.

On the way to Pottenstein pass through **Tüchersfeld**, where houses have been built right against bizarre shaped dolomite cliffs. Also worth noting is the Fränkische-Schweiz-Museum. **Pottenstein** has a Schloss and church that are of interest but the greatest attraction is the Teufelshöhle, just out of town. This cave is supposed to be the most impressive of them all. With over 150km (93 miles) of way-marked trails in the vicinity Pottenstein makes an excellent base for walking excursions. Among the things to be discovered in the surrounding countryside are wild orchids, rare butterflies and a wide variety of birdlife.

Return back along the B470 to Behringersmühle. Follow the turn-off marked Bayreuth/Oberailsfeld into the Ailsbach-Ahorntal. Near

Burg Rabenstein (not open to the public) is the **Sophienhöhle**. In this cave it is possible to see 40,000-year-old cave-bear skeletons and the fossilised bones of a mammoth. While travelling through visitors will have noticed lots of Gaststätte, not only in this valley but also in the Wiesenttal, offering dishes of fresh trout (*Forelle*). This is something of a speciality here and the numerous streams running through Franconian Switzerland are kept well stocked by several trout hatcheries. The route continues on via Glashütten and Mistelgau, after which a turn-off to Eckersdorf on the B22 returns it to Bayreuth. It would also be possible to turn west on the B22, connect with the B505 going south and join the start of Route 24 at Bamberg.

# Route 24 • From Bamberg into the Upper Main Valley and Coburger Land 135km (84 miles)

Located in the Main valley the town of **Bamberg** is over 1,000 years old. The Altstadt as a whole has been described as a collective work of art with superb examples of Romanesque and Baroque architecture. Of all the many sights the Kaiserdom (cathedral) from the early thirteenth century is the most outstanding. This Romanesque building is in fact one of the most important examples of medieval architecture in Germany. Among the cathedral's many treasures the most famous is the *Bamberger Reiter* (Bamberg Horseman), a stone sculpture from around 1240.

In the Domplatz (Cathedral Square) are the palaces of the Alte Hofhaltung (1571-6) and the Neue Hofhaltung (1695-1704). The latter is a Baroque masterpiece by Johann Leonhard Dietzenhofer and contains over forty rooms furnished in the styles of the seventeenth and eighteenth centuries. The Staatsgalerie housed within the palace contains a collection of European painting from the fifteenth to the eighteenth centuries.

There are more churches in Bamberg than most people have the energy to visit, but St Michael's with its 'Botanic Garden' fresco and the Gothic Obere Pfarrkirche are especially worth a visit, all on the cathedral side of the Regnitz river. Perhaps the most picturesque sight is, however, the Altes Rathaus (1744-56). Set upon a tiny island it straddles the middle of an ancient bridge (1453-6) crossing the river.

An excursion south of Bamberg can be made along the B505 to **Pommersfelden**. Schloss Weissenstein (1711-16) stands as the first great palace complex of the eighteenth century in Germany. In spite of its size it was built in the record time of 5 years and one month. Of

*The Sun Temple of the Neues Schloss at Eremitage*

*The Neue Residenz at Bamberg*

*Detail of a half-timbered house in Franconia*

particular interest inside is the famous monumental staircase. For a small fee it is possible to walk in the spacious Schloss deer park.

From Bamberg follow the B173 north to Ebensfeld, then the minor road to Staffelstein. By taking the road north-west across the Main river, it is possible to visit **Kloster Banz** (1695-1719). This important Baroque monastery was largely the work of the Dientzenhofer brothers, although another great architect, Balthasar Neumann, contributed the gate-house wing in the main courtyard. In the former monastery is a museum with a fossil collection, of which the most interesting exhibit is a 2m (6.5ft) long ichthyosaurus head.

Return to Staffelstein and then continue in the direction of Lichtenfels. The pilgrimage church of Vierzehnheiligen (1743-72) is virtually opposite Kloster Banz and is considered one of Balthasar Neumann's greatest achievements. The church exterior is dominated by the two high sandstone towers in front. Every year, on the fourth Sunday after Easter, a large pilgrimage festival is held here.

Take the B289 around the basket-making town of Lichtenfels to Untersiemau, then follow the B4 to **Coburg**. Veste Coburg dates back to the eleventh century and is certainly one of the largest and most beautiful of Germany's castles. Within the fortress is a priceless art collection, including paintings (some by Cranach) and copper-etchings. A large weapon collection also deserves mention. Below the castle, on the eastern edge of the Altstadt, Schloss Ehrenburg (1816-38) was originally built as a Franciscan monastery in the thirteenth century now houses a museum and art gallery. The Altstadt, as a whole, is very picturesque with the Rathaus in the Marktplatz being particularly noteworthy. In the Hofgarten, a park which climbs towards the fortress, is the excellent Natur-Museum (Natural History Museum).

It might seem curious to many people that there is a statue of Queen Victoria in Coburg. The solution to the puzzle of an English queen in the depths of Germany is that her husband, Prince Albert, came from this area. He was born a short distance from Coburg in Schloss Rosenau, recently opened to the public. After his death in 1861 Queen Victoria quite often spent time here. About 10km (6 miles) south-west of Coburg, on the B303, is Schloss Tambach with its Wildpark containing a wide variety of European wildlife.

Return a few kilometres south on the B4, then turn east along the B303, via Sonnefeld and the winter sports resort of Mitwitz, to **Kronach**. The pretty Altstadt is situated below the Veste Rosenburg, another well preserved fortress which dates back to the twelfth century, though it was extended as a residential palace in the sixteenth century. Other historic sights include the Haus zum scharfen Eck (sixteenth century), where the Renaissance painter Lucas Cranach the Elder was supposed to have been born, the Rathaus (1583) and the parish church of St Johannes der Täufer (John the Baptist). Spreading to the east of Kronach the Naturpark Frank-enwald is a mountainous, forested area, ideal for outdoor activities in both winter and summer.

From Kronach continue south on the scenic B85 to **Kulmbach**. Just before town are the best views of Kulmbach's castle, the Plassenburg. It dates back to the twelfth century and though rather plain from outside it has an impressive Renaissance courtyard known as the Schöner Hof. Housed in the castle is the Zinnfigurenmuseum, a collection of over 300,000 tin-soldiers and other figures arranged in impressive dioramas. It is possible to drive up to the Plassenburg, otherwise it is a steep 20 minute walk from the town directly below.

As is only proper in a town that lies on the Bier-und Burgenstrasse (Beer and Castles Road) there are several local breweries and a beer festival called the Kulmbacher Bierwoche — a smaller version of Munich's Oktoberfest that takes place during the first week of August. An interesting fact for American visitors is that there is only one brewery for every 200,000sq km (124,000sq miles) in the USA whereas there is one for every 33sq km (20sq miles) in Upper Franconia! Those who are keen on knowing more about the Bierstrasse should inquire at the tourist office in the Stadthalle, Sutte 2.

A worthwhile detour for anybody fascinated by old steam trains is to the Dampflokmuseum (Steam Locomotive Museum) at **Neuenmarkt**. To get there go east on the B289 to Untersteinach, then south on the B303 to near Wirsberg, where a turn-off to the right leads to Neuenmarkt. The museum has around twenty locomotives on display and there is also a miniature railway.

From Kulmbach the main route continues west along the B289. A pause in **Burgkunstadt** is worth it as there are a number of old houses here that are typical for the area — this is also the case in nearby Altenkunstadt. By making a detour south via the pretty village of Weismain, a very scenic excursion could be made through the Kleinziegenfelder valley. By continuing further south it should not be difficult to link with Route 23 at Hollfeld. Shortly after Burg-kunstadt the main route joins the B173, passes around Lichtenfels and then returns south to Bamberg.

# Additional Information

## Places of Interest in Nürnberg

**Dürer Haus**
Open: Tuesday to Sunday 10am-5pm, Wednesday to 9pm.

**Germanisches Nationalmuseum**
Kornmarkt/Kartäusergasse
Open: Tuesday to Friday 9am-5pm, Thursday also 8-9.30pm, Saturdays and Sundays 10am-5pm. Closed Mondays.

**Kaiserburg**
Open: 1 April to 30 September daily 9am-12noon and 12.45-5pm. 1 October to 31 March daily 9.30am-12noon and 12.45-4pm. Guided tours of the interior daily 9.30am-12noon and 12.45-4pm.

**Nürnberger Tiergarten**
Open: March to October daily 8am-7.30pm. November to February daily 9am-5pm.

**Spielzeugmuseum**
Karlstrasse 13
Open: Tuesday to Sunday 10am-5pm. Closed Mondays.

**Verkehrsmuseum**
Lessingstrasse 6
Open: daily 9.30am-5pm.

## Useful Information

**Area Code** ☎ 0911

**Hospital**
Flurstrasse 17
☎ 3980

**Medical Emergencies**
Kesslerplatz
☎ 533771

**Tourist Information Centre**
Hauptbahnhof
Open: Monday to Saturday 9am-8pm, Friday until 9pm.
☎ 233632

## Other Places of Interest

**Ansbach**
*Markgrafenschloss* (Residenz)
Open: April to end September daily 9am-12noon and 2-5pm. October to end March daily 10am-12noon and 2-4pm. Closed Mondays.

**Bamberg**
*Neue Hofhaltung/Residenz*
Open: April to end September daily 9am-12noon and 1.30-5pm. October to end March daily 9am-12noon and 1.30-4pm.

**Bayreuth**
*Eremitage: Altes Schloss*
Open: April to end September daily except Mondays 9-11.30am and 1-4.30pm. October to end March daily except Mondays 10am-11.30am and 1-2.30pm. Fountains play from May to mid-October daily from 10am every hour, on the hour.

*Markgräfliches Opernhaus*
Opernstrasse
Guided tours 9-11.30am and 1.30-4.30pm.

*Neues Schloss*
Ludwigstrasse
Open: Tuesday to Sunday. Guided tours 10-11.30am and 1.30-4.30pm.

*Richard Wagner Museum*
Richard-Wagner-Strasse 48
Open: daily 9am-5pm.

## Coburg
*Natur-Museum*
Open: April to September daily
9am-6pm, October to March daily
9am-5pm, except Monday.

*Schloss Ehrenburg*
Open: 1 April to 30 September
daily, except Monday 10am-
12noon and 1-5.30pm, 1 October to
31 March daily, except Monday
10am-12noon and 1-4.30pm.
☎ (09561) 7767

*Schloss Rosenau*
Open: 1 April to 30 September
daily, except Monday. 1 October to
31 March daily, except Monday
10am-12noon and 1-4.30pm.

*Veste Coburg*
Open: April to October daily
except Mondays 9.30am-1pm and
2-5pm. November to March daily
2-4pm. Closed Mondays.

## Dinkelsbühl
Guided tours through Dinkelbühl's
historic Altstadt
Start: Münster St Georg
Times: April to October daily 2pm
and 8.30pm.

## Heiligenstadt
*Burg Greifenstein*
Open: guided tours May to
September daily 8.30-11.15am (last
tour) and 2-5.15pm (last tour).
October to April same times but
closed Mondays.
☎ (09198) 423

## Heroldsbach
*Erlebnispark Schloss Thurn*
Schlossplatz 4

☎ 09190/555
Open: Easter to end October daily
9am-6pm.

## Hersbruck
*Deutsches Hirtenmuseum*
Eisenhüttlein 7
Open: tours Tuesday to Sunday
10am-12noon and 2-4pm.
☎ (09151) 2161

## Kulmbach
*Plassenburg*
Open: 1 April to 30 September,
Tuesday to Sunday 10am-4.30pm.

*Zinnfigurenmuseum*
Open: April to September, Tuesday
to Sunday 10am-4.30pm, October
to March 10am-3.30pm.

## Kronach
*Veste Rosenburg*
Open: guided tours daily, except
Mondays 11am and 2pm. Also by
prior arrangement.
☎ (8640) 97312

## Lauf an der Pegnitz
*Wenzelschloss with Wappensaal*
Open: on request, inquire at the
Stadtarchiv
Spitalstrasse 5
Open: Tuesday to Thursday 9am-
12noon and 2-4pm.
☎ (09123) 184166

## Neuenmarkt
*Dampflokmuseum*
Open: May to October, Tuesday to
Friday 9am-12noon and 1-5pm;
November to April, Tuesday,
Friday, Saturday and Sunday
10am-12noon and 1-4pm.
☎ (099227) 5700

**Plech**
Fränkisches Wunderland Plech
☎ 09244 (451)
Open: Easter to mid-October daily
9am-6pm, ticket office only until
5pm.

**Pommersfelden**
*Schloss Weissenstein*
Open: guided tours April to
October daily 9am-10am, 11am,
2pm, 3pm and 4pm, except
Monday.
☎ (09548) 203

**Pottenstein**
*Burg Pottenstein*
Open: Easter to October daily
10am-5pm, except Monday.
☎ (09243) 274

*Teufelshöhle*
Open: Easter to October 9am-5pm.
☎ (09243) 208 or 833

**Rothenburg ob der Tauber**
*Former Dominikanerinnenkloster*
(Reichsstadtmuseum)
Klosterhof 5
Open: daily 10am-5pm, from
1 November to 31 March daily
1-4pm.

*Mittelalterliches Kriminalmuseum*
(Medieval Museum of Crime)
Burggasse 3
Open: daily 9.30am-6pm, 1
November to 31 March daily 2-
4pm. Closed January and February.
☎ (09861) 5359

*Rathaus*
Open: April to October daily
9.30am-12.30pm and 1-5pm.

*Guided Tours*
Start: Rathaus
Times: May to October daily
around 11am and 2pm, April and

December daily 2pm
Duration: $1^1/_2$ hours
Minimum size of group: 10 persons

**Sanspareil**
*Burg Zwernitz*
Open: 1 April to 30 October daily,
except Monday 9am-12noon and
1.30-5pm. Closed in winter
(1 October to 31 March).

**Sophienhöhle**
Open: 1 April to 31 October
9.30am-5pm, except Monday.

**Streitberg**
*Binghöhle*
Open: 15 March to 31 October daily
8am-5pm.

**Tüchersfeld**
*Fränkische-Schweiz-Museum*
Open: 1 April to 30 October daily
10am-5pm, except Monday.
Winter, Sunday 1.30-5pm, Tuesday
and Thursday 1.30-3.30pm.
☎ (09242) 1640

**Wildgehege Egloffstein-
Hundshaupten**
Open: 23 March to 31 October daily
9am-5pm. Otherwise Saturdays,
Sundays and public holidays
11am-3pm. Children up to 5 free.
Facilities for disabled. Refreshments in summer.
☎ (09197) 202 or 241

## *Tourist Information Centres*

**Altenkunstadt**
Gemeindeverwaltung
Marktplatz 2
☎ (09572) 641

**Ansbach**
Städtisches Verkehrsamt
Rathaus
☎ (0981) 51243

**Bamberg**
Hauptwachstrasse
Open: Monday to Friday 8am-5/
6pm according to season. Saturday
8am-12.30pm.
☎ (0951) 21040

**Bayreuth**
Verkehrsverein
Luitpoldplatz 9
☎ (0921) 88588

**Behringersmühle**
(district of Gössweinstein)
Verkehrsamt D-8556
Open: Monday to Friday 10-
11.30am and 2.30-4.30pm, Saturday
10-11.30pm.
☎ (09242) 840

**Burgkunstadt**
Stadtverwaltung
Vogtei 5
☎ (09572) 38818

**Coburg**
Tourist Information
Herrngasse 4
☎ (09561) 7418-0

**Dinkelsbühl**
Tourist-Information Verkehrsamt
Marktplatz
☎ (09851) 90240

**Ebermannstadt**
Städtisches Verkehrsamt
Bürgerhaus
☎ (09194) 8128

**Egloffstein**
Fremdenverkehrsamt
Felsenkellerstrasse 20

D-8551
Open: 2.30-6.30pm, Saturday 9am-
12noon.
☎ (09199) 586 (mornings) and 202
(afternoons).

**Feuchtwangen**
Kultur- und Fremdenverkehrsamt
Marktplatz 1
☎ (09852) 90444

**Gössweinstein**
Verkehrsamt
D-8556
Open: Monday to Friday 8am-
12noon and 2-5pm, Saturday 9am-
12noon.
☎ (09242) 456

**Heiligenstadt**
Verkehrsbüro
Am Marktplatz
D-8551
Open: Monday to Friday 8am-
12noon, Saturday 10am-12noon.
☎ (09198) 721 or after office hours
462.

**Heilsbronn**
Stadtverwaltung
☎ (09872) 423

**Hersbruck**
Verkehrsamt
Stadthaus am Schlossplatz
☎ (09151) 4755

**Kronach**
Städtisches Verkehrsamt
Marktplatz 5
☎ (09261) 97236

**Kulmbach**
Fremdenverkehrsbüro
(in the Stadthalle)
Sutte 2
☎ (09221) 802216

**Lauf an der Pegnitz**
Stadtverwaltung
Urlasstrasse 22
☎ (09123) 184-0

**Lichtenfels**
Städtisches Verkehrsamt im
Rathaus
Marktplatz 1
☎ (09571) 7950

Tourist Information
Oberes Maintal-Coburger Land
Kronacher Strasse 30
Landratsamt, Zimmer (room) 20
Open: Monday to Thursday 8am-
12noon and 2-4pm, Friday 8am-
12noon.
☎ (09571) 18283

**Pottenstein**
Städtisches Verkehrsbüro
Kurverwaltung
Gästezentrum am Rathaus
D-8573
Open: Monday to Thursday 8am-
12noon and 1-5pm, Friday 8am-
12noon and 1-4pm.
☎ (09243) 833835

**Rohrbrunn** (see Chapter 1)
Tourist Information Franken
Am Rasthof im Spessart-Süd
Open: Easter to mid-October daily
10am-1pm and 2-7pm.
☎ (06094) 220
(This information centre covers all
Franconia)

**Rothenburg ob der Tauber**
Marktplatz
Open: Monday to Friday 9am-
12noon and 2-6pm, Saturday 9am-
12noon.
☎ (09861) 40492

**Staffelstein**
Fremdenverkehrsamt Alte Darre
Bamberger Strasse 25
☎ (09573) 4144

**Streitberg**
Verkehrsamt Muggendorf-
Streitberg
☎ (09196) 717 and 346

**Weismain**
Städtisches Fremdenverkehrsamt
Rathaus
Am Markt 19
☎ (09575) 1224

# Southern Germany: Fact File

## Accommodation

A booklet listing some 300 typical German hotels is published by the German National Tourist Office. Lists containing a wider variety of accommodation such as camping grounds (Campingplätze) and the many privately run small hotels or inns (Gasthöfe) can be obtained in Germany from regional or local tourist offices. Many local tourist offices will reserve rooms but not every office will do this over the 'phone.

### Camping

A free list of camp sites is available from the German National Tourist Office. There are some fairly expensive books listing camping grounds put out by the German Automobile Club (ADAC) and the Deutscher Camping Club. Both are available in larger bookshops and are updated annually.

Note that most camping grounds are open only between April to October, though near major cities or resorts with summer and winter seasons they remain open throughout the year.

Camping rough has been made illegal in the interests of protecting the environment.

### Hotels

The German Hotel Reservation System (ADZ) is a department of the German National Tourist Board (DZT) through which accommodation can be conveniently booked in all hotels, inns and boarding-houses.

Contact:
DZT-Serviceabteilung ADZ
Corneliusstrasse 34
D-6000 Frankfurt am Main 1
☎ (069) 740767

**Youth Hostels**
German Youth Hostels are listed in the International Youth
Hostels *Guide to Budget Accommodation Handbook, Volume 1,
Europe and the Mediterranean.*
For further information contact:
Deutsches Jugendherbergswerk (DJH)
Hauptverband
Bismarckstrasse 8
Postfach 1455
D-4930 Detmold
☎ 05231/7401-0
Hostels in Germany are identified by a green triangle with
the letters DJH.

## Arrival and Customs

Nationals of the UK and other EEC countries require no visa
but a valid passport. Holders of Australian, USA, Canadian
and New Zealand passports do not need a visa provided they
do not take up employment and their stay does not exceed 3
months.

### Customs Regulations
All personal belongings needed for a visit are duty-free.

If wine is intended for personal consumption and the
imported value does not exceed 250DM, duty will be
charged at an overall rate of 15 per cent.

Tobacco and alcoholic beverages are only duty-free for
persons over 17 years of age and coffee only for persons over
15. In respect of goods bought in a tax/duty-free shop, only
the regulations for imports from non-EEC countries apply.
Duty-free allowances only apply when the goods are carried
in the visitor's personal luggage.

# Banks

Banks are usually open weekdays 8.30am-1pm and from 2.30-4pm (Thursday to 5.30pm). They are closed at weekends.

The Deutsche Verkehrsbank has branches in railway stations of most main cities and are sometimes open all week and until quite late in the evening.

# Business Hours

Shop opening times vary somewhat between the various Federal States. In general shops are open between 9am-6.30pm during the week, Saturdays until 2pm and they are closed Sundays.

On the first Saturday of every month, known as Langer Samstag, and in the 4 weeks before Christmas, shops may remain open until 6pm.

Museums and historic monuments are usually closed Mondays and admission charges for museums vary greatly. For the most part village churches are open during the day, if locked then check the notice board for the address of the Küster or whoever else might hold the key (Schlüssel). Large churches, cathedrals, and monasteries may have set opening times and if they are not pinned up by the main entrance then inquire at the Verkehrsamt. Visitors should refrain from taking photos during services; especially with a flash. At some of the more important places there are often booklets or leaflets available in English.

# Chemists

Open during normal business hours. Usually clearly visible at the shop front are details of which chemist is on night or Sunday duty (Apothekennotdienst or simply Notdienst). This information is also found in the local newspapers.

Medicines are only available on doctor's prescription from the chemist. No prescription is necessary for aspirins & other mild medication. A Drogerie (Drug Store) sells things like insect repellents, vitamin tablets etc.

# Climate

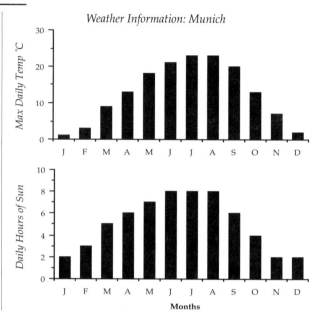

*Weather Information: Munich*

# Consulates

The main German consulates are:

**CANADA**
German Consulate General
77 Admiral Road
Toronto
Ontario M5R 2L4
☎ (416) 925-2813

**USA**
German Consulate General
New York
NY
460 Park Ave
☎ (212) 308-8700

**UK**
German Consulate General
16 Eglinton Crescent
Edinburgh EH 12 5D9
☎ (031) 337 23 23

The main consulates in Germany are:

**CANADA**
Consulate
Godesberger Allee 119
5300 Bonn 2
☎ (0228) 8100630

**USA**
German Consulate
Siesmayerstrasse 21
6000 Frankfurt am Main
☎ (069) 75350

**UK**
General Consulate
Triton House
Bockenheimer Landstrasse 42
6000 Frankfurt am Main
☎ (069) 1700020

## *Currency and Credit Cards*

The German unit of currency is the Deutsche Mark (DM). 100 Pfennigs (Pf) = 1DM. It is freely convertible ie, it can be exchanged for any foreign currency at any time at the going rate. You can bring as much currency as you wish into Germany.

The Deutsche Mark comes in **notes** of DM10, DM20, DM50, DM100, DM200, DM500 and DM1,000; **coins** of DM0.01 (one pfennig), DM0.02, DM0.05, DM0.10, DM0.20, DM0.50, DM1, DM2 and DM5.

Credit cards are not so widely accepted as in some other countries, especially outside large cities and major tourist centres. In smaller towns banks only accept American Express or Euro-Cards.

All banks exchange traveller's cheques. If the cheques are in Deutschmarks the full face value will be given. If they are in a foreign currency the bank will make a service charge of around 2 per cent.

Eurocheques, together with a cheque card, are used like ordinary domestic cheques and must be made out in the local currency. Eurocheques can be used for all business transactions but petrol stations make a small additional charge. These cheques can only be cashed up to a value of 400DM per transaction. Scottish bank notes are not accepted for exchange nor are foreign coins.

Bureaux de change: at airports, main railway stations and

border crossings. Open: usually 6am-10pm.

The Deutsches Verkehrsbank (see Banks) will give a cash advance against major credit cards, subject to a DM100 minimum.

## Electricity

Electricity operates at 220 volts AC 50 Hertz. Round ended, two pronged continental adaptors are needed for UK/USA appliances. Note that the adaptor should be constructed so as to fit into recessed sockets. The 'Traveller Super-Plug International Adaptor' is a multi-purpose plug that fits German electrical sockets. For further information contact:
Traveller International Products
51 Hays Mews
London W1X 5DB

## Embassies

The main embassies in Germany are:

**Australia**
2 Godesberger Allee 107
5300 Bonn
☎ (0228) 8103-0

**New Zealand**
Bonn Centre
5300 Bonn
☎ (0228) 214021

**Canada**
Friedrich Wilhelm Strasse 18
5300 Bonn
☎ (0228) 231061

**USA**
2 Deichmanns Aue
5300 Bonn
☎ (0228) 339-1

**UK**
1 Friedrich Ebert Allee 77
5300 Bonn
☎ (0228) 234061

Other embassies are listed in the telephone book under 'Botschaften'.

*Other German embassies are:*

**Australia**
119 Empire Circuit
Yarralumla, ACT 2600
Canberra
☎ (062) 701911

**Canada**
1 Waverley Street
Ottawa
Ontario K2P OT8
☎ (613) 232-1101

**Britain**
23 Belgrave Square
London
SW1 X8PZ
☎ (071) 2355033

**New Zealand**
90-92 Hobson Street
Thornton
Wellington
☎ 85 02 89

**USA**
4645 Reservoir Road N.W.
Washington DC
☎ (202) 298-4000

## *Facilities for the Disabled*

Facilities for the disabled are fairly good in Germany. Facilities are usually indicated by the blue pictogram of a person in a wheelchair. Most motorway service stops have toilet facilities for the handicapped and there are usually reserved parking places for people in wheelchairs in multi-storey car parks and elsewhere. Most important museums and public buildings are accessible for the handicapped. Town guides for the handicapped are available (free) at tourist offices in major cities and are mostly bilingual.

The information from some of the following addresses may only be in German:

Infozentrale für Behinderte
(Information Centre for the Disabled)
8000 Munich
☎ (089) 21171

Club der Behinderten un ihrer Freunde
Eupenerstrasse 5
D-6500 Mainz
☎ (06131) 225514
Very good for general information on travel etc, but when writing be prepared to allow for a bit of time before getting an answer (this organisation is run on a honorary basis).

Reisebüro für Behinderte BTS
Behinderten Touristic Service
(Travel Agent for the Disabled)
D-6700 Ludwigshafen/Rhein

Handicapped Reisen
Am Markt 33
5300 Bonn 1

Behindertenreisen
Jahn Reisen
(Travel company)
Elsenheimer Strasse 61
D-8000 Munich 21

Zentrale Verkaufsleitung der Deutschen Bundesbahn
(Kontaktstelle für Behindertenfragen)
Rhabanusstrasse 3
D-6500 Mainz
☎ (06131) 1552 16
Contact the above address for information about the
facilities offered by German Federal Railways for the
handicapped. They put out the *Reiseführer für unsere
behinderten Fahrgäste* (*Travel Guide for Disabled Passengers* —
partly in English). It is available at train stations, DB
(Federal Rail) agencies and DER travel bureaux.

Gesellschaft für Nebenbetriebe der Bundesautobahn (GfN)
Poppelsdorfer Allee 24
D-5300 Bonn 1
☎ (0228) 7090
For the pamphlet *Autobahn-Service für Behinderte* (*Motor-
way-Service for the Disabled*).

## *Festivals*

There are many more festivals and local events than can be
listed here. A calendar of events should be obtainable from
the National Tourist Office or at the various regional and
local tourist offices.

### Bad Dürkheim
Dürkheimer Wurstmarkt: second and third weekends in
September. This is just one of the wine festivals that take
place in Germany's wine-growing regions during autumn.

### Everywhere in Southern Germany
Carnival (Karneval, Fastnacht, Fastnet): period before Lent

(January/February). Especially famous in Rottweil and Villingen-Schwenningen.

**Furth im Wald**
Drachenstich: second Sunday in August.

**Grafenau**
Salzsäumerfest: first Sunday in August.

**Kötzting**
Pfingstritt: Whit Monday. One of Bavaria's many colourful horse-back processions with religious background.

**Landshut**
Landshuter Hochzeit: four weekends in July/August, every 3 years (next in 1993).

**Munich**
Oktoberfest: September/October.

**Nürnberg**
Christkindlesmarkt: from end November to 24 December. One of the most famous of the many Christmas fairs held in Germany.

**Oberammergau**
Passion Play: May to September, every 10 years (next in 2000).

**Stuttgart**
Folk festival 'Cannstatter Wasen': September/October.

# *Further Reading*

*A Concise History of Germany* Mary Fulbrook (Cambridge).
*Germany: A Short History* Donald S. Detwiler (Southern Illinois University Press).
*Germany 1866-1945* Gordan A. Craig (History of Modern Europe series, Oxford University Press).
*The German People: Their History* Veit Valentin (AMS). For those with a good knowledge of German there is an updated paperback edition published by Knaur and available in Germany titled: *Geschichte der Deutschen.*
*The Rise and Fall of the Third Reich (A History of Nazi Germany)* William L Shirer (Simon and Schuster).

*Off the Beaten Track West Germany* (Moorland Publishing Co. Ltd).
*The Visitor's Guide to the Black Forest* George Wood (Moorland Publishing Co. Ltd).
*The Visitor's Guide to Bavaria* George Wood (Moorland Publishing Co. Ltd).

## *Health Insurance*

Visitors from the UK are covered by reciprocal agreements when in Germany. They require an E111 form which can be obtained from their local post office or DHSS office. Nationals of other countries should ensure that they have adequate medical cover before departing.

## *Language*

Although English is quite widely spoken it is a good idea to get a decent phrase book such as *Berlitz Language Guide: German for Travellers* or *Language Guide Germany* by Polyglott. Even mastery of the very simplest phrases produces a positive response. Note that 'ß' is sometimes used in German to represent a double 's'. Double 's' is used in this book. What follows is a list of names frequently used in the text and encountered when touring.

*Abtei* — abbey
*Altstadt* — old quarter of town
*Autobahn* (A-) — motorway
*Bad* — spa
*Berg* — mountain
*Bundesstrasse* (B-) — Federal Road
*Burg* — castle or fortress
*Dom* — cathedral
*Freibad* — outdoor swimming pool
*Fremdenverkehrsamt/Verkehrsamt* — tourist office
*Gaststätte* — restaurant
*Gondelbahn* — cable railway
*Hallenbad* — indoor swimming pool
*Hauptbahnhof* — main railway station
*Heimatmuseum* — local museum
*Kapelle* — chapel

*Kirche* — church

*Kloster* — monastery, nunnery or convent

*Marktplatz* — market square

*Münster* — minster; in Southern Germany can also mean
cathedral

*Naturlehrpfad* — nature trail

*Naturschutzgebiet* — nature reserve

*Rathaus* — town hall

*Ried* — moor or marsh

*Schloss* — castle or residential palace

*See* — lake

*Seilbahn* — cable railway

*Strasse* — street

*Tal* — valley

*Tierpark* — zoo

*Tor* — gate

*Veste* — fortress

*Wanderparkplatz* — car park specially situated near
walking area

*Wallfahrtskirche* — pilgrimage church

*Wasserfall* — waterfall

*Wasserschloss* — moated castle

*Wildgehege* — forest enclosure usually for native animals

## *Maps*

A good map of Germany is well worth the price. Maps to the
scale of 1:700,000 or 1:800,000 are useful as they give a good
overall view, while still including enough detail to make
following the routes described relatively easy. Excellent
choices obtainable in Germany are *Deutschland 1:800,000* in
the *Euro-Länderkarte* series — also available as 1:500,000 —
published by the RV Verlag and *Germany 1:700,000* with
Distoguide in the *Euro-Map* series published by Hallwag.
Both show Germany's many tourist roads and the Hallwag
even has a little booklet attached with plans of the major cities
and other practical information. For more detailed explora-
tion of a particular region individual sheets on a scale of
1:200,000 are ideal. Maps to this or similar scales are published by the fuel companies and are available at most filling
stations. This guide was compiled using the *RV Auto Atlas*

*Bundesrepublik Deutschland 1:200,000.* For those spending more time in Germany and covering wide areas of the country it is a good investment and includes useful plans of Germany's main cities.

## Measurements

The metric system is used in Germany.
1 kilogram (1,000 grams) = 2.2lb
1 litre = $1^3/_4$ pints
4.5 litres = 1 gallon
1 kilometre = 0.62 miles (10km = approximately 6 miles).

## Medical Treatment

Doctors' (Arzt) and Dentists' (Zahnarzt) consulting hours are normally 10am-12noon and 4-6pm, except Wednesdays, Saturdays and Sundays. Note that in some cases they could be open earlier and longer — it depends on the doctor. To call an ambulance dial 110. For the ADAC Ambulance Service Munich and Telephone Doctor (Telefonarzt) ☎ (089) 76762244. This service is offered daily 8am-8pm and during the main holiday season 7am-11pm. The Telephone Doctor gives advice on medicaments for less serious problems.

## Pets

Permits are not required to bring in pets — up to 3 dogs and/or cats — however evidence must be produced to show that the animals have been vaccinated against rabies between 12 months and 30 days prior to entry. Accepted proof is an international vaccination pass or a veterinary vaccination certificate with a certified German translation. Other kinds of domestic animal require a special permit. Further information is available at German consulates and veterinary authorities.

## Photography

All the main brands of film (Agfa, Fuji, Kodak) are readily available in Germany. Prices for all brands of film are reasonable but the cheapest name-brand is Agfa. Shops belonging to the chains of Porst and Quelle sell even cheaper 'no-name' film.

The best time of the day for photos is the early morning or late afternoon. In summer the light can be very hazy, some of the clearest weather being in autumn and spring.

# Post Offices

Post Offices (die Post) are usually open Monday to Friday 8am-6pm, Saturdays 8am-12noon. At railway stations in larger cities they are open during the week until late in the evening. Post offices can also change currency.

# Public Holidays

1 January *Neujahr* (New Year's Day)
6 January *Heilige Drei Könige* (Epiphany)
*Karfreitag* (Good Friday)
*Ostermontag* (Easter Monday)
1 May *Tag der Arbeit* (May Day, Labour Day)
*Pfingstmontag* (Whit Monday)
*Fronleichnam* (Corpus Christi. In Baden-Württemberg, areas of Bavaria with mainly Catholic population, Hesse and Rhineland-Palatinate)
15 August *Mariae Himmelfahrt* (Assumption of Mary. In areas of Bavaria with mainly Catholic population and Saarland)
3 October *Tag der deutschen Einheit* (Day of German Unity)
1 November *Allerheiligen* (All Saints Day. In Baden-Württemberg, Bavaria and Rhineland-Palatinate)
*Buss- und Bettag* (Repentence Day. In all Federal States; in Bavaria only those areas with mainly Protestant populations)
*Weihnachten* (Christmas)

# Public Transport

Bus services run jointly by the railway and postal authorities, as well as by other operators, supplement the rail network. The Europa-Bus Service runs tours along particularly inter-

esting routes for visitors.
Reservations:
Deutsche Touring GmbH
Am Römerhof 17
D-6000 Frankfurt am Main
To make reservations from overseas contact your local
travel agent, offices of the Deutsche Touring GmbH or a
Europa-Bus agent.

## *Smoking*

Some restaurants have non-smoking *(Nichtraucher)* sections.
The car hire firm Inter Rent/Europcar offers a 'No-Smoking'
car which is available at all German airports.

## *Sports and Pastimes*

### Angling

Permits are required for fishing in Germany.

1. National permit — obtainable from appropriate district
   administration (Landratsamt) or town council (Stadtverwaltung — Ordnungsamt).
2. Permits from the fishing water owner or lease-holder
   (Fischwasserbesitzer or Fischwasserpächter). Tourist
   offices should be able to help visitors with this.

Stocks of fish to be found in Germany include carp, pike,
perch, pike-perch, sheat-fish, eels, bream, barbel, chub,
rudd, trout, char, and salmon.
Details of facilities, etc, can be obtained from:
Verband Deutscher Sportfischer (VDSF)
Bahnhofstrasse 37
D-6050 Offenbach

### Boat Trips

During the peak season boat trips take place regularly on the
following rivers and lakes.
*Rivers:* Donau (Danube), Main, Neckar and Rhein (Rhine).
*Lakes:* Ammersee, Bodensee (Lake Constance), Chiemsee,
Königssee, Starnberger See, Titisee and a number of smaller
lakes.
  For exact details about short excursions inquire at the local

tourist offices. Information about longer cruises on the Rhein should be available at most travel agents or from the various German National Tourist Offices overseas.

## Cycling

From April to October bicycles can be hired at many railway stations in Germany and can be returned to any other station that offers this service. For a list of those stations where cycles can be hired it is best to inquire at a Hauptbahnhof (main railway station) in one of the larger cities. Tourist offices have lists of other places hiring out bicycles and sometimes they even have maps. Detailed *Radwanderkarten* (maps showing cycling routes) are available at many bookshops. If you are in an area which does not have a cycle hire station look in a phone book under Fahrradverleih to find addresses of local bike rental outlets.

To take your own bike on a train you need to purchase a 'bicycle ticket' or Fahrrad-Karte. You have to take the bike to the luggage carriage yourself.

For further information contact:
Bund Deutscher Radfahrer
Otto-Fleck-Schneise 4
D-6000 Frankfurt 71
☎ (069) 678 92 22

## Flying and Gliding

There are more than 50 flying-schools and some 1,000 gliding clubs in Germany. For detailed information write to:
Deutscher Aero Club
Lyoner Strasse 16
D-6000 Frankfurt am Main

## Mountaineering

The German Alpine Club maintains 252 huts in the Alps and Germany's upland regions (Mittelgebirge) which are available to all mountaineers. Introductory courses in mountaineering and week-long tours involving summer and winter climbing are run by the club's mountaineering and skiing school. They also conduct guided tours in nearly every Alpine range. The address for further information is:
Deutscher Alpenverein (DAV), Praterinsel 5
D-8000 Munich 2

## Walking

Walking is one of Germany's great national pastimes. The number and length of waymarked trails in the south is immense. For the motorist the numerous Wanderparkplätze (walkers' car parks) are ideal. They are almost always marked by the pictogram of a couple walking, are free, and there is usually an information board with a map, including length and duration of the walks. These trails or Wanderwege are mostly of a circular nature and might take from an hour to a full day at the most. For longer walks a map (Wanderkarte) showing the various trails is recommended, as the many different symbols used along some trails can get confusing. The best scales are from 1:75,000/1:50,000 for covering a fairly large area and 1:25,000 for those who want to do a lot of walking in the area where they are based. Walking guides such as the *Kompass Wanderführer* are useful for visitors with a good knowledge of German, as they give very detailed descriptions of walks and cover virtually all Germany.

### LONG DISTANCE WALKS (A SELECTION)
#### Black Forest
Westweg Pforzheim-Basel about 275km (170 miles)
Mittelweg Pforzheim-Waldshut about 230km (143 miles)
Ostweg Pforzheim-Schaffhausen about 237km (147 miles)

#### Swabian Jura
Albrandweg about 570km (354 miles)
North edge Bopfingen-Gosheim. South edge Tuttlingen-Harburg (along Donau).

#### Bavarian Alps/Alpine Plateau
König Ludwig Weg: Berg on Starnberger See via Ammersee to Füssen, about 110km (68 miles)
Prälatenweg: Marktoberdorf-Kochel am See, about 140km (87 miles)
Über den Grat: Alpine route (for the experienced), Oberstdorf-Hindelang, about 60km (37 miles)

For further information contact:
Europäische Wandervereinigung/Verband Deutscher Gebirgs-und Wandervereine, Reichsstrasse 4
6600 Saarbrücken, ☎ (0681) 390070

This was first offered in the Black Forest over 17 years ago, but now there is hardly an area in Southern Germany that does not offer this service. What it basically involves is a hike along a specific route where certain Gasthöfe not only offer accommodation but also transfer luggage to the next Gasthof on the route. Organised tours of this type — where hotel reservations, etc, are all taken care of — often have to be booked at least 3 weeks in advance and can be quite cheap if undertaken in spring or autumn. It is often much more comfortable at this time of the year anyway.

Wandern ohne Gepäck and Radeln ohne Gepäck (Cycling without Baggage) are not organised on a national basis but on a regional and local basis. If DER travel offices or German National Tourist Offices overseas cannot provide sufficient information then it is best to write to the regional tourist offices. They should be able to provide specific information on the nature of the walk — pamphlets with route descriptions, sometimes route maps and costs. To be sure of a reply it is best to include an International Reply Coupon. Some tourist offices will actually help visitors organise such a walk within their region and reserve rooms in the various Gasthöfe. Note that individual hikers usually have to pay a bit more for the transport of their luggage than groups — in some cases two people already qualify as a group.

The Verband Deutscher Gebirgs and Wandervereine (see address under Long Distance Walks) also offers information on organised walks (with and without backpack) and cycling tours (Rad-Wanderung). They definitely require an International Reply Coupon for a reply.

Some suggestions for Wandern ohne Gepäck are:

### The Burgenweg (Castles Path)
In the Oberpfälzer Wald (Upper Palatinate Forest)
*Length:* 180km (112 miles)
*Route:* From Marktredwitz to Waldmünchen
*Time*: 9 days
*Waymark:* yellow-blue-yellow striped rectangle

### Pandurensteig (Path of the Pandurs)
In the Bayerischer Wald (Bavarian Forest)
*Length:* 160km (99 miles)

*Route:* Waldmünchen to Passau
*Time:* 8 days
*Waymark:* varies as this route is made up of several different paths.

For information on the above walks contact:
Fremdenverkehrsverband Ostbayern e.V.
Landshuter Strasse 13
D-8400 Regensburg
☎ (1941) 560260

**Auf Schusters Rappen im Land des Blauen Löwen (On Shank's Pony through the land of the Blue Lion)**
Hunsrück
*Length:* the daily stages are between 15 and 25km (9 and 15 miles).
*Route:* Idar-Oberstein — Stipshausen — Idar-Oberstein
*Time:* 7 days (maps are provided)
Information on this walk and also riding tours, cycling tours and covered waggon safari from:
Fremdenverkehrsamt Idar-Oberstein
Postfach 01 1480
D-6580 Idar-Oberstein
☎ (06781) 27025

**Schwarzwälder Mühlentour (Black Forest Mill Tour)**
*Length:* 80km (50 miles)
*Route:* in the Achertal and Sasbachtal
*Time:* 5 days

**Schwarzwald, Wutachtschlucht, Rundwanderweg (Black Forest, Wutach Gorge Circular Walk)**
*Length:* 150km (93 miles)
*Route:* Marbach — Wutach Gorge — Marbach
*Time:* 6 days

For information about walking guides, maps, 'hiker's hostels' etc contact:
Fremdenverkehrsverband Schwarzwald
Postfach 1660
D-7800 Freiburg im Breisgau
☎ (0761) 31317

## Winter Sport

The following areas are generally suitable for winter sports. Information about resorts and facilities are available at regional and local tourist offices.

### Bavaria

Fichtelgebirge (Fichtel Ranges)
Oberpfälzer Wald (Upper Palatinate Forest)
Bayerischer Wald (Bavarian Forest)
Bayerische Alpen (Bavarian Alps)
Allgäu

### Baden-Württemberg

Schwäbische Alb (Swabian Jura)
Schwarzwald (Black Forest)

### Rhineland-Palatinate

Hunsrück (in good winters)
For further information contact:
Deutscher Skiverband (German Ski Association)
Hubertusstrasse 1
D-8033 Planegg
☎ (089) 85 70 00-9
or
DSV
Postfach 20 18 27
D-8000 Munich 2
The ADAC Skiatlas and the DSV Skiatlas have useful information about skiing in Germany and are available in local bookshops (Buchhandlungen). They are updated annually.

## Yachting

A list of schools can be obtained from:
Verband Deutscher Segelschulen e.V.
Varlar 86
D-4428 Rosendahl 1

# *Taxis*

Fares are made up of a basic flat rate plus a charge per kilometre, and vary from place to place. Surcharges for luggage also vary. Meters are obligatory.

# *Telephones*

In the main post offices you can use the direct phone service. Ask at the counter marked Ferngespräche for a phone booth. You pay at the counter when you have finished your phone call. This is much more convenient than queuing for a pay phone and saves having to find change.

Every telephone booth has a local directory. Phone books covering all Germany are found in the post offices. Local and national calls may be made from all post offices and coin/card-operated phone booths. Unit fees for calls from hotels are about twice as expensive as the standard call units. International calls can be made from post offices and phone booths with a phone marked 'Auslandsgespräche'.

Coins that can be used in a phone booth are: 10 Pfennig, 1DM, 5DM. A much more comfortable way of telephoning is with a Telefonkarte. These cards are available at post offices and obviously solve the problem of small change. Telephone booths which accept these cards are usually marked 'Kartentelefon' — they are becoming more widespread but may not yet exist in smaller towns or villages.

You can only reverse charges (R-Gespräch, ring collect) to the USA. To do this look up the number of the international Fernamt under the heading Telefon-Sonderdienste in the telephone book. This number is usually 0010 but it can vary from region to region. The person at reception will then give further details. You cannot ring collect within Germany.

Instructions on how to use payphones are written in English in phone booths for international calls. Otherwise the principle is simple. Lift up the receiver, insert the coins and dial the number. A meter shows how much credit is left.

For international directory inquiries dial 0 01 18. This number will also help if you have language difficulties in finding a number in an emergency.

**Emergency Numbers**
Police and accidents 110
Fire brigade 112
National directory inquiries dial 11 88 or 0 11 88

Main international direct dialling codes are:
Australia 00 61

Britain 0044
Irish Republic 00 353
New Zealand 00 64
USA and Canada 00 1
For international directory phone 400 118.
Telephone call rates are cheaper after 8pm and at weekends.
This does not apply to calls outside Germany.

When dialling from Germany remember after dialling the national code to omit the first zero of the number you are ringing.

# Tipping

Not a must but is customary for good service. Small sums are rounded off, large sums over 100DM might include a tip of around 2DM.

# Tourist Offices

The main German National Tourist Offices are:

**Australia**
German National Tourist Office: Lufthansa House
12th Floor
143 Macquarie Street
Sydney 2000
☎ (02) 221-1008

**Canada**
175 Bloor Street East
North Tower, 6th Floor
Toronto
Ontario M4 W3R8
☎ (416) 968-1570

**UK**
Nightingale House
65 Curzon Street
London
W1Y 7PE
☎ (041) 4953990 or 91

**Germany**
Deutsche Zentrale für Tourismus e.V. (DZT)
Beethovenstrasse 69
6000 Frankfurt am Main
☎ (069) 7572-0
(general information)

Deutsche Fremdenverkehrsverband
Niebuhrstrasse 16b
5300 Bonn 1
☎ (0228) 214071-72
(general information)

**USA**

444 South Flower Street
Suite 2230
Los Angeles CA 90071
☎ (213) 688-73 32

747 Third Avenue
33rd Floor
New York, NY 10017
☎ (212) 308-3300

## *Travel*

### By Air

Lufthansa German Airlines link more than 1,000 cities throughout the world with Germany. The following airlines also have direct services:

**Australia**
Qantas

**Canada**
Air Canada, Wardair, CP Air

**New Zealand**
Air New Zealand

**UK**
British Airways, Lufthansa, Air UK, TWA, United Airlines

**USA**
LTU American Airlines, Pan Am, TWA, Delta, World, Condor, Northwest.

For exact schedules and air fares contact any Lufthansa office or travel agent.

**Lufthansa Offices**
**Canada**
55 Yonge Street
Toronto, Ontario M5E IJ4
☎ (416) 3 60-36 00
Reservations ☎ (414) 2 83-77 00
(also in Montreal, Ottawa, Calgary and Vancouver)

**Germany**
Deutsche Lufthansa AG
Von-Gablenz-Strasse 2-6, D-5000 Köln 21
International Airports in Southern Germany are Frankfurt, Munich, Nürnberg, Stuttgart and Saarbrücken.

**UK**
23-26 Piccadilly
London W1V 0EJ
(also in Birmingham, Bristol, Glasgow, and Manchester)

**USA**
680 Fifth Avenue
New York NY 10019
☎ (212) 357-8400
(and many other American cities)

**Domestic Air Services**
There are regular flight connections between all German airports. As a supplementary service to the existing flight schedule the Lufthansa Airport Express Train links the airports of Düsseldorf, Cologne, Bonn and Frankfurt.

All airports are linked to their local urban transport network. Some even have their own shuttle service — eg bus or direct trains to the city centre. There are DB (German Rail) offices at all airports.

Frankfurt Airport has its own railway station directly beneath the terminal building. There are direct Inter City services to and from Koblenz, Bonn, Cologne, Düsseldorf, Dortmund, Würzburg, Nürnberg, Augsburg and Munich. Trains run between Frankfurt's main railway station at 10 minute intervals; length of journey is around 11 minutes.

# By Road

**Breakdown**
The German motoring organisation is the ADAC, which also helps members of foreign organisations. A 24-hour breakdown service exists in most large cities, first dial the relevant area code and then 19211. On motorways and some main roads help can be called from one of the orange emergency telephones. Motorway telephones are clearly indicated and may be used by the motorist in distress to communicate with the police who will, if appropriate, inform the ADAC patrol. Emergency telephones are now gradually being installed on other main roads.
ADAC, AM Westpark 8
D-8000 Munich 70. ☎ (089) 76 76-0

The brochure *Autobahn Service* contains detailed information about motorway petrol stations, service areas and motels. It is available from all tourist offices.

## Parking

Free parking is rare in German towns and cities. Time is saved by going direct to a multi-storey car park (Parkhaus). They are always clearly signposted by a 'P' with an inverted 'v' top. The hassles of driving into many cities can be avoided by using the 'P+R' (Park and Ride) system; a large car park outside the city centre from where regular trains or buses depart for the inner-city. Parking is forbidden on main roads or those with fast moving traffic, on or near tram lines, near bus or tram stops, traffic lights, taxi ranks and intersections. It is also forbidden to park on the 'wrong' side of the road, except in one-way streets.

The whole idea of the P+R system is to provide a cheap and convenient alternative to parking in the cluttered inner-cities. The large car parks are free of charge. The bus/train that travels a short distance into the inner-city is quite modest in price compared to the cost of a multi-storey car park. Not every city, however, offers this service. Note also that in order to discourage parking in the inner-city the parking metres sometimes only have a duration of thirty minutes. Some of the larger towns, especially a spa, offer free parking outside the town centre but still within walking distance.

## Driving Regulations

UK, American and Canadian citizens only require their valid national driving licences or an international driver's licence. This enables the motorist to drive for a period of up to 1 year in Germany. National or international vehicle registration papers should also be carried.

Third party insurance is compulsory in Germany and foreign visitors, other than nationals of EEC countries, must have an international insurance certificate (Green Card) or take out third party insurance at the border. This is obtainable for 15 days or 1 month. On expiring this temporary insurance can be extended — as is also the case with the Green Card — at any office of the Automobile Association (ADAC).

Germans drive on the right-hand side of the road. Speed

limits are as follows: in towns and villages 50km (31mph); outside built up areas 100km (62mph); on motorways 130km (81mph) is recommended. These speeds are not indicated by signs but variations from them are shown in km per hour. The rectangular yellow sign bearing the place name denotes the entrance to a built up area and the similar sign with a diagonal stripe indicates the exit from this place. Place names on a green sign do not constitute a speed restriction.

Other than on minor roads in rural areas, priority is always indicated on signs approaching a junction. Traffic on a Bundesstrasse (state main road) always has priority. Bundesstrassen are recognised by a small rectangular yellow plate bearing the road number. Priority is shown elsewhere by a yellow square with white border set on its corner while the same sign with diagonal black line indicates the end of priority. Standard 'Give Way' or 'Stop' signs will be found on converging roads.

The German police are very strict on tyre condition and a vehicle found with less than 2mm tread depth over the whole surface will not be allowed to proceed until the tyres have been replaced. Spikes on snow tyres are prohibited.

Warning triangles are compulsory and must be placed 100m (109yd) behind a broken down vehicle and 200m (219yd) on an Autobahn.

Seat belts are compulsory for those riding in the front seat and children under 12 years must sit in the back. There are on the spot fines for speeding and other offences.

Blood alcohol levels must not exceed 0.8 per mille (80mg/100ml). If caught drinking and driving the penalties are stiff.

### Fuel
Though leaded fuel is available everywhere the trend is to unleaded (Bleifrei) — this is always indicated on the pumps, so check first! Note that although Super grade is available in leaded (Verbleiter) form, normal grade fuel (Benzin) is only available in unleaded form.

### Useful Road Signs
*Ausfahrt* — Exit from motorway or dual carriageway
*Bankett nicht befahrbar* — Soft verges
*Einbahnstrasse* — Nothing to do with the railway, but a one-way street

*Einordnen* — Get in lane
*Freie Fahrt* — End of restrictions, usually after passing roadworks
*Gegenverkehr* — Oncoming traffic
*Glatteisgefahr* — Danger of icy road
*Langsam fahren* — Drive slowly
*Rollsplit* — Loose chippings
*Umleitung* (on yellow arrow) — Not the way to the next village but a traffic diversion
*Links/Rechts fahren* — Drive on the left/right

## Vehicle Lights
Left-dipping headlights must be adjusted to dip to the right. Cars may not be driven on sidelights and headlights must be used, even during daylight hours, if visibility is impaired by fog, snow, rain, etc. Rear fog lights may be used if visibility is less than 50m (160ft) but not in built-up areas.

## Tourist Roads
There are many tourist roads in Southern Germany, some of which are clearly sign-posted. Good maps usually indicate these roads. They always follow scenically attractive or historically interesting routes, though using them means, for the most part, following a well-beaten path. Here is a list of some of the better known roads.

### Burgenstrasse (Castles Road)
Stretches are touched upon: Mannheim — Heidelberg — Mosbach — Bad Wimpfen — Heilbronn — Öhringen — Rothenburg ob der Tauber — Ansbach — Bürnberg
*Sign*: castle tower (but infrequent)
*Length:* 290km (180 miles)

### Deutsche Alpenstrasse (German Alpine Road)
Large stretches are described in this book
Lindau — Sonthofen — Garmisch-Partenkirchen — Rottach-Egern — Reit im Winkl — Berchtesgaden
*Sign:* German name written on blue ground
*Length:* 400km (248 miles)

### Deutsche Weinstrasse (German Wine Road)
Described virtually in its entirety
Schweigen — Bad Bergzabern — Edenkoben — Neustadt an der Weinstrasse — Bad Dürkheim — Bockenheim

*Sign:* blue bunch of grapes on yellow ground
*Length:* 100km (62 miles)

**Oberschwäbische Barockstrasse
(Upper Swabian Baroque Road)**
Large stretches touched upon
Ulm — Ehingen — Zwiefalten — Bad Waldsee —
Ravensburg — Friedrichshafen — Isny — Bad Wurzach —
Ulm
*Sign:* German name with angel's head
*Length:* 440km (273 miles)

**Schwäbische Albstrasse (Swabian Jura Road)**
Followed quite closely
Nördlingen — Heidenheim — Geislingen — Urach —
Burladingen — Tuttlingen — Trossingen
*Sign:* carline thistle on blue ground
*Length:* 380km (236 miles)

**Romantische Strasse (Romantic Road)**
Stretches are touched upon
Würzburg — Tauberbischofsheim — Rothenburg ob der
Tauber — Nördlingen — Augsburg — Landsberg —
Füssen
*Sign:* not consistent, usually written in German
*Length:* 370km (230 miles)


**Car Hire** (Autovermietung)
This is available at most airports and major train stations.
Generally speaking you have to be 21 years old to hire a car.
For small model cars (VW Polo, VW Golf) 19 years is accepted
at InterRent/Europcar; for a big Mercedes they want you to
be at least 25 years old. A valid national driving licence that
has been held for at least 1 year is required. Major credit cards
and cash are accepted.

**Avis**
Central Reservation Service (all Germany at local rates)
☎ (0130) 7733. In Frankfurt ☎ 730081

**Hertz**
Central Reservation Service (all Germany and free of
charge) ☎ (0130) 2121. In Frankfurt ☎ 73 04 04

### InterRent
Central Reservation Service (all Germany at local rates)
☎ (0130) 2211 and 3151

### Sixt/Budget
Central Reservation Service (all Germany at local rates)
☎ (0130) 3366

### *Head Offices*

**ai/Ansa International Rent-a-Car**
Savignystrasse 71
D-6000 Frankfurt am Main 1
☎ (0469) 75 61 00-20

**Avis Autovermietung**
Eschersheimer Landstrasse 55
D-6000 Frankfurt am Main 1
☎ (069) 15 37-0

**Europcar Autovermietung**
Frankfurter Ring 243
D-8000 Munich 40
☎ (089) 3 23 09-0

**Hertz Autovermietung**
Schwalbacher Strasse 47-49
6000 Frankfurt am Main 1
☎ (069) 75850

**Inter Rent Autovermietung**
Tangstedter Landstrasse 81
D-2000 Hamburg 62
☎ (040) 52 01 80

**Sixt/Budget Rent-a-Car**
Dr-Carl-von-Linde-Strasse 2
D-8023 Pullach
☎ (089) 79 10 71

## By Sea
Motorists travelling from Scotland or northern England may find the North Sea Ferries services from Hull to Rotterdam or Zeebrugge (14 hours) a convenient connection. On the east coast there are the shorter Felixstowe to Zeebrugge and Harwich to the Hook of Holland lines (7-8 hours), operated by P&O Ferries and Sealink respectively. South of the Thames overnight crossings can be made from Sheerness to Vlissingen (Flushing, around 8 hours) with Olau Lines and from Ramsgate to Dunkirk with Sally Viking. There are day and night crossings from Folkestone or Dover to Ostend and Zeebrugge with P&O Ferries taking about 4 hours. Finally there are many sailings on the short sea route from Dover to Calais with P&O Ferries.

The majority of rail travellers will no doubt go via London and cross from Harwich to the Hook of Holland or from Dover to Ostend. If the overnight sailings are used the western areas of Southern Germany (Saarland, Rhineland-

Palatinate, Black Forest and the region around Frankfurt) can be reached by the following afternoon.

The European ports have good motorway connections to Southern Germany. For those who wish to start their touring with chapter 1 or 2 a suitable entry point is Aachen. To get close to Bad Kreuznach (Route 5) or Heidelberg (Route 2) drive a few kilometres east on the A4/E40 and at Autobahn Kreuz (motorway junction) Kerpen proceed south on the A61/E31. To get to Frankfurt (Route 1) continue on the A4 to Köln and at Autobahn Dreieck Heumar take the A3 south. Go via Luxembourg to start with the tours in the Saarland (Saarbrücken).

Some distances are:
Dunkirk to Frankfurt am Main 578km (359 miles)
Hook of Holland to Baden-Baden (Black Forest) 713km (443 miles)
Dunkirk to Munich 969km (602 miles)

Some addresses:

*Sally Line*

| | |
|---|---|
| UK | Germany |
| Argyle Centre | Münchener Strasse 48 |
| York Street | D-6000 Frankfurt am Main 1 |
| Ramsgate CT11 9DS | ☎ (069) 250197 or 236798 |
| ☎ (0843) 595566 | |

*P&O European Ferries*

| | |
|---|---|
| UK | Car Ferry Terminal |
| Russell Street | The Docks |
| Dover | Felixstowe |
| Kent CT16 1QB | Suffolk IP11 8TB |
| ☎ (0304) 203388 | ☎ (0394) 604802 |

| | |
|---|---|
| The Continental Ferry Port | Germany |
| Mile End | Graf-Adolf-Strasse 41 |
| Portsmouth | D-4000 Düsseldorf 1 |
| Hampshire PO2 8QW | ☎ (0211) 387060 |
| ☎ (0705) 827677 | |

## By Train

It is possible to get to just about every city or town in Germany by train. The quickest way to travel between major cities is on the Intercity-Eurocity (IC/EC) trains. A good bargain is the German Federal Railway's DB Tourist Card (Touristenkarte) which can be bought outside the country. The tourist cards offer unlimited travel around Germany within a specified period of time (up to 16 days). There are special reductions for groups (large or small) people up to the age of 26 and senior citizens. These cards can be bought at any DER (Deutsches Reisebüro) office, German Lufthansa offices and agencies of German Federal Railways overseas.

You can plan your route by train using the free national timetable (Städteverbindungen) which can be obtained from the German National Tourist Office and the DER travel service. These are also available at information counters at any big railway station.

Most trains have First and Second Class compartments, as well as Smoking/Non-Smoking compartments (Raucher/Nichtraucher). All have toilets (WC). Trains in Germany are not particularly cheap but there are many special reduced fares. The booklet *Happy Days in Germany* available from tourist offices has details of several bargain rail tickets.

Children up to 4 years of age may travel free of charge. Those between the ages of 4 and 11 and younger children occupying a sleeping-car berth or couchette pay half fare only and half the Intercity and Eurocity train supplements.

**Nah-Schnellverkehrszug** (local train): stops nearly everywhere, therefore comparatively slow. Good for visiting smaller towns and villages.

**Eilzug** (express): faster than latter. Stops at bigger stations.

**D-Zug/FD-Zug/Interregio** (through-trains): even faster. Only stops at larger towns or cities. For journeys under 50km (31 miles) an additional 3DM has to be paid. The Interregio train is a bit more comfortable than the D/FD-Zug.

**Intercity/Eurocity:** fastest of the lot and most comfortable. Travel only between the main cities. Additional 6DM has to be paid on top of fare. Only worthwhile for long distances and for people who are really in a hurry.

**Autoreisezug** (Motorail): German Federal Rail's service links up with the European network. By night passengers travel in sleeping-cars or couchettes and by day in first class carriages. Cars are carried on the same train. An overall charge is made for car and driver, with reduced rates for accompanying passengers.

Destinations in Germany can be reached by Motorail from the following countries: Holland, Belgium and France.

Special concessionary fares are available on these Motorail services: Auto-Traum-Express (Hamburg/Bremen/Hanover-Munich); Hochrhein-Auto-Express (Hamburg-Karlsruhe) and all DER Motorail services. There are substantial reductions if return tickets are bought and if visitors travel in a group.

The advantages of this form of long distance travel are as follows: drivers arrive at their destinations refreshed and relaxed. Clogged motorways and unpleasant driving conditions are avoided. The kids have plenty of room to get rid of excess energy and last but not least; the environment will have been spared the extra pollution.

### Luggage Services
Luggage services are provided by Federal Railways in Germany.

*Door to door luggage service (Haus-und-Gepäckservice)*

Contact the railway station (ask for the Gepäckannahmestelle) from where you plan to depart a few days before you actually leave. Your luggage will be collected and awaits you in the hotel at your destination.

*Porter and taxi service (Gepäckträgerservice und Taxiservice)*

A person who wears a green jacket with the badge 'DB Gepäckträger-Service' carries hand-luggage from and to the platform or from platform to platform.

If a taxi is also required the taxi driver will collect passengers and their hand-luggage directly from the train and drive them to their hotel. All the traveller has to do is book the Gepäckträgerservice beforehand.

*For further information about rail tours etc contact:*

**Canada**
DER Travel Service Ltd
1290 Bay Street
Toronto — Ontario
M5R2C3

**Germany**
Deutsches Reisebüro GmbH
Eschersheimer Landstrasse 25-27
Postfach 100701
D-6000 Frankfurt (Main)
☎ (069) 1566-289 or 345

**UK**
DER Travel Service
18 Conduit Street
London W1R 9TD

**USA**
DER Travel Service Inc
230 Park Avenue
Suite 1511
New York

New World Travel Inc
747 Third Avenue
18th Floor
New York NY 10017

*Mitfahrzentrale*
This is an institutionalised form which many young travellers find a more pleasant alternative to hitch-hiking. By going to one of the 'Mitfahr' travel offices in most large cities it is possible to get lifts with private motorists going in the same direction. A modest fee is payable to the office for booking rides and they also advise passengers on the maximum fee to be paid to drivers. There is a valuable safety factor in this system as all drivers have to notify agencies of their addresses and car registration numbers. Female passengers can, if they wish, choose female drivers.

Some useful addresses are:
Mitfahrzentrale (MFZ)
Gutleutstrasse 125
6000 Frankfurt am Main 1
☎ (069) 230291

MFZ
Amalienstrasse 87
8000 Munich 40
☎ (089) 280124

MFZ
Lerchenstrasse 65
7000 Stuttgart
☎ (0711) 613015

## Steam and Other Trains

Most of the oldtimer trains are operated by private clubs and run during the summer. As the timetables are quite often subject to variation it is best to inquire at the relevant tourist offices or to contact the following addresses. For a reply include a self-addressed envelope and sufficient International Reply Coupons to cover return postage.

### Baden-Württemberg

*Achern-Ottenhöfen* (Achertalbahn)
Achertäler Eisenbahnverein
c/o Willi Reichert
Josef-Gottwald-Strasse 6
D-7600 Offenburg

*Ettlingen-Busenbach-Bad Herrenalb* (Albtalbahn)
Ulmer Eisenbahnfreunde
Arbeitsgruppe Karlsruhe
Kaiserstrasse 17a
D-7500 Karlsruhe 1
☎ (0721) 848109

*Möckmühl-Dörzbach* (Jagsttalbahn)
SWEG - Südwestdeutsche Verkehrs-AG- Jagsttalbahn
Bahnhofstrasse 8
D-7119 Dörzbach
☎ (07937) 277

*Ochsenhausen-Warthausen* (Öchsle-Schmalspurbahn)
Öchsle-Schmalspurbahn
Postfach 1228
D-7955 Ochsenhausen
☎ (07352) 2203 and 3866

Öchsle-Schmalspurbahn-Betriebsgesellschaft
Lessingstrasse 20
D-7953 Bad Schussenried
☎ (07583) 1342

*Zollhaus-Blumberg-Weizen*
(Wutachtalbahn or Sauschwänzlesbahn)
Stadt Blumberg, Verkehrsamt
D-7712 Blumberg 1
☎ (07702) 5127 (8am-12noon)

**Bavaria**

*Blaibach-Viechtach-Gotteszell*
Regentalbahn AG
D-8374 Viechtach
☎ (09942) 750
and Bayerischer Localbahn Verein
Postfach 1311
D-8180 Tegernsee

*Ebermannstadt-Behringersmühle*
Dampfbahn Fränkische Schweiz
Postfach 1
D-8553 Ebermannstadt
☎ (09131) 65873

*Nördlingen-Dinkelsbühl*
Bayerisches Eisenbahnmuseum
Oderstrasse 4
D-8000 Munich 80
☎ (089) 915462

**Hesse**
*Frankfurter Feldbahnmuseum*:
Dampfbahn Rhein-Main/Feldbahnmuseum am Rebstock
Am Römerhof 15a
D-6000 Frankfurt am Main 90
☎ (069) 709292

**Rhineland-Palatinate**
Neustadt an der Weinstrasse-Lambrecht-Elmstein
Deutsche Gesellschaft für Eisenbahngeschichte
Postfach 100318, Hindenburgstrasse 12
D-6730 Neustadt an der Weinstrasse 1
☎ (06321) 32572 or (063225) 8626

**Saarland**
*Merzig-Losheim-Wadern-Nunkirchen*
(Saar-Hochwald-Museumsbahn)
MECL-Eisenbahnfreunde
Tulpenstrasse 6, D-6646 Losheim
☎ 06872/3592 and 4248
also *Verkehrsverein*
Postfach 1169, D-6646 Losheim
☎ 06872/6169

# INDEX